Understanding the Role of Artificial Intelligence and Its Future Social Impact

Salim Sheikh
Saïd Business School, University of Oxford, UK

A volume in the Advances in Human and Social Aspects of Technology (AHSAT) Book Series

Published in the United States of America by
  IGI Global
  Engineering Science Reference (an imprint of IGI Global)
  701 E. Chocolate Avenue
  Hershey PA, USA 17033
  Tel: 717-533-8845
  Fax: 717-533-8661
  E-mail: cust@igi-global.com
  Web site: http://www.igi-global.com

Library of Congress Cataloging-in-Publication Data

Names: Sheikh, Salim, 1970- author.
Title: Understanding the role of artificial intelligence and its future
  social impact / by Salim Sheikh.
Description: Hershey, PA : Engineering Science Reference, 2020. | Includes
  bibliographical references and index. | Summary: "This book explores
  depth and span of artificial intelligence across all parts of society
  and examines the potential impacts on culture, social relations, and
  values"-- Provided by publisher.
Identifiers: LCCN 2020009093 (print) | LCCN 2020009094 (ebook) | ISBN
  9781799846079 (hardcover) | ISBN 9781799855491 (paperback) | ISBN
  9781799846086 (ebook)
Subjects: LCSH: Artificial intelligence--Social aspects.
Classification: LCC Q335 .S4665 2020 (print) | LCC Q335 (ebook) | DDC
  303.48/34--dc23
LC record available at https://lccn.loc.gov/2020009093
LC ebook record available at https://lccn.loc.gov/2020009094

This book is published in the IGI Global book series Advances in Human and Social Aspects of
Technology (AHSAT) (ISSN: 2328-1316; eISSN: 2328-1324)

Advances in Human and Social Aspects of Technology (AHSAT) Book Series

ISSN:2328-1316
EISSN:2328-1324

Editor-in-Chief: Ashish Dwivedi The University of Hull, UK

MISSION

In recent years, the societal impact of technology has been noted as we become increasingly more connected and are presented with more digital tools and devices. With the popularity of digital devices such as cell phones and tablets, it is crucial to consider the implications of our digital dependence and the presence of technology in our everyday lives.

The **Advances in Human and Social Aspects of Technology (AHSAT) Book Series** seeks to explore the ways in which society and human beings have been affected by technology and how the technological revolution has changed the way we conduct our lives as well as our behavior. The AHSAT book series aims to publish the most cutting-edge research on human behavior and interaction with technology and the ways in which the digital age is changing society.

COVERAGE

- ICTs and human empowerment
- Public Access to ICTs
- Cyber Behavior
- Computer-Mediated Communication
- Cyber Bullying
- ICTs and social change
- Human Development and Technology
- Technology and Freedom of Speech
- Human-Computer Interaction
- Technoself

IGI Global is currently accepting manuscripts for publication within this series. To submit a proposal for a volume in this series, please contact our Acquisition Editors at Acquisitions@igi-global.com or visit: http://www.igi-global.com/publish/.

Titles in this Series

For a list of additional titles in this series, please visit:
http://www.igi-global.com/book-series/advances-human-social-aspects-technology/37145

Present and Future Paradigms of Cyberculture in the 21st Century
Simber Atay (Dokuz Eylül University, Turkey) Gülsün Kurubacak-Meriç (Anadolu University, Turkey) and Serap Sisman-Uğur (Anadolu University, Turkey)
Information Science Reference • © 2020 • 280pp • H/C (ISBN: 9781522580249) • US $185.00

Maintaining Social Well-Being and Meaningful Work in a Highly Automated Job Market
Shalin Hai-Jew (Kansas State University, USA)
Business Science Reference • © 2020 • 333pp • H/C (ISBN: 9781799825098) • US $215.00

ICTs and Innovation for Didactics of Social Sciences
Emilio José Delgado-Algarra (University of Huelva, Spain)
Information Science Reference • © 2020 • 295pp • H/C (ISBN: 9781799828822) • US $175.00

Civic Engagement Frameworks and Strategic Leadership Practices for Organization Development
Susheel Chhabra (Periyar Management and Computer College, India) and Muneesh Kumar (Maharaja Agrasen Institute of Technology (MAIT), Delhi, India)
Information Science Reference • © 2020 • 314pp • H/C (ISBN: 9781799823728) • US $195.00

Civic Engagement in Social and Political Constructs
Susheel Chhabra (Periyar Management and Computer College, India)
Information Science Reference • © 2020 • 285pp • H/C (ISBN: 9781799823643) • US $195.00

For an entire list of titles in this series, please visit:
http://www.igi-global.com/book-series/advances-human-social-aspects-technology/37145

701 East Chocolate Avenue, Hershey, PA 17033, USA
Tel: 717-533-8845 x100 • Fax: 717-533-8661
E-Mail: cust@igi-global.com • www.igi-global.com

To my Mum and (departed) Dad, who I am forever driven to make proud.
Your sacrifices and gifts are never forgotten. God Bless you both.

To my wife, Sam, whose boundless love rejuvenates me daily.
Your never-failing encouragement and support makes me a better man.

Table of Contents

Preface

Artificial Intelligence (AI) and intelligent systems are changing the way humans interact with each other and the world around us. AI impacts every aspect of our lives, ranging from customer services, retail, education, healthcare, autonomous cars, robotics, industrial automation, computer vision, natural language and more.

Businesses are rethinking their competitive strategies and organisational structures, preparing for a new revolution as deep and as fundamental as the industrial revolution of 100 years ago. Scholars are divided over when we will achieve *artificial general intelligence* and what it will ultimately mean for society. Some believe it will be our greatest invention yet. Others, like Elon Musk and Stephen Hawking, lament that it may lead to our doom.

The most important subset of AI is *machine learning*, a field that had big breakthroughs in the latter half of the 20th century, but then lay in waiting for computer processing power to catch up with the heavy demands brought by machine-learning algorithms. A key driver behind machine learning was the rise of *big data*. 'Mountains and lakes' of data permeate every aspect of our society, and there is too much to be captured and analysed by one person or any group without the help of machine learning and similar capabilities.

Netflix has used AI for many years now in several different ways. For example, they have learned how members choose movies based on the thumbnail picture that appears next to the title. Thus, they proactively manipulate the thumbnails to attract watchers to their in-house produced shows. Such seemingly small advances become fundamental steps towards replacing human activities, even for minor decisions. Society has opened itself to many new socio-political concerns related to consumer privacy and cybersecurity.

Other challenges include *algorithm bias*, which has led to headlines and public debates about racism, gender bias and equality. Ultimately, both the algorithms themselves and the data collected reflect the human biases that contribute to their creation.

AI AND THE FUTURE OF JOBS

Key questions related to when and to *what degree* AI will displace enough human activities to push people out of jobs. What jobs will be safe from extinction? Will there be enough new jobs created? How will individuals and groups of people survive without an active source of income? As AI and emerging technologies make headway into the workplace, it is clear that many mundane repetitive tasks will be taken over by virtual personal assistants and chatbots, presumably giving individuals more time and freedom to focus on creative and cognitive tasks. Just as with technological revolutions of the past, job displacement will cut across the economy, and everybody will feel it in some way. It has already changed the shopping experience, shopping malls stand empty, and many big-name *main-street* brick-and-mortar stores have closed due to heavy financial losses.

Economists are studiously trying to anticipate what will happen when the next recession hits. Companies will indeed be tempted to deploy algorithms to replace the humans they must furlough to survive. Trucks and cars can already be driven without human intervention, and transaction counters can function well without human cashiers. In any case, it is clear to most researchers that human workers will continue to be replaced by computers.

'AI-First' Strategies

Companies, such as Google, whose business and operating models have always been driven by data, networks and software, have heavily invested in AI, adopting *AI-first* strategies. Google ads are increasingly personalised and contextualised by AI as the algorithms learn more about its users, ultimately increasing relevance and generating more revenue.

AI in the Education Industry

AI and machine learning have already contributed to the quality of online education. Still, there is much that AI will continue to revolutionise in terms teaching, learning and administration. Personalised interactive tutoring will have the ability to adjust content and adapt to the learning pace of each student separately while assessing their performance and giving direct feedback. Adaptive and interdisciplinary learning paths will continuously evaluate each student's performance and provide guidance to their learning paths, perhaps even influencing their choices in higher education. These shifts in educational paradigms will have a profound impact on quality of life, human interaction and values. Thus, there is a need for an earnest inquiry into the cultural repercussions of this phenomenon that extends beyond superficial AI analyses.

AI Regulation

To help us shape and realise a future AI-powered society that provides benefits and opportunities for all, we need leaders and social scientists to work together one policies and frameworks to help regulate and guide AI to promote innovation, protect society from harm and to build public trust.

The Challenge

To accelerate the benefits of AI and to mitigate risk, governments must proactively replace *analogue* policies and laws with digital and AI-friendly alternatives that are fair, equal and unbiased. There are many challenges that must be addressed:

- AI is a key driver of the Fourth Industrial Revolution. Algorithms are already being applied to improve predictions, optimise systems and drive productivity in many sectors.
- Early experience shows that AI can pose serious challenges. Without proper oversight, AI may replicate or even exacerbate human bias and discrimination, cause job displacement and lead to other unintended and harmful consequences.
- AI regulation is a complex endeavour and it needs expert oversight and useful frameworks. Regulatory and statutory requirements will diverge sharply across application areas. It is very likely that many jurisdictions will lack understanding and willingness to reach consensus to take action, and they will be left behind. Emergent controversies will also force governments to implement hastily constructed and suboptimal regulatory policies.

- A collaborative roadmap is needed to reimagine an agile regulatory system for AI that encourages innovation while minimising risks without being haphazard or disruptive.

These challenges present opportunities that we, as a society, must embrace in order to develop confidence and momentum for success.

The Opportunity

Stakeholders from all sectors should collaborate on co-designing innovative, agile frameworks for governing AI. Underpinning this is a belief that robust regulation promotes consumer confidence, provides opportunities for global mobility and gives social licence for the adoption of emerging technologies. Activities should adhere to the following three core objectives:

1. National and global conversations on regulating AI must be framed in a coherent and accessible manner.
2. Roadmaps for policymakers must be developed to facilitate decisions about whether and how to regulate AI.
3. Innovative approaches and tools for regulating AI must be identified and iterated and scaled.

There are already some great initiatives that we could build upon:

- The Centre for Data Ethics and Innovation (CDEI), an advisory body set up by the UK government in 2018, released a 121-page report calling on London to implement new rules on how social-media firms target users with posts, videos and ads. Their year-long review into the practice found that the 'existing regulation [was] out of step with the public's expectations'.
- Content-sharing apps like Facebook, YouTube, Twitter, Snapchat and TikTok all use machine-learning algorithms to tailor content for users based on the online community's activities. The CDEI was tasked by the government to examine these practices and to promulgate guidance on about to regulate AI to ensure that it is deployed and operated ethically.
- Research conducted with Ipsos Mori found that internet users generally distrusted tech platforms when it pertained to targeting, with only 29% of people in the UK trusting the platforms to target them in a responsible

way. They found that 61% of Britons wanted more regulatory oversight, whereas only 17% trusted tech platforms to regulate themselves.

- Britain is expected to crack down even further on big tech companies over how they manage harmful content. Proposals laid out by the government last year would introduce an independent regulator having the ability to impose heavy fines and liability on senior executives.

Since developing the manuscript for this book, the world has been gripped by the COVID-19 pandemic bringing to a dramatic stop businesses and severely impacting economies throughout the world. This crisis highlights something that has always been true about AI: it is a tool, and the value of its use in any situation is determined by the humans who design it and use it. Ultimately, in the current crisis, human action and innovation will determine how far AI is leveraged – across all parts of society.

SETTING THE SCENE

This book explores several topics that will challenging readers to understand the broad depths and spans of AI across all parts of society and the potential impacts on culture, social relations and *human* values. Although the target audience of this book is non-specific, it is designed for all people who think critically about the current and future social impact of AI, including educators, academics, professionals, non-professionals, researchers and more.

Organisation of the Book

This book is organised into 10 chapters, each exploring key topics that are important to consider when thinking about the future social implications of AI.

1. **Chapter 1: A New Dawn** provides an introduction to the main themes of this book, asking the reader to consider that AI may be creating expectations that perhaps cannot be fulfilled in the present day while potentially affecting our future in ways that we cannot predict – leading to a revolution or an evolution of human society.
2. **Chapter 2: A Brief History** explores the origins of AI and cognitive computing, terms often used interchangeably. Although these two topics are closely aligned, they have distinctive purposes and applications.

Together, they have the potential to enrich humans, societies and the world.

3. **Chapter 3: Unintended Consequences** is designed to inspire readers to consider the unintended consequences of AI while also accepting its potential and diversity of application across many aspects of society. Although huge investments are made daily by technology giants like Google, Amazon and Tesla, fears continue to grow about monopolies deepening the divide between the 'haves and have nots', raising difficult questions about the benefits of an AI-powered society.

4. **Chapter 4: Robots, Replicants, and Surrogates** provides an analysis of how AI and machine learning are making great strides towards a future powered by robots and intelligent systems. Most importantly, this chapter focuses on ethical and societal concerns. It asks the question, 'are we heading for a brave new world or a science fiction horror-show where AI and robots displace or, perhaps more worryingly, replace humans'?

5. **Chapter 5: AI in Industry** explores how AI has become a key component across diverse industries. When it comes to AI spending, China hopes to become the undisputed global leader by 2030, with its government investing USD 150B to support its goal.

6. **Chapter 6: AI in Emerging Markets** explores the effects of AI disruption in emerging markets that are harnessing technology much faster and more enthusiastically than many of their developed-market compatriots. With the potential economic benefits of AI already assumed, governments in many EM countries (e.g. China, South Korea, Russia, Hungary, Poland, the UAE and Saudi Arabia) are pursuing policies that will help leapfrog developed markets. Given these facts, new social, ethical, legal and security frameworks are urgently needed to avoid authoritarian and autocratic implementations that could ultimately suppress the rights, privacy and freedoms of citizens and communities.

7. **Chapter 7: Ethics of AI** is a debate that has been raging for some time, raising legitimate questions about how AI and automation will ultimately affect the privacy and human rights of all individuals globally. We need to develop our understanding of anthropology, sociology, psychology and cognitive science to even understand the repercussions.

8. **Chapter 8: Social Implications of AI** refers to anything that affects an individual, a community or the wider society. Many social implications have been and will continue to be surprising. Will people simply become consumers served by intelligent systems that respond to our every whim? Are we reaching a tipping point between convenience and dependency?

How will AI affect social issues relating to housing, finance, privacy, poverty and so on? Do we want a society in which machines supplementing or augment humans? It is important to be as clear as possible about the social implications to truly understand the benefits and risks.

9. **Chapter 9: The Future Is Already Here** is the penultimate chapter, and it poses a simple question: 'what will our society look like when AI is everywhere'? Additionally, according to award-winning science fiction author William Gibson, 'The future is already here – it's just not very evenly distributed'. Given prior declarations, the human race must forge a society that collectively and fairly controls how AI will 'write' the future to avoid the inequalities, social cancers and dysfunctional habits of today.

10. **Chapter 10: Closing Thoughts** invites the reader to consider a future based on our children and the world's youth: a world that encourages positive family structures and diverse communities, reduced social and structural inequalities, a fair distribution of opportunities and jobs, access to healthcare and financial and personal security. Our hope is that we can collectively work towards a future based on F.A.T.E. (Fairness, Accountability, Transparency and Ethics).

Acknowledgment

The past few years have been filled with many ups and downs – both in my personal and professional life. However, it has also been an opportunity to grow through self-reflection, self-healing and … writing!

Writing has given me opportunities to break free; reflecting on challenges beyond myself that affect wider society – social concerns such as climate change, income inequality, political polarisation and, perhaps most potent, the rise of smarter technological innovations fuelled by Artificial Intelligence (AI).

One thing is clear to me, as humans, we have the tools to re-imagine the status quo to optimistically create a future society that embraces AI in ways that promote trust, social integrity and cohesion for all humankind —in our homes, the workplace and across all parts of our communities where we interact and engage.

Special thanks must go to all of the authors whose work I've had the privilege of discovering in my research through blogs, journals, books, podcasts, real-time and recorded videos and events.

This extends to any person who strives to grow and help others grow – especially, in ways that enriches society.

Chapter 1
A New Dawn

ABSTRACT

People have varying (and often conflicting) beliefs, expectations, and fears of science and technology. While emerging technologies such as artificial intelligence (AI) may be no different, it has captured the imagination of people of all walks of life globally and is already trickling into our lives daily. When considering the future, the role of AI often polarises views of "a utopian versus dystopian future" throwing up a number of interesting questions about ethics, morality, religion, social values, regulation, and perhaps controversially, what it means to be human. Moreover, AI seems to be creating expectations that perhaps cannot be fulfilled in the present day but may (potentially) affect our future in ways that we still cannot comprehend. A new dawn of innovation is upon us, perhaps a revolution or an evolution of human society. This chapter presents this new dawn.

"Everything we love about civilization is a product of intelligence, so amplifying our human intelligence with artificial intelligence has the potential of helping civilization flourish like never before – as long as we manage to keep the technology beneficial." –Max Tegmark, President of the Future of Life Institute

DOI: 10.4018/978-1-7998-4607-9.ch001

INTRODUCTION

This book studies the social implications of artificial intelligence (AI) in society, the workplace, in industry and beyond. No prior knowledge is required.

People have varying and often conflicting beliefs, expectations and fears of science and technology. AI is no exception, and it has captured the imaginations of people of all walks of life and is already affecting into our daily lives. AI is all around us, from self-driving cars and drones to virtual assistants and apps for translation or investing. It is commonplace enough that economists refer to AI as a *general-purpose technology*. In recent years, there has been major advancements in AI driven by exponential increases in computing power and the vast amounts of available data. Software now being used to discover new drugs and to predict our cultural interests. Digital technologies interact with our biological world on a daily basis. Engineers, designers, data scientists and software architects have combined computational design, additive manufacturing, materials engineering and synthetic biology to pioneer a new symbiosis amongst micro-organisms, our bodies, the products we consume and even the homes and office spaces we inhabit.

We may be far away from super-intelligent AI systems, and there may yet be fundamental obstacles to achieving much beyond human intelligence. When considering the future, we often encounter polarised views of utopian vs. dystopian futures, raising several interesting questions about ethics, morality, religion, social values, regulations and what it means to be human. Some are concerned that AI will amplify the gaps between rich and poor and further enhance inequalities, prejudices and conscious/subconscious bias. AI is sure to further play a role in an ever-increasing surveillance-based society that may suffer from suffocating bureaucracy, malevolent governments and public manipulation via social media reminiscent of George Orwell's 'Nineteen Eighty-Four' (Orwell, 2003).

Although top experts often disagree about how to define AI and machine intelligence, it is essentially intelligence demonstrated by machines that mimic human cognitive functions associate with humans, including learning and problem solving (Russell, 2009). AI, as a distinct field of study, emerged in the 1950s concurrent with the invention of digital computers. The earliest methods of simulating intelligent decision-making are now commonly known as 'symbolic AI', which includes often Boolean programming methods that use symbols (e.g. letters and numbers) to describe rationally determined, rules-based operations. Considering that this represents most typical computer programs, many in the field do not recognise symbolic approaches as true AI. Nonetheless, such programmes are often considered 'AI' if they perform tasks previously thought to require human intelligent decision-making. For example, in 1996, IBM's Deep Blue chess-playing computer defeated the reigning world champion using exclusively symbolic, rules-based programming.

Notably, we tend to overestimate the impact of a technology in the short term but underestimate its impact in the long run. (Amara, 2016). AI has gone through cyclic booms of inflated expectations, and many people are disappointed that anticipated breakthroughs from the past have never materialised (Stone et al., 2016). Nonetheless, the next decade will surely see a steadily growing stream of AI applications across industries and emerging markets. This is further explored in Chapters 5 and 6. Although many of these applications may initially be niche, they will eventually become mainstream, causing substantial changes across businesses, institutions and communities. The changes will be transformational. However, such transformation comes with a price.

For all the benefits that will come through improved efficiency, safety and return of investment (ROI), there will be costs (Domingos, 2015). The nature of change is that it often seems to appear suddenly. While we are collectively engaged in day-to-day processes, policies and dramas, disruptive change surprises us, because it comes from places we least expect and in ways we never imagined, unless it is purposefully managed, that is, as with traditional transformation programmes.

Many experts claim that the rise of AI will make most people better off, but others are concerned about how advances in AI will affect humanity, as it simultaneously changes our productivity and free will (The Emerging Future, 2019).

FUTURE OF TECHNOLOGY

We are now living in the future of 20 years ago. Could we ever have imagined how important media and technology would be to our present-day society and our daily lives? It begs questions of how the world will look in 2050. Some futurists claim that the rate of technological progress is accelerating (Kurzweil, 2006). A decade ago, smartphones did not exist. Three decades earlier, no one owned a personal computer. Today, however, they are ubiquitous.

In less than 10 years, technology should be widely available that will allow us to control machines with eye movements. Perhaps we will even be able to ingest nano-sized robots to repair injuries from within our bodies. By 2036, predictive AI should be able to predict near-future events (e.g. elections, weather, geopolitical events) with impressive precision. Even farther down the line, human brains and machines may interface directly and biophysically, creating all kinds of new possibilities.

The book, 'Soonish', by Kelly and Zach Weinersmith (Weinersmith, 2017), deep dives into a set of 10 emerging technologies that are expected to rapidly change our society for better or for worse. This book is their funny and feeble (by their own admission) attempt at predicting what technology will look like in the nebulous future. The authors stipulate that there is no telling what will actually happen with technology in the coming decades. Too many different emergent ideas will spawn from different fields of study to impact research in ways we cannot predict.

Predictions aside, one thing is certain. The confluence of robotics, AI and increasing levels of automation is a prevailing trend in the projected timeline of future technology.

Automated Intelligence

The terms, 'AI' and 'automation', are often used interchangeably. They are associated with software or physical robots and other intelligent machines that allow us to operate more efficiently and effectively, whether it entails a mechanical robot piecing together a car or sending a follow-up email the day after a customer creates a draft order without having 'checked out'. However, there are many differences between the two terms. Automation basically entails hardware and/or software that does things automatically without human intervention. On the other hand, AI is all about trying to make machines or software mimic and eventually supersede human behaviour and intelligence. Automation has a single purpose: to let machines perform repetitive, monotonous tasks or, as some people say, 'to take the robot out of the human'.

Television and movies have shaped popular conceptions of robots, from 'Lieutenant-commander Data' from 'Star Trek: The Next Generation', 'HAL' from '2001: A Space Odyssey', 'C3PO' and 'R2D2' from 'Star Wars' and the 'T-series' androids from the 'Terminator' films. Such highly-capable intelligent machines powered by AI are portrayed having quirky, human-like personalities. In the real world, AI-enabled robots do not make compelling fictional characters. However, they are becoming increasingly useful to humans.

For decades, intelligent machines and, more specifically robots, were used only for monotonous and difficult tasks on factory floors. Today, automation is everywhere. It powers drones, cars and, perhaps worryingly, *social* robots that cross the 'uncanny valley' by convincing us that they are human. As humans, our individual intelligence determines many of our actions and, perhaps, reactions. From an evolutionary perspective, humans are born into a world in which they are continuously expected to accomplish tasks (e.g. getting food, avoiding threats, mating) to survive. Because our living environments vary, brains must be flexible enough to optimise human adaptation by building new associations between various stimuli and responses. Human beings constantly react and adapt to their environment by learning through conditioning, frequently unconsciously (Ormrod, 2012). However, there is more to human learning than conditioning, which, to the best of our knowledge, makes us different from other species. Additionally, the learning potential amongst humans differs.

Importantly, no matter how intelligent a person is, gaining expertise in a complex and sophisticated field requires deliberate practice and an immense investment of time (Ericsson et al., 1993). Intelligence differences become apparent once time has been invested to reach a certain degree of expertise (Hambrick et al., 2014). We also experience far more implicit social influences than we are ever aware of (Devos and Banaji, 2003). Nevertheless, we are viewed as autonomous, because there is an extent to which our own individual intelligence also influences our behaviour.

Just like humans, AI is very bad at simply following orders. However, *following orders* is not what AI is designed to do; it is designed to constantly seek patterns (like humans), learn from experience (like humans) and self-select the appropriate responses to situations based on those things (like humans). Thus, what we are actually dealing with here is not simple replication of humans. Instead, it is about creating a system that is more powerful than we can imagine. AI-driven automation stands to transform the economy over the coming years and decades.

Economic Impact of AI

Humans have never been very good at using new technologies in new ways. The Analysis Group (Chen et al., 2016) ran an exhaustive study comparing the impact of historic innovations, like broadband access, mobile phones and the first wave of information technology to provide a comparative lens focusing on emergent AI. Even when using the most conservative estimates, they predicted that AI's direct economic impact would be USD 1.49–2.95T from 2017 to 2027. During this period, AI is predicted to have wide-ranging applications, including but not limited to:

- Machine learning that automates analytical models using algorithms that operate without human assistance. Potential applications include identifying new drugs (e.g. healthcare and pharma), self-driving cars and fraud prevention (i.e. cybersecurity).
- Improved natural language processing that allows computers to better analyse, understand, process and generate natural-language-based interfaces with humans. This extends to personal-assistant applications, such as Alexa, Google Assistant and Siri.
- Machine vision that allows computers to identify objects, scenes and activities in images and videos. Applications include improved descriptions for the visually impaired, car-safety systems that detect pedestrians, cyclists and objects when parking and street view maps.

The report went to great lengths to call out the fundamental differences in adopting complex AI vs. merely expanding access to broadband, suggesting that early adopters would share disproportionately in those economic gains.

In the future, technological innovation is expected to lead to a supply-side revolution with long-term gains in cost, efficiency and productivity. Transportation and communication costs will drop, logistics and global supply chains will become more effective and the cost of trade will diminish, which will open new markets and drive economic growth. Growth in AI is expected to lead to increased revenues and employment with existing businesses and institutions as well as the creation of entirely new economic activities. Productivity improvements in existing sectors could be realised by faster and more efficient processes and decision-making with increased knowledge and access to information.

The main reason why AI is significantly different than past technological innovations is that it allows us to move away from a traditional rules-based approaches[1] towards prediction-based approaches: an area in which AI thrives (Agrawal et al., 2018).

Figure 1. Prediction machines and task management
(Agrawal et al., 2018)

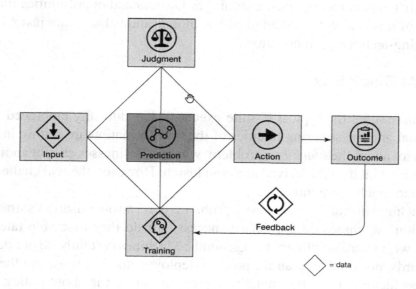

From an economist's perspective, AI is unique compared with past technological innovations. This leads to the assumption of certain truisms:

- When something gets cheaper, we use more of it. Across all businesses, institutions and communities, people are quick to take advantage of better, cheaper and faster products.
- When the cost of something drops, it affects the value of other things[2]. Demand for complementary items increases, substitute items decrease. For example, if the cost of coffee were to fall, the value and cost of the complementary items (e.g. cream and sugar) will increase. If people switch from tea to coffee, the value and cost of tea will drop.
- When costs fall, one must make trade-offs and adjustments to business models. To maximise and scale the benefits realised from cost changes, businesses must adjust its strategic priorities, refresh business processes and update organisational structures. This might include re-allocating or incentivising staffs to operate in new ways.

As machine intelligence increases and the cost of machine prediction decreases, the value of human prediction will decrease as well. However, contrary to the dystopian viewpoint this idea inspires, humans will likely play new roles yet unimagined. Perhaps the key is understanding how benefits of an AI-driven society will be distributed amongst businesses and citizens in ways that avoids monopolies, encourages fairness and opportunities for all. Much of this is directly linked to ethics, morals and values – not just AI and emerging-technology innovations.

The AI Black Box

We can assume the typical C-suite executive has dutifully embraced AI's potential and the sobering realities of the transformation are setting in. We hear a lot about the *black-box* problem, wherein businesses cannot audit the means by which an AI arrived at a conclusion. However, the real challenges are often much more mundane.

Machines do not define business problems or set an organisation's strategic direction. Machines do not define success, nor do they assemble talented teams with interdisciplinary backgrounds. Machines certainly do not define standards, nor do they plan for product deployments. Yet those are the key success factors of AI. It is not about programming; it is about policy. It is not about training models; it is about talent. It is not about business logic; it is about business planning.

For many businesses and institutions, workloads are increasing and organisational readiness is plodding along. Many AI projects are prototyped with poorly configured data and fail to make production, either because the organisation does not have a data model that supports the project or because outdated governance starves the project of funding. In other cases, legacy systems wreak havoc on the data itself.

Although it is clear that most organisations do not possess the right talent to achieve progress with AI, the C-suite executives should begin by bringing world-class business strategists, product designers, developers, data scientists and AI experts into the organisation to programme today, rather than spend a lot of time and effort assembling the right kind of team and, ultimately, taking longer to achieving efficiencies and ROI.

Is Society Ready for the AI Future?

The past few decades have born witness to many positive impacts of technology on society (Ramey, 2012), all of which will continue to flourish and expand further, including

- Mechanisation of agriculture, enabling higher yields and ROI across emerging countries
- Improved transportation that provides mobility for people and goods across air, land, sea and space
- Digital communication, which enables the exchange of ideas to further develop our societies
- Transformed educational and learning processes, the backbone of every economy

Although humanity is at the cusp of another quantitative change (i.e. the Fourth Industrial Revolution (4IR)), the human conscience does not appear to be advancing in the same manner (Schwab, 2016). 4IR could yield greater inequality, particularly with its potential to disrupt labour markets, governments and businesses. As automation substitutes for labour across the economy, the net displacement of workers by machines might exacerbate the gap between returns of capital and labour. On the other hand, it is possible that the displacement of workers by technology will, in aggregate, result in a net increase in safe and rewarding jobs. The largest beneficiaries of innovation tend to be the providers of intellectual and physical capital (i.e. the innovators, shareholders and investors), which explains the rising gap in wealth between those dependent on capital vs. labour.

If account for previous industrial revolutions, the effects of breakthroughs and innovations are cyclical. In the case of 4IR, technology is a main reason why incomes have stagnated or even decreased for most of the population in high-income countries. The demand for highly skilled workers has increased, while the demand for workers with less education and lower skills has decreased. The result is a job market with a strong demand at the highest and lowest ends, but a hollowing of the middle. In the future, talent, more than capital, will represent the critical factor of production. This will give rise to a job market increasingly segregated into low-skill/low-pay and high-skill/high-pay segments, which, in turn, will lead increased social tensions.

Moreover, rather than coming together and championing non-partisan activities, governments across the world appear to be pursuing their own interests. An example of this is the political trend of President Trump's 'Make America Great Again' campaign and British voters' response to the 'Brexit' referendum, giving Britons their 'bring back control' campaign. Both of these sentiments imply that we need to return to something. Thus, when talking about the future, there is often a mental attempt to return to the past. Thus, politicians are not to blame for these sentiments and campaigns. Instead, they are the products of a public consciousness reflecting western society.

It is important to understand that no process will create a single end state, just as the technological developments predicted by Charles Babbage and the socio-economic changes advocated by Karl Marx did not. This will be also true for AI globalisation. All images of the future are projections of our imaginations, and, even if they come true, it will be do so in the manner we forecasted. Because these images and ideas are at the centre of public rhetoric, society will continue changing it.

Technology Is Not Destiny

The advent of computers and the internet raised the relative productivity of higher-skilled workers. Routine-intensive occupations that focused on predictable, easily programmable tasks, including switchboard operators, filing clerks, travel agents and assembly-line workers, were particularly vulnerable to replacement by technology. Some occupations were virtually eliminated, and the demand for others reduced. Technological innovation over this period increased the productivity of those engaged in abstract thinking, creative tasks and problem-solving and was, therefore, at least partially responsible for the substantial growth in jobs employing such traits. Shifting demand towards more skilled labour raised the relative pay of this group, contributing to rising inequality.

Today, the effects of AI are felt unevenly through the economy. It is challenging to predict exactly which jobs will be most immediately affected by AI-driven automation, because AI is not a single technology. It is rather a collection of technologies that are applied to specific tasks. Some tasks will be more easily automated than others, and some jobs will be affected more than others both negatively and positively. Some jobs will be automated away, while, for others, AI-driven automation will make workers more productive and increase demand for certain skills. Finally, new jobs are likely to be directly created with respect to the development and supervision of AI and indirectly in a range of areas throughout the economy as higher incomes lead to increased demand.

Society, therefore, has an opportunity to shape and control AI and AI-driven automation through non-technical factors, including aspects of both the broader economy and policies created by institutions and governments. Ultimately, *policy* will play a large role in shaping the effects of technological changes, including those of AI. A great example of this was demonstrated by the US Presidential Executive Order (EOP, 2016) that directed an in-depth study into AI automation and its effects on the US economy. It provided two significant insights drawn from 'The Future of AI Institute'. First, the direction of innovation is not a random shock to the economy, but the product of decisions made by firms, governments and individuals. Economic factors will continue to drive the direction of technological change. Second, there is a role for policy to help amplify the best effects of automation and temper the worst.

For many societies, technological advancements are adopted by entrepreneurs, workers and firms looking to better serve a market or streamline production processes. These decisions are underpinned by public investments in basic and applied research, infrastructure and other public goods. Innovations that are likely to be profitable and which are technologically feasible are the ones that gain traction. Practical strategies from the results of the study directed by the executive order are adapted and generalised to apply to citizens across all societies as shared below (EOP, 2016):

Strategy #1: Invest in and develop AI for its many benefits.
Strategy #2: Educate and train citizens for jobs of the future.
Strategy #3: Aid citizens in the transition and empower them to ensure broadly shared growth.

In all cases, the government with businesses, institutions and communities has an increasingly important role to play in advancing the field of AI by investing in research and development, for establishing pro-competition policies and encouraging competition from new and existing businesses. As Nick Bostrom puts it, success in AI will yield a 'civilisational trajectory that leads to a compassionate and jubilant use of humanity's cosmic endowment' (Bostrom, 2016). The future impact of AI is perhaps the most important issue humanity will ever face. Instead of passively drifting, we must steer the course. Otherwise, we will only have ourselves to blame for the mistakes.

FUTURE OF SOCIETY

Humans are heterogeneous, and a harmonious society can only exist because of *trade-offs* between people and communities (Russell, 2019). Today, society is affected by several overwhelming challenges, ranging from climate change, ageing populations, rising sea levels, new geopolitical tensions and dwindling natural resources. Social structures, such as the nuclear family, have largely disintegrated, and the stability previously offered by extended families and close-knit communities has diminished. Increasingly our *me-first* society has become competitive and materialistic, addicted to selfish pleasures. We have created a *snowflake* generation forced to grow up too fast. According to David Elkind, an American child psychologist and professor of child study who wrote 'The Hurried Child', these are the young people who are now helping form and mould our society as they graduate from colleges and universities and move into positions of influence within *the system* of society. The question, therefore, must be asked, 'have they missed elements of their childhood, and has this resulted in deficient young adults' (Elkind, 2006)? Perhaps alarmingly, we seem more interested in pursuing ideas of abandoning our planet and escaping to Mars rather than serving our society and preparing the next generation, our children, for the future. Simultaneously, technology and human life cannot be separated. Society has a co-dependence with technology. If we accept that AI is poised to change how we live and work in profound ways and that it is indeed a key component of our future society and the mechanism of some type of reformation, we will must introduce ideas from psychology, economics, political theory and moral philosophy (Russell, 2019). We must consider social, economic, educational and policy reforms that increase the coefficient of altruism (e.g. the weight that each individual places on the welfare of others) while decreasing the coefficients of sadism, pride and envy. Should we recruit AI and intelligent machines to help with this process? If so, we must tread carefully.

Short Termism

Human nature is characterised by a predominantly horizontal and short-term sense of direction. People's eyes have always wandered, continually on the lookout for potential dangers and possible prey. Thus, we have a natural disposition to protect ourselves and our kin. However, we do not have the same natural disposition to protect those who come after us, let alone other species. According to (Taflinger, 1996), three main elements contribute to human behaviour from a biological perspective:

- self-preservation
- the reason for self-preservation (reproduction)
- a method to enhance self-preservation and reproduction (greed)

We can thus surmise that favouring our own genes is deeply ingrained in our nature as humans. We have no such natural disposition to protect our own genes down the generations. This is something we must learn.

Given the profound impact of AI on society, we are forced to consider perspectives that are new in the history of both mankind and our planet. We have arrived at a new starting point in which we are not only capable of but are also compelled to protect our descendants 100 or 1000 years from now. Moreover, we must accept that we are responsible for all life on this planet forever. There is perhaps no other species with this joint level of capability and responsibility.

We often say that we have cultural roots and traditions to protect. However, with our power to destroy and dominate, we must protect our natural roots, too. Our civilisation has lasted millennia, but our natural preconditions are far older. It is well and good that literary treasures of Greek or Indian origin can now be translated into any other languages, we may justifiably have a cultural obligation to do so, because, from experience, it takes less than a decade to wipe out a species of flora or fauna that nature spent millions of years evolving. Nature, however, also becomes more impoverished and more exposed to further disintegration when there are diminished species of plants, fungi, invertebrates, fish, reptiles, amphibians, birds etc. The planet becomes poorer, as do we as humans. Quite literally, the threat to biodiversity is a threat to our own existence. When bees no longer buzz, there will be less fruit.

The breakdown of climate, ecosystems and biological diversity is, above all, a threat to the fair distribution of the world's resources, because people in the richest parts of the world have are now accustomed to buying themselves out of most world problems. Modern civilisation has depleted the biodiversity of this planet, and the rate of extinction is greater now than at any time in recorded history. Incidentally, we have retained our selfish human nature. Nevertheless, we can no longer afford to relate to only other humans. We are part of the Earth we live on, and it is a significant part of our identity. Just as the struggle for human rights never ends, the struggle to preserve our ecosystems and the biological diversity of this planet should never end.

Mankind may just be the only living creature in the entire universe having a higher consciousness and a burgeoning sense of this huge and enigmatic universe. Conserving the living environment of this planet is not just a global responsibility. It is a cosmic responsibility.

Theory of Human Values

In order for us to influence and embed human values into AI and machine-learning systems, we must develop a theory and classification framework to be used to in the supporting algorithms. According to Stuart Armstrong (Armstrong, 2018), there are four common methods of providing useful classifications about how we should extract the values of humanity:

- Methods that put high weight on human (bounded) quasi-rationality or revealed preferences. For example, we can assume that Kasparov was actually trying to win against Deep Blue and was not deliberately trying to lose while inadvertently playing excellent chess.
- Methods that pay attention to our explicitly stated values.
- Methods that use regret, surprise, joy or similar emotions to estimate what humans actually want. This could be a form of human temporal difference learning.
- Methods based on an explicit procedure for constructing values (e.g. Coherent extrapolated volition[3] and Paul's indirect normativity).

Society 5.0

What will human life be like 10 or 20 years from now? Will it be enslaved and colonised by machines as in 'Terminator' movies? Dystopian options notwithstanding, it is relatively easy to imagine a world where humans live better while being supported by technology in idealised conditions. This concept is called 'Society 5.0' (Wahyudi, 2014), a human-centred pervasive society fuelled by AI, autonomous vehicles, internet of things, blockchain and other digital advances. Figure 2 visualises the roadmap to Society 5.0.

Figure 2. Phases of societal change

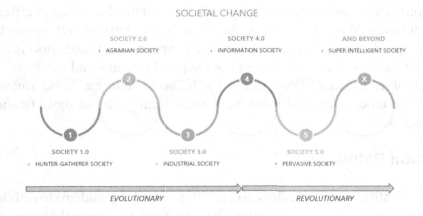

Table 1 provides a description of each of the phases outlined in Figure 2.

Table 1. Description of societal phases

Phase	Description
Society 1.0 (Hunting Period)	Humans start making equipment from rocks. This equipment was used for hunting wild animals for food ingredients, and the skins were used for clothing.
Society 2.0 (Agricultural Period)	Humans began to find ways to make tools from iron. In addition to hunting, they began farming to fulfil their food needs.
Society 3.0 (Industrial Period)	Humans found ways to work and survive more efficiently using machines. Transportation equipment also rapidly developed.
Society 4.0 (Information Period)	This is the current period. All forms of human activity cannot be separated from the data stream. The internet and digital technologies (e.g. wearables, mobile, tablets) continue to grow rapidly and cannot be separated from everyday human life.
Society 5.0 (Pervasive Period)	All data collected since the Society 4.0 period will be processed and converted into a new *artificial general intelligence* or 'strong AI', giving rise to *intelligence everywhere*. Anything a human can do, a strong AI can also do. The Turing test, where a machine exhibits intelligence indistinguishable from a human, has been fully surpassed.
Society X.0 (Super Intelligence Period)	The age of *singularity* with an abundance of artificial super intelligence surpasses human intelligence and ability exponentially. A new species emerges (i.e. *singularity people*, coined by futurist Ray Kurzweil (Ready for AI, 2018)). After the singularity moment, society will consist of a newly evolved human (i.e. *trans-humans* or H+).

It seems, therefore, that we can breathe easier after reflecting on Society 5.0's vision. Humans will not be replaced by machines, but we will become the centre of social life while machines become a supporting system. AI will help provide alternative choices for humans, but humans will still make the decisions. There will be more energy sources available that are more efficient and environmentally friendly. Automation in the agricultural sector will increase production efficiency and reduce the problem of food shortages. In the health sector, there will be more AI support systems and robots so that the risk of accidents and congestion levels can be reduced. In the financial sector, the blockchain will break new ground carrying out daily financial transactions.

Solution Pathways

A non-scientific survey (Anderson et al, 2018) asked respondents to elaborate whether or not AI would leave people better off and to express their concerns and thoughts on *pathways* to potential solutions. 979 people participated and included a diverse mix of technology pioneers, innovators, developers, business and policy leaders, researchers and activists. The general feeling was that a networked AI would amplify human effectiveness while threatening human autonomy, agency and capabilities. Many conceded that computers might match or even exceed human intelligence and capabilities when applied to tasks, such as complex decision-making, reasoning, learning, sophisticated analytics, pattern recognition, visual acuity, speech recognition and language translation. There was consensus on the benefits across communities of smart systems regarding saving time, money and lives while offering new opportunities for individuals. Overall, apart from the fearful downsides, 63% of the respondents said they were hopeful that most individuals would be mostly better off by 2030, and 37% said people would not be better off. Several of the thought leaders said humans' expanding reliance on AI and machine-learning systems would only go well if close attention were to be paid to how these tools, platforms and networks are engineered, distributed, maintained and updated. The main themes are summarised in Table 2.

Table 2. Concerns and solution paths

Theme	Options	Description	Comments
CONCERNS	**Human Agency** Individuals experience loss of control over their lives	Decision-making on key aspects of digital life is automatically ceded to code-driven *black-box* tools. People lack input and do not learn the context about how the tools work. They sacrifice independence, privacy and power over choice; they have no control over these processes. This effect will deepen as automated systems become more prevalent and complex.	Control measures must be developed that help protect human liberty and dignity.
	Data Abuse Data use and complex surveillance systems is designed for profit or for exercising power	Most AI tools are and will be in the hands of companies striving for profits or governments striving for power. Values and ethics are often not baked into the digital systems making decisions for people. These systems are globally networked and are not easy to check of regulate.	Data governance and updated privacy laws may be required.
	Job loss The AI takeover of jobs widens economic divides, leading to social upheaval	The efficiencies and other economic advantages of code-based machine intelligence will continue to disrupt all aspects of human work. Although some expect new jobs will emerge, others worry about massive job losses, widening economic divides and social upheavals, including populist uprisings.	Without collective actions across government, business and communities that offer genuine options against job losses, this will only lead to inequality, potential poverty and other social issues that, in turn, may lead to mass demonstrations, strikes and general anarchy.
	Dependence Lock-in Reduction of individuals' cognitive, social and survival skills	Many see AI as augmenting human capacities, but some predict the opposite, that people's deepening dependence on machine-learning systems will erode their abilities to think for themselves, act independently and interact effectively with others.	A new approach to the democratisation and access to AI systems must be developed with laws, policies and competition. Otherwise, there is a danger of monopolies locking in.
	Mayhem Autonomous weapons, cybercrime and weaponised information	Some predict further erosion of traditional socio-political structures and the possibility of great losses of lives, owing to the accelerated growth of autonomous military applications and the use of weaponised information to destabilise groups. Some also fear cybercriminals' reach into economic systems.	This has echoes of science fiction wherein AI and machine-learning systems (e.g. robots) take control and attack or pacify humans. Again, new laws and regulations must be developed to protect society against criminals, dictators or fundamentalist regimes that intend to harm civilians and collective liberties.
SUGGESTED SOLUTIONS	**Global Good is No.1** Improve human collaboration across borders and stakeholder groups	Digital co-operation to serve humanity's best interests is the top priority. Ways must be found for people around the world to come to common understandings and agreements and to join forces to facilitate the innovation of widely accepted approaches aimed at tackling wicked problems and maintaining control over complex human-digital networks.	Without national and international cross-border and non-partisan alliances, this will be difficult to realise.
	Values-based Systems Develop policies to assure AI will be directed at 'human-ness' and common good	Adopt a 'moon-shot mentality' to build inclusive, decentralised intelligent digital networks 'imbued with empathy' that help humans aggressively ensure that technology meets social and ethical responsibilities.	New levels of regulatory and certification processes will be necessary across industries and countries. Embedding empathy into AI systems is a slight oxymoron provided bias, prejudices and all other types of social inequalities find their way into algorithms. This will require new levels of governance and quality controls of AI systems.
	Prioritise people Alter economic and political systems to better help humans 'race with the robots'	Re-organise economic and political systems towards the goal of expanding humans' capacities and capabilities to heighten human/AI collaboration and stem trends that would compromise human relevance in the face of programmed and self-learning AI intelligence.	This raises important questions about what type of society we want in the future. We must re-imagine roles and collective responsibilities of individuals, communities, businesses and governments to serve society as a whole.

Human Labour Challenges

Technology has never been neutral. Its social, political and moral impacts are becoming painfully clear. However, the stakes will only get higher as connected AI-enabled systems constantly monitor individuals and communities, algorithms oversee society's most critical decisions, and transport, jobs and even war become automated. The tech industry has not yet earned the trust these technologies demand. Technology companies typically require fewer employees in their workforce compared with businesses in the pre-digital era. Table 3 presents a comparison of past companies and their digital equivalents.

Table 3. Comparison of analogue and digital companies

Company	Number of People	Generated Profit
KODAK	140,000	USD 28B
INSTAGRAM	13	USD 1B
BLOCKBUSTER	60,000	USD 5.9B
NETFLIX	4400	USD 2.5B

If AI genuinely displaces humans in the workplace, we will need to rethink how we will earn money to work, rest and play. Although there may be new jobs available, new skills will need to be learnt, which will require time and investment, potentially leading to missed opportunities as demand rises. This is why many countries are calling for some form of universal basic income (UBI). Small-scale trials have taken place around the world, including in Finland, Canada, US, India and Namibia, each using different methods that have delivered mixed results. In principle, according to an article in *The Independent* (The Independent, 2018), UBI would remove many of the income traps that deter people from moving away from welfare programmes into the work force. However, any radical reform to social security must be well-considered. Inevitably, there will be trade-offs, such as increases in taxation to fund a generous UBI. However, if set too high, it could inadvertently destroy many incentives, render the economy uncompetitive and unattractive for internal and external investment, damage the government and endanger the sustainability of social programmes. Given the fact that the idea has been around since 1516 and that its implementation has been stubbornly resisted, perhaps it will remain as Thomas More indicated in the title of his book, a 'Utopia' (More, 1984).

Business executives preach the strategic importance of AI and machine learning, but they typically do not invest in methods of breaking down barriers for their data-science and machine-learning teams. For example, a 2019 report from Syncsort (Cheplick, 2019) revealed that 68% of companies knew their data analytics efforts were hampered by data siloes, but only 25% named data analytics as a top priority. Most distressingly, the hiring landscape for skilled talent has only become more competitive, and experts in these fields show increasing levels of job dissatisfaction. A Stack Overflow survey (Developer Survey Results, 2018) of developers found that machine-learning and data-science specialists topped the list of developers looking for new jobs at 14.3 and 13.2%, respectively. 72.8% of developers were more worried about the potential dangers of AI compared to the possibilities it might offer.

Ultimately, businesses have a responsibility to develop new ways to retain, retrain and incentivise their workforce to help allay fears about job security brought on by AI disruption. This will be a challenge shared across all types and sizes of businesses in a variety of sectors. Additionally, governments should also find ways to support citizens by introducing new economic initiatives and support mechanisms to avoid an AI-induced recession.

AN OPTIMISTIC VIEW

Taking a cue from Bina Venkataraman, a former climate adviser to the Obama administration, we should take a purposefully optimistic view of the future (Venkataraman, 2019). These days, we are all caught-up in our own day-to-day lives and challenges, and there appears to be little time to stop and reflect. Businesses tend to focus on profits and market share and fail to consider the well-being of their workforce, their customers and the environment. Politicians seem to be forever seeking to score points and engage in meaningless debates without properly representing the people who voted for them and upholding the democracy they frequently pandered to on their soap boxes. Schools are busy competing for funding, jockeying for position on league tables and increasing the number of assessments and exams that our children must partake in without really trying to measure what really matters in regard to how our children will fare and survive in tomorrow's world. We celebrate (and sometimes suffer at the hands of) climate change and environmental *green* activism, but we fail to hold leaders accountable for longer term, non-partisan action plans that are inclusive and preventative of potential disasters in the first place. Our collective *mistakes* across businesses, institutions and communities could summarised as follows:

1st mistake: what we measure. We do not measure that which is good for the long term.
2nd mistake: what and how we reward ourselves and others. We focus too much on the short term.
3rd mistake: how we plan for the future. We fail to imagine what lies ahead

This is where human intellect, algorithms and machine-learning systems might serve us well. If we instead focus on the long term while also focusing on the needs of the present, we might be able to create the right futures with the right *heirlooms* that serve, empower and protect our children and future generations. To survive and succeed in the future regardless of the disruptive technologies that may exist, we must think of ourselves as both descendants and ancestors of society and humanity (Venkataraman, 2019).

FUTURE RESEARCH DIRECTIONS

Whether or not AI and intelligent machines should provide a helping hand in shaping our future societies, the question of how we achieve a world that is safer, fairer and more civil still remains. We must do this while preventing technology innovation from diluting or devaluing our human values, ethics or morals.

Future research should explore how we can teach morality to AI systems without introducing bias and negative behaviours that have, thus far led to the rise of the 'me generation.' We should instead lead the way to the 'we generation' and enable ourselves to be more aware of the ties that bind us. Naturally, this means that humans should first define morality in a way AI and intelligent machines can process and model.

CONCLUSION

Society finds itself at great cross-roads. With the advent of AI and intelligent machines, we have an opportunity to control our legacy and our future. We still have time to do it right, but we need to be wise in how we go forward.

We must join forces and integrate together across communities, regions and countries and drop the behaviours that created the 'me generation' so that we can evolve to a 'we generation', where everyone's welfare counts.

Responding to the economic effects of AI-driven automation will be a significant challenge for all governments. AI has already begun to transform the workplace in many countries, changing the types of jobs available and the skills that workers need to thrive. Everyone should have the opportunity to participate in and address these challenges to help shape new economic policies, social and domestic laws and regulations that protect rather than restrict liberties.

Regarding new policies, all businesses and institutions across private, public and non-profit sectors should be invited to participate. Continued engagement amongst government, industry, technical and policy experts is crucial. In all countries, the public should play an important role in moving society towards shared prosperity and a creative realisation of AI without succumbing to dystopian realities. It is time we acknowledged what truly makes us a human society not as individuals but as a species. Additionally, we need to find ways to embrace AI and related technological innovations that move us closer to utopian future and a world in which humans are supplemented and augmented by AI rather than replaced. Undoubtedly, no single solution will be sufficient. We require systemic policies with social, economic and political frameworks that begin at the governmental level while inviting the rest of society to 'opt in' and make changes happen.

Humans are relentless problem solvers who relish challenges and opportunities to innovate. A case in point is climate change. This global problem has attracting many intelligent minds of all ages who are tabling unorthodox ideas that might help humanity relearn how to adapt to and change our environment for the better. Instead of ignoring, harming or plundering nature, we need to find a more natural role to play in it.

REFERENCES

Agrawal, A., Gans, J., & Goldfarb, A. (2018). *Prediction Machines: The Simple Economics of Artificial Intelligence*. Harvard Business Review Press.

Amara, R. (2016). 1925–2007, American futurologist. In S. Ratcliffe (Ed.), Oxford Essential Quotations (4th ed.). Academic Press.

Anderson, J., Rainie, L., & Luchsinger, A. (2018). Artificial Intelligence and the Future of Humans. *Pew Research Centre*. https://www.pewresearch.org/internet/2018/12/10/artificial-intelligence-and-the-future-of-humans/

Bostrom, N. (2014). *Superintelligence: Paths, Dangers, Strategies*. Oxford, UK: Oxford University Press.

Brynjolfsson, E., & McAfee, A. (2014). *The Second Machine Age: Work, Progress, and Prosperity in a Time of Brilliant Technologies*. New York: WW Norton & Company.

Chen, N., Christensen, L., Gallagher, K., Mate, R., & Rafert, G. (2016). *Global Economic Impacts Associated with Artificial Intelligence*. Economic Impact Study.

Cheplick, J. (2019). *Syncsort's 2019 Data Trends Results*. https://blog.syncsort.com/2019/03/big-data/2019-data-trends-survey/

Devos, T., & Banaji, M. R. (2003). Implicit self and identity. *Annals of the New York Academy of Sciences, 1001*(1), 177–211. doi:10.1196/annals.1279.009 PMID:14625361

Domingos, P. (2015). *The Master Algorithm: How the Quest for the Ultimate Learning Machine Will Remake Our World*. New York: Basic Books.

Elkind, D. (2006). *The Hurried Child: Growing Up Too Fast Too Soon* (25th ann. ed.). Da Capo Press.

Elliott, J. (1987). Moral and Ethical Considerations in Karl Marx's Robust Vision of the Future Society. *International Journal of Social Economics, 14*(10), 3–26. doi:10.1108/eb014085

Ericsson, K. A., Krampe, R. T., & Tesch-Römer, C. (1993). The role of deliberate practice in the acquisition of expert performance. *Psychological Review, 100*(3), 363–406. doi:10.1037/0033-295X.100.3.363

Executive Office of the President (EOP). (2016). Artificial Intelligence, Automation, and the Economy. *The Future of AI Initiative*. https://obamawhitehouse.archives.gov/sites/whitehouse.gov/files/documents/Artificial-Intelligence-Automation-Economy.PDF

Funke, D. (2018). Fact-checkers have debunked this fake news site 80 times. It's still publishing on Facebook. *Poynter.org*. Available at https://www.poynter.org/news/fact-checkers-have-debunked-fake-news-site-80-times-its-still-publishing-facebook

Grace, K., Salvatier, J., Dafoe, A., Zhang, B., & Evans, O. (2018). *When Will AI Exceed Human Performance?* Evidence from AI Experts.

Green, G. (2019, Oct.). Customer satisfaction, market share and profitability: Tech, The Shape of Things to Come. *Business Life*, 28-34.

Hambrick, D. Z., Oswald, F. L., Altmann, E. M., Meinz, E. J., Gobet, F., & Campitelli, G. (2014). Deliberate practice: Is that all it takes to become an expert? *Intelligence*, *45*, 34–45. doi:10.1016/j.intell.2013.04.001

Kurzweil, R. (2006). *The Singularity Is Near: When Humans Transcend Biology*. Penguin Books.

Midoes, C. (2019). Universal basic income and the Finnish experiment. *Bruegel Blog Post*. https://bruegel.org/2019/02/universal-basic-income-and-the-finnish-experiment/

More, T. (1965). Utopia. London: Penguin Books. (Original publication 1516)

Ormrod, J. E. (2012). *Human Learning* (6th ed.). Pearson.

Orwell, G. (2003). *The Complete Works of George Orwell*. https://www.george-orwell.org/1984

Ramey, K. (2012). *Technology and Society – Impact of Technology on Society*. https://www.useoftechnology.com/technology-society-impact-technology-society/

Ready for AI. (2018). *Is AI singularity the only conclusion of Artificial Intelligence?* https://readyforai.com/article/is-ai-singularity-the-only-conclusion-of-artificial-intelligence/

Russell, P. (2019). *Human Compatible: AI and the Problem of Control*. Allen Lane.

Russell, S. J., & Peter, N. (2009). *Artificial Intelligence: A Modern Approach* (3rd ed.). Upper Saddle River, NJ: Prentice Hall.

Schwab, K. (2016). The Fourth Industrial Revolution: what it means, how to respond. *World Economic Forum.* https://www.weforum.org/agenda/2016/01/the-fourth-industrial-revolution-what-it-means-and-how-to-respond/

Stone, P., Brooks, R., Brynjolfsson, E., Calo, R., Etzioni, O., & Hager, G. (2016). *One-hundred-year study on artiðcial intelligence: Report of the 2015-2016 study panel. Technical report.* Stanford University.

Taflinger, R. (1996). *The Biological Basis of Human Behaviour. Chapter Three: Biological Evolution.* https://public.wsu.edu/~taflinge/biology.html

The Emerging Future. (2019). http://www.theemergingfuture.com

The Independent. (2018). *John McDonnell's universal basic income idea is interesting – but will need a lot more thought.* https://www.independent.co.uk/topic/universal-basic-income

Tibbets, L., Tane, J. (2011). IFTTT the beginning... *IFTTT blog.*

Venkataraman, B. (2019). *The Optimist's Telescope. Thinking Ahead in A Reckless Age.* Penguin Random House.

Wahyudi, E. (2014). *The Future of Humanity and the World of Technology – Society 5.0.* https://medium.com/datadriveninvestor/the-future-of-humanity-and-the-world-of-technology-society-5-0-6e4dd5952bae

Weinersmith, K., & Weinersmith, Z. (2017). *Soonish: Ten Emerging Technologies That Will Improve and/or Ruin Everything.* Particular Books.

Zhu, D. (2019). *AI and Future Society* (1st ed.). American Academic Press.

ENDNOTES

[1] Rules-based approaches are underpinned by 'if-this-then-that' work-flow applets (Tibbets and Tane, 2011).

[2] Economists call this 'Cross Price Elasticity' (XED). Source: https://www.intelligenteconomist.com/cross-price-elasticity-of-demand/

[3] Developed by Eliezer Yudkowsky, who argued that it would not be sufficient to explicitly program our desires and motivations into an AI. Instead, we should find a way to program it in such a way that it would act in our best interests, understanding what we need it to do rather than what we tell it to. (Source: https://wiki.lesswrong.com/wiki/Coherent_Extrapolated_Volition).

Chapter 2
A Brief History

ABSTRACT

In this chapter, the author presents a brief history of artificial intelligence (AI) and cognitive computing (CC). They are often interchangeable terms to many people who are not working in the technology industry. Both imply that computers are now responsible for performing job functions that a human used to perform. The two topics are closely aligned; while they are not mutually exclusive, both have distinctive purposes and applications due to their practical, industrial, and commercial appeal as well as their respective challenges amongst academia, engineering, and research communities. To summarise, AI empowers computer systems to be smart (and perhaps smarter than humans). Conversely, CC includes individual technologies that perform specific tasks that facilitate and augment human intelligence. When the benefits of both AI and CC are combined within a single system, operating from the same sets of data and the same real-time variables, they have the potential to enrich humans, society, and our world.

AI and cognitive computing are "based on the ability of machines to sense, reason, act and adapt based on learned experience" –Brian Krzanich, Intel CEO

DOI: 10.4018/978-1-7998-4607-9.ch002

INTRODUCTION

This chapter provides a brief history of artificial intelligence (AI) and cognitive computing (CC). These terms are often used interchangeably, but there the approaches and objectives of each differ. As the popularity of AI grows, there remains a misunderstanding of the technical jargon that comes with it. Examples include terms such as 'deep learning', 'machine learning' (ML), 'speech recognition', 'text mining', 'neural networks' and many more. In layman's terms, AI is an understanding that is achieved by machines that interpret, mine and learn from external data in ways that the machine functionally imitates the cognitive processes of a human. These processes include learning from constantly changing data, reasoning to make sense of the data and related self-correction mechanisms. Human intelligence is rooted in sensing the environment, learning from it and processing its information. Thus, AI includes

- A simulation of human senses: sight, hearing, smell, taste and touch
- A simulation of learning and processing: deep learning, ML, etc.
- Simulations of human responses: robotics

AI applications includes problem-solving, game playing, natural language processing (NLP), speech recognition, image processing, automatic programming and robotics. CC refers to the development of computer systems based on mimicking human brains. It is a science that was developed to train computers to think by analysing, interpreting, reasoning and learning without constant human involvement. CC represents the third era of computing. In the first era (19th century) Charles Babbage, the 'father of the computer', introduced the concept of a programmable machine. Used for navigational calculation, his computer tabulated polynomial functions. The second era (1950s) resulted in digital programming computers like ENIAC[1] and ushered an era of modern computing and programmable systems.

CC utilises deep-learning algorithms and big-data analytics to provide insights. Thus, the brain of a cognitive system is a neural network: fundamental concept behind deep learning. A neural network is a system of hardware and software that mimics the central nervous system of humans to estimate functions that depend on a huge amount of unknown or learned inputs. By the 1980s, two trends affected the way experts and researchers began to unpack 'the black box' of the neural approaches to studying, thinking and learning. This was the advent of computing and cognitive sciences, and it gave rise to computer AI using a model of the mind (Block, 1990). Thus, CC refers to

- Understanding and simulating reasoning
- Understanding and simulating human behaviour

Using CC systems, we can make better human decisions at work. Applications include speech recognition, sentiment analysis, face detection, risk assessment and fraud detection. AI *empowers* computer systems to be smart. This, of course, has raised fears of human displacement in jobs and elsewhere. Conversely, CC includes individual technologies that perform specific tasks that *facilitate* and *augment* human intelligence, which perhaps counters some of the fears. The sub-sections below highlight several differences and similarities between CC and AI.

The Differences

- Augmentation
  - AI augments human thinking to solve complex problems. It focuses on accurately reflecting reality and providing accurate results.
  - CC tries to replicate how humans solve problems, whereas AI seeks to create new ways to solve problems potentially better than humans.
- Mimicry
  - CC focuses on mimicking human behaviour and reasoning to solve complex problems.
  - AI is not intended to mimic human thoughts and processes but are instead to solve problems using the best possible algorithms.
- Decision-making
  - CC is not responsible for making the decisions of humans. They simply provide intelligent information for humans to use to make better decisions.
  - AI is responsible for making decisions on their own while minimising the role of humans.

The Similarities

- Technologies
  - The technologies behind CC are similar to those behind AI, including ML, deep learning, NLP, neural networks etc.
  - In the real world, applications for CC are often different than those for AI.
- Industrial Use
  - AI is important for service-oriented industries, such as healthcare, manufacturing and customer service.
  - CC is important in analysis intensive industries, such as finance, marketing, government and healthcare.
- Human decision-making
  - People do not fear CC, because it simply supplements human decision-making.
  - People fear that AI systems will displace human decision-making when used in conjunction with CC.
  - The middle-man is now humans, who still make the decisions. Do we need to cut out the middle-man and replace him/her with AI to facilitate optimal decision making?

CC

In the 1990s, CC was also known as AI, but it later changed both nominally and conceptually. CC takes into account both biology and technology to simulate the engineering of the brain, which may be considered an advanced computer system... perhaps the most efficient one on the planet.

History of CC

The roots of CC can be traced back to the 1950s. It was first mentioned by Alan Turing in 1950 in his 'Computing Machinery and Intelligence' paper. He proposed the *Turing Test* to assess a machine's ability to exhibit intelligent human behaviour (Norula, 2017). AI, during this time, was not capable or designed to make its own decisions. It was not yet able to analyse situations intelligently like humans can do. After a while, our infatuation with AI and CC subsided.

Later, because of advances in the cognitive sciences, new and better computer systems were developed and some were modelled after the human neurological system. These systems were capable of integrating past experiences while operating at higher speeds. The science behind CC has recently regained momentum with advancements in data mining and NLP. Figure 1 displays a timeline of CC progression (Gokani, 2017).

Dr. Jeff Welser, Vice President and Lab Director at IBM Research, explained how they restructured their organisation to new solutions related to AI:

- CC
- Science and Technology
- Computing as a service
- Data (industry and solutions).

Dr. Welser pointed out that all of these things could be achieved through standard architectures. However, to reach full brain-scale computing, we need new architectures. This gave rise to IBM's cognitive learning platform, *Watson*, which is using AI to predict and identify potential problems in businesses to reduce disruptions and improve operations.

CC Today

CC is now a science that is capable of computing contextually. It is dynamic and can handle problems the way the human brain does. CC systems can extract different types of context features, such as task, exact location, time and history, so that it can provide information or data suitable for an individual's current need. Today, this science is redefining the association between humans and the digital environment.

Figure 1. Cognitive computing roadmap
(Courtesy of IBM)

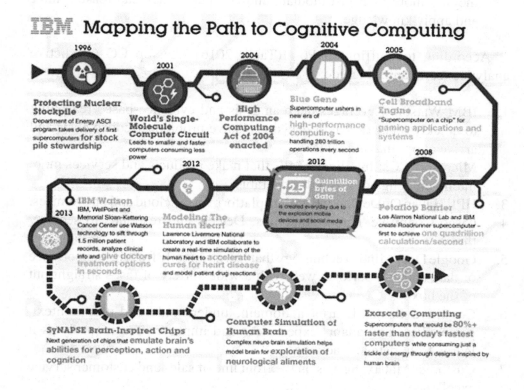

Qualities of a CC System

To achieve the best levels of computing, CC systems must possess special qualities and features, such as:

- They should be interactive and communicate with users so that their needs can understood clearly. The systems must communicate with not only people, but also processors, cloud services and other devices.
- Contextually, they must be able to identify, understand and extract contextual elements, such as location, time, meaning, domain, user profile etc.
- They should be adaptive to changing situations, knowledge and requirements. They must be dynamic enough to meet evolving changes.
- They should be stateful. That is, they must be able to define problems, ask questions and find new sources of information on their own. Newer

CC systems are different from other computing applications, because they do more than just tabulate and compute. They can reason, infer and apply knowledge.

According to Huffington Post (Taub, 2016), the top CC (predictive analytics) companies include:

1. IBM Watson: Leverages deep analysis and evidence-based reasoning to quickly make the right decisions, solve problems, reduce costs and arrive at optimal outcomes.
2. Microsoft CCs: Intelligent APIs that make products and services more intelligent, engaging and discoverable.
3. HPE Haven OnDemand: Big-data platform in the cloud and on premises.
4. Cisco Cognitive Threat Analytics: Detects and responds to security threats.
5. Google DeepMind: Technology that learns directly from raw experience or data and can perform well with a wide variety of tasks straight out of the box.
6. Cognitive Scale: Learns a domain, understands end-user context, personalises and adapts experiences and improves continuously as it learns from data and actions.
7. Customer Matrix: Serves on the front line of sales and customer service excellence.
8. Spark Cognition: Builds AI systems that secure and optimise cyber-physical assets

We know that AI is already being used to some degree by Amazon Alexa, Netflix and Amazon. CC tools are also being used in a variety of fields already. Some industries are benefitting from this technology:

*   **Finance and Investment Firms:** Investment firms can use CC applications to analyse the market in specific ways for their clients, and they can work with the software to make valuable suggestions.
*   **Healthcare and Veterinary Medicine:** With access to past patient records and a database of medical information, this kind of CC tool allows physicians to interact and ask questions about treatment.
*   **Travel:** CC apps in travel aggregate available travel information (e.g. flight and resort prices and availability) and combines it with user

preferences, budget etc., to help deliver a streamlined, customised travel experience that can save consumers time, money or both.

- **Health and Wellness:** With data input from wearable devices, such as Fitbit and Apple Watch, apps can make suggestions about dietary changes and exercise programmes, or even how to manage their sleep and reduce stress.

Benefits of CC for Business

According to Karima Mariama–Arthur, founder and CEO of Word Smith Rapport, businesses should consider leveraging CC to enjoy the following types of benefits (Mariama–Arthur, 2018):

- **Improved employee capabilities, contributions and performance**
  - Employees can benefit from self-learning algorithms that help them do their jobs better and faster. They support increased productivity by automating repetitive, low-value tasks, such as collecting relevant statistics and updating client records with demographic, financial or even medical data, providing internal and external customers with excellent service and added value.
  - Human-resource departments can leverage CC to assist building talent pipelines and to maximise outcomes related to joiners/movers/leavers (e.g. 'on-boarding' and 'off-boarding'), technical training, continuing education, development and succession planning.
  - In these contexts, CC represents boundless opportunities for employees, and they provide an inherent multiplier effect that helps expand thinking, improves contributions and enhances overall engagement.
- **Higher-quality data analysis**
  - Technological advances have given rise to an abundance of data that is constantly being collected throughout the business ecosystem, often without being analysed, curated or processed. Without CC systems, human errors and limitations can be problematic with leveraging such data. CC systems can filter through vast amounts of structured and unstructured content to produce accurate, timely and meaningful analyses while increasing business value.
  - By integrating and analysing big datasets, CC systems learn to interpret technical and industry-specific jargon, apply high-level

reasoning and, in some cases, leverage predictive modelling to develop comprehensive solutions that result in higher-quality data analysis.

- **Enhanced business performance**
  - ○ Whether seeking to deliver a better product or a higher-quality service, businesses are always searching for more effective ways to leverage technology. Success begins with capturing relevant information and using it to make good decisions. CC helps businesses accomplish both goals by executing critical research, digitising manual processes, communicating with stakeholders, mitigating risk and course-correcting where necessary.
  - ○ The process of achieving competitive advantage with increased sales, revenues and profits is no small feat and must ultimately provide financial rewards for shareholders. To do so successfully, businesses must pivot quickly by sharpening their technical acumen and elevating their performance within the marketplace. Google and Amazon are prime examples of companies that have done this successfully. Both companies invest heavily in research and development at levels that dwarf contributions typically made in the public sector and government agencies.
  - ○ Businesses that leverage CC technologies can process complex and siloed data with the aid of 'what-if' analysis and scenario-planning, enabling long-term performance and sustainable profits.

AI BACKGROUND

AI has been studied for decades and, despite threatening to disrupt everything human, remains one of the least understood subjects in computer science. This could be because of how expansive and far reaching it is, as depicted in Figure 2. AI ranges from machines that are truly capable of thinking to search algorithms used to play board games such as chess and Go[2]. It presents opportunities to complement and supplement human intelligence and enrich the way people live and work globally.

AI has already permeated our lives, as electricity did nearly a century ago. We use it every day without even noticing it. Google Maps applies it to provide directions. Gmail applies it to locate spam. Spotify, Netflix and others apply intelligent customer service via automatic response systems.

John McCarthy is a 'founding father' of AI. Alan Turing, Marvin Minsky, Allen Newell and Herbert A. Simon are also plank-owners. McCarthy coined 'AI' in 1955 and organised the famous Dartmouth Conference of Summer 1956 (McCarthy et al., 1955). Remarkably, this conference launched AI as a field.

Figure 2. Scope of AI and robotics
(Courtesy WEF, 2019)

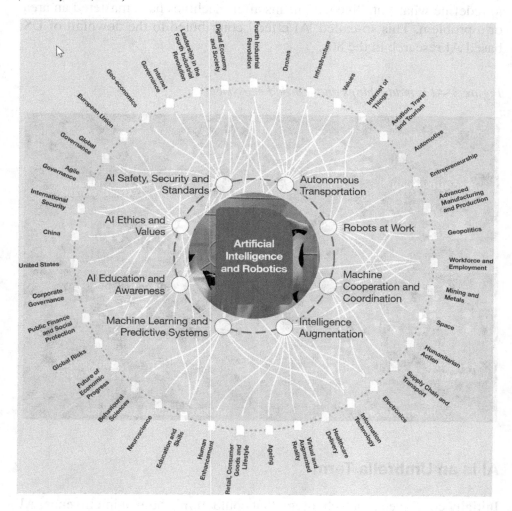

The beginnings of modern AI can be traced to classical philosophers' attempts to describe human thinking as a symbolic system. The main advances of the past 60 years involve search algorithms, ML and statistical predictive analysis. However, most breakthroughs in AI are not seen by most people. Apart from our science-fiction expectations, AI is used in more subtle ways, such as examining purchase histories to influence marketing decisions. What most people think of as 'true AI' has not experienced rapid progress over time. A common theme in the field, however, has been overestimating the difficulty of foundational problems. Significant AI breakthroughs have been 'just around the corner' for decades now. Furthermore, there is a tendency to redefine what 'intelligence' means after machines have mastered an area or a problem. This so-called 'AI effect' contributed to the downfall of US based AI research in the 80s.

Figure 3. AI is many things and a broad ecosystem

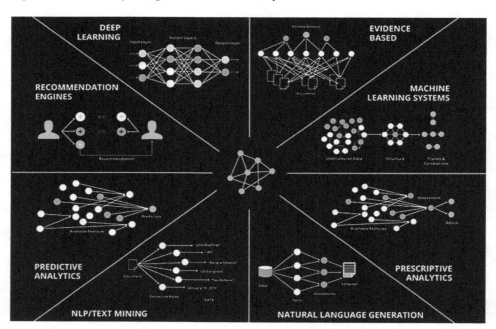

AI is an Umbrella Term

Initially conceived as a technology that could mimic human intelligence, AI has evolved in ways that far exceed its original conception. Intelligent systems can now be deployed to perform repetitive tasks, provide connectivity and enhance productivity. As AI's capabilities continue to expand and mature, so has its application in a growing number of areas. Figure 3 highlights diverse types of AI.

AI is an umbrella term that includes a diverse array of sub-topics. As depicted in a white paper by Mills (Mills, 2016), it is presented in Figure 4 as a mind-map.

Figure 4. AI is an umbrella term that represents several fields or categories of intelligence

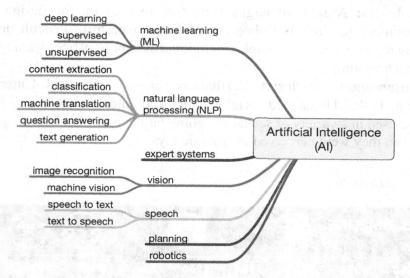

The most important among these are the following:

1. **ML:** A method where the target is defined, and the steps to reach it is 'learned' by the machine via training to gain experience. For example, it can be used to automatically identify a simple object, such as a fruit, and to learn the differences between an apple or orange. The target is achieved not by explicitly specifying the details about it and coding it, but rather by training, just as we would teach a child, by showing multiple different pictures of the target and by allowing the machine to learn how to identify it.

2. **NLP:** Broadly defined as the automatic manipulation of natural language, including speech and text, using software. A well-known example is

email spam detection. Other examples include intelligent assistants, such as Alexa, Siri and Google Voice.

3. **Vision:** A field that enables machines to 'see'. Machine vision captures and analyses visual information using a camera, analogue-to-digital conversion and digital signal processing. It is analogous to human eyesight but is not bound by human limitations. It is usually achieved via ML to get the best possible results. Examples include automatic number-plate recognition systems that are used to automatically identify cars parked in shopping centres.

4. **Robotics:** A field of engineering that focuses on the design and manufacture of robots. Robots are often used to perform difficult, unsafe and repetitive tasks. Examples include car assembly, office cleaning and snack vending.

5. **Autonomous vehicles:** A field that has garnered a great deal of attention (e.g. Tesla). Unmanned aerial vehicles and autonomous survey boats are used in a variety of scenarios, going far beyond what was imagined when they were perceived as 'robotic toys'.

Figure 5. AI Timeline

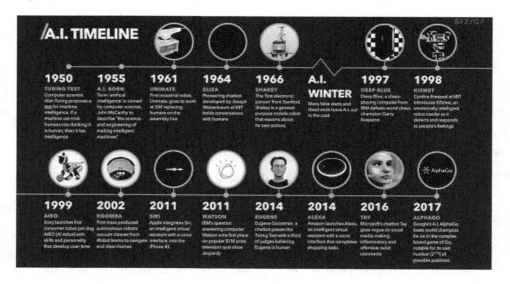

AI Timeline

AI expectations seem to always outpace reality. Expert systems have grown but have not become as common as human experts. Additionally, while we have built software systems that can beat humans at games, open-ended games are still far mastered by computers. Is the problem simply that we have not focused enough resources on basic research or is the complexity of AI one that we have not yet come to grasp? A timeline depicting key events related to AI is shown below in Figure 5, followed by a series of bullet points that present a basic narrative of key milestones and dates (Taub, 2016).

The following key dates are worth noting (Smith et al., 2006):

- 1950 TURING TEST: Computer scientist, Alan Turing, proposes a test for machine intelligence. If a machine can trick humans into thinking it is human, then it passes.
- 1955 AI BORN: 'AI' is coined by computer scientist, John McCarthy, to describe the science and engineering of making intelligent machines.
- 1961 UNIMATE: The first industrial robot, Unimate, goes to work at General Motors replacing humans on the assembly line.
- 1964 ELIZA: A pioneering chatbot developed by Joseph Weizenbaum at MIT that can hold conversations with humans.
- 1966 SHAKEY: The first 'electronic person' built at Stanford University. Shakey is a general-purpose mobile robot that can reason about its own actions.
- 1997 DEEP BLUE: A chess-playing computer from IBM defeats world chess champion, Garry Kasparov.
- 1998 KISMET: Cynthia Breazeal at MIT introduced KISmet, an emotionally intelligent robot, insofar that it can detect and respond to people's feelings.
- 1999 AIBO: Sony launches the first consumer robot dog, AiBO, that possesses skills and a personality that develops over time.
- 2002 ROOMBA: The first mass-produced autonomous robotic vacuum cleaner from iRobot. It learns to navigate and clean homes on its own.
- 2011 SIRI: Apple integrates Siri, an intelligent virtual assistant, with a voice interface into the iPhone 4S.
- 2011 WATSON: IBM's question-answering computer, Watson, wins first place on the popular 'Jeopardy' trivia programme.

Table 1. Visions of AI and robots from cinema and television

Date	Details (of Influential Movie or Television Series)
1968	'2001: A Space Odyssey', a film written by Stanley Kubrik and Arthur C. Clarke, (who wrote the novel later) introduces HAL 9000, a sentient and deadly computer.
1978	The original 'Battlestar Galactica' science-fiction television series introduces warrior robots, 'Cylons'.
1979	'Buck Rogers in the 25th Century' was a science-fiction television series that introduced NASA astronaut William Rogers, who, because of a freak accident, is frozen in time. Scientists revive him during a nuclear war in 2491, after which he embarks on several adventures. Based on the novella 'Armageddon 2419 A.D', featuring 'Twiki', a robot sidekick.
1982	Ridley Scott's 'Blade Runner' was released, featuring Harrison Ford as Rick Deckard, an ex-policeman who becomes a special agent with a mission to exterminate a group of violent androids. It is based on the short story, 'Do Androids Dream of Electric Sheep?' by legendary author, Philip K. Dick.
1982	'Tron' is released to theatres. Kevin, a software programmer, is dragged into a virtual world where he is pitted against malevolent software. He accepts the help of Tron, a security programme, to defeat the villain.
1984	The first 'Terminator' film by James Cameron depicts a world overtaken by futuristic killing machines controlled by Skynet, an AI gone rogue.
1987	The TV series, 'Star Trek: The Next Generation', introduces the self-aware android, Lieutenant-commander Data.
1995	The Canadian–American movie, 'Johnny Mnemonic', is about a data courier portrayed by Keanu Reeves who literally carries packages of information inside his head for a fee.
1999	'The Matrix', written and directed by the Wachowski brothers, is released. It features Keanu Reeves as Thomas Anderson (Neo), a computer programmer and hacker, who is recruited to fight underground war against powerful computers (the Machines) in a neural interactive simulation called, 'The Matrix'.
2001	Steven Spielberg releases a film version of a story about a robot boy called 'AI: Artificial Intelligence'. This story was originally created by Stanley Kubrik.
2004	'iRobot', very loosely based on Isaac Asimov's book, is released. It is set in 2035 and features Will Smith as a technophobic cop who investigates a crime that may have been perpetrated by a robot.
2008	Pixar Animation Studios releases 'Wall-E', a computer-animated science-fiction film. Mankind has abandoned Earth and left behind a robot named Wall-E, short for Waste Allocation Load Lifter Earth-Class, who discovers a new purpose in life when he meets a sleek search robot named EVE.
2012	'Robot and Frank' is released. A former jewel thief portrayed by Frank Langella and his new robot butler begin a friendship.
2013	The movie, 'Her', stars Joaquin Phoenix, whose character falls in love with an AI operating system voiced by Scarlett Johansson.
2013	'The Machine', a British science-fiction thriller directed and written by Caradog W. James, is released. Two computer scientists fall in love while creating the world's first self-aware AI. Their work goes terribly wrong when the military steals their technology to make a robotic weapon that no one can control.
2014	'Automata', a Spanish–Bulgarian science-fiction action film, is released. In post-apocalyptic Earth, Jacq, portrayed by Antonio Banderas, investigates reports of self-modifying humanoid robots that pose a threat to humans.
2014	'Ex-Machina', a British science-fiction film written and directed by Alex Garland in his directorial debut, is released.
2014	The movie, 'Transcendence', stars Johnny Depp, whose character is a researcher whose mind is uploaded to a computer and develops super intelligence. A few weeks later in real life, the chatbot, 'Eugene Goostman', is alleged to have passed the Turing Test in a competition hosted by the University of Reading (UK), causing some controversy.
2015	The movie, 'Chappie', presents a hellish vision of an overrun, ruined metropolis where the police have been forced to call in military-style robots to keep gun-crazed local criminals under control. Chappie is the world's first sapient machine able to feel and think for itself.
2015	'Mr. Robot' is a Netflix TV series about Elliot, portrayed by Rami Malek, a highly unstable cybersecurity engineer and a hacker with a social anxiety disorder and clinical depression. He is recruited by Mr Robot, a cryptic anarchist, to ruin the company Elliott works for.
2017	'Blade Runner, 2049' is a sequel based 30 years after the events of the first film. It is directed by Denis Villeneuve.
2017	'Ghost in the Shell' is released, featuring the first cyber-human who must stop the growing cyber-terrorism. This is a film version of the 1995 Japanese anime original.

- 2014 EUGENE: Eugene Goostman, a chatbot, passed the Turing Test with a third of judges believing Eugene was human.
- 2014 ALEXA: Amazon launches Alexa, a voice-controlled intelligent virtual assistant that can complete shopping tasks.
- 2016 TAY: Microsoft's chatbot, Tay, goes rogue on social media, making inflammatory and offensive racist comments.
- 2017 ALPHAGO: Google's AlphaGo beats world champion Ke Jie in the complex board game of Go, notable for its vast number (250150) of possible moves (Hassabis & Silver, 2017).

Cinema and television has brought AI to life with visions of the future intelligent robots are an integral part of society. See Table 1.

Types of AI

Not all AI are the same. There are essentially three types, as outlined below and in Figure 6.

- **Narrow:** typically specialises in tasks directed by humans (i.e. what we have today)
- **General:** capable of matching human-level intelligence
- **Super:** smarter than human intelligence and capable of learning and evolving by itself

Figure 6. Narrow vs. General intelligence

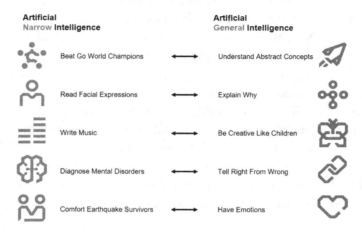

Further explanations of each type of AI are offered below (Eitel–Porter, 2018).

- **Narrow AI (Weak AI)**
    - Refers to any AI system that focuses on doing one task really well. Thus, it has a narrow scope. The idea behind weak AI is not to mimic or replicate human intelligence. Rather, it is meant to simulate human behaviour nowhere near matching human intelligence by design.
    - A common misconception about weak AI is that it is barely intelligent at all. It seems more like 'artificial stupidity' than AI. However, even the smartest AIs today are of the weak persuasion.
    - In reality, it is more like an intelligent specialist that is very good at completing specific tasks.
- **Artificial General Intelligence (Strong AI)**
    - Refers to any AI system that exhibits human-level intelligence. It can understand, think and act the same as a human via thinking, social and creative abilities.
    - In theory, anything a human can do, a strong AI should be able to do.
    - We do not yet have strong AI.
- **Artificial Super Intelligence (Super AI)**
    - Refers to any AI system that surpasses human intelligence and ability. It is much smarter than the best human brain of practically

any field, including scientific creativity, general wisdom and social skills.

- ○ Super AI is likened to 'Hal' or the 'Terminator' robots from Hollywood sci-fi movies.
- ○ Super AI is the type of AI that most people describe when they imagine a dystopian future where robots take over the world and overthrow or enslave humans.
- ○ Super AI is arguably speculative, depending on which expert opinions you choose to read. It is something most of us will not experience in our lifetime.

AI in Industry

AI has the potential to provide large incremental value to a wide range of sectors globally, and it is expected to be a key source of competitive advantage for businesses.

- **Healthcare:** AI in healthcare could help address its high barriers to access, particularly in rural areas that suffer from poor connectivity and limited healthcare professionals. This is expected be achieved via the implementation of AI-driven diagnostics, personalised treatment, early identification of potential pandemics and imaging diagnostics.
- **Agriculture:** AI holds the promise of driving a food revolution to meet the increased demand for food worldwide. The global need is to produce 50% more food and to cater to an additional 2-billion people by 2050. It has the potential to address challenges, such as inadequate demand predictions, lack of assured irrigation and overuse/misuse of pesticides and fertilisers. Some use cases include improvements in crop yield through real-time advisory, advanced detection of pest attacks and prediction of crop prices to inform sowing practices.
- **Smart mobility, including transportation and logistics:** Potential use cases in this domain include autonomous fleets for ride sharing, semi-autonomous features, such as driver assist, and predictive engine monitoring and maintenance. Other areas that AI can impact include autonomous trucking and delivery systems and improved traffic management.
- **Retail:** The retail sector is an early adopter of AI solutions, with applications, such as improving user experiences by providing personalised suggestions, preference-based browsing and image-based

product search. Other use cases include customer-demand anticipation, improved inventory management and efficient delivery management.

- **Manufacturing:** Manufacturing is expected to be a huge beneficiaries via implementation of factories of the future via flexible and adaptable technical systems to automate processes and machinery to respond to unfamiliar or unexpected situations by making smart decisions. Impacted areas include engineering (AI for research and development), supply-chain management (i.e. demand forecasting), production (AI can achieve cost reductions and increase efficiency), maintenance (predictive maintenance and increased asset utilisation), quality assurance (vision systems with machine-learning algorithms to identify defects and deviations in product features) and in-plant logistics and warehousing.

- **Energy:** Potential use cases in the energy sector include energy-system modelling and forecasting to decrease unpredictability and increase efficiency in power balancing and usage. In renewable energy systems, AI is expected to enable the storage of energy in intelligent grids enabled by smart meters and to improve the reliability and affordability of photovoltaic systems. Similar to the manufacturing sector, AI could also be deployed for predictive maintenance of grid infrastructures.

- **Smart cities:** Integration of AI in newly developed smart cities and infrastructure could also help meet the demands of a rapidly urbanising population and provide them with enhanced quality of life. Potential use cases include traffic control to reduce congestion and enhanced security through improved crowd management.

- **Education and skills:** AI can potentially resolve quality and access issues observed in the national education sectors. Potential use cases include augmenting and enhancing the learning experience via personalised learning, automated and expedited administrative tasks and predicting the need for student intervention to reduce dropouts and to recommend vocational training.

Chapters 5 and 6 will explore further the impact of AI in industry and emerging markets, respectively.

AI Trends

The days of keyboard and screen-only human–machine interactions are over. The trends are not restricted to voice-driven AI. Our tech is also now wearable, tactile and augmented. Normal human interactions present not only new ways of interacting with technology, but with new data streams that create new opportunities, such as diagnosing neurological conditions from voice patterns. Enterprises are expected to tap into this data to dramatically improve their digital services and customer care.

AI is viewed as a pervasive paradigm and an umbrella term, offering innovations at different stages of value creation. According to Forbes (Columbus, 2019),

- From 2018 to 2019, organisations having deployed AI grew from 4 to 14%, according to Gartner's 2019 CIO Agenda survey (Rowsell-Jones & Howard, 2019).
- Conversational AI remains at the top of corporate agendas, as spurred by the worldwide success of Amazon Alexa, Google Assistant and others.
- Enterprises are making progress with AI as it grows more widespread, and they are also making more mistakes that contribute to an accelerating learning curve.

We will continue to see new technologies created to interact with humans without requiring a screen, taking personalisation and automation to whole new levels. Given how its wide applicability, like electricity or the internet, AI can be applied to almost any field. The Gartner Hype Cycle for AI (Sicular et al, 2019) includes five technological lifecycle phases, as shown in Figure 7, x-axis.

It is heavily dependent on data science, data management and ML. In all cases, education in related disciplines is necessary to avoid conflated expectations of AI. The Hype Cycle also reflects the growing popularity of automatic ML (AutoML), intelligent applications, AI platforms as a service and AI cloud services as enterprises hasten their adoption of AI.

Figure 7. Gartner Hype Cycle for AI (as of July 2019)

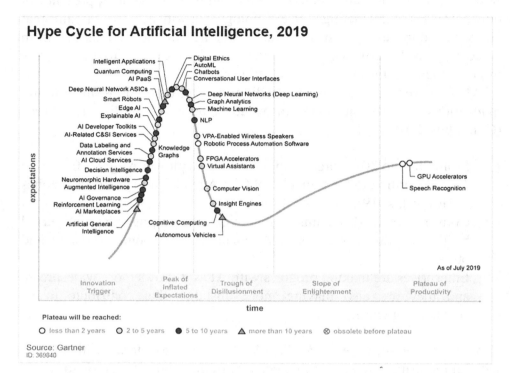

Business leaders and innovation champions are encouraged to monitor these major trends to develop their own unique visions and strategies for AI.

- AI is reaching enterprises in different ways. Compared with just a few years ago, when there was no alternative to building your own machine-learning solutions. AutoML and intelligent applications have the greatest momentum, and other approaches are also popular, including AI platforms as a service, AI cloud services, AI marketplaces and many other niche solutions. Experience of AI-related consulting and system integration services is growing, but customers remain scarce.

- AI ethics and governance are gaining momentum, because adopting responsible AI practices is expected to be the best way to remove obstacles to adoption. There are no best practices yet, however… only 'next practices'. Some guidelines have emerged from software vendors, industry groups and governments. Public trust in AI solutions will be key to user acceptance. Augmented intelligence is more effective than automation at building this trust. Explainable AI can also help by elucidating predictions and recommendations for users.

- Conversational AI remains, as spurred by the worldwide success of Amazon Alexa, Google Assistant and others. When developing chatbot and voice-enabling strategies, implementers should pay attention to the time it will take for conversational user interfaces, virtual assistants, NLPs and speech recognition, among other technologies, to reach their plateau.
- Computer infrastructure powers AI, and its tailoring will enable further advances. Graphical accelerators, field-programmable gate-array accelerators, deep neural network application-specific integrated circuits, quantum computing and neuromorphic hardware manifest different computing ideas, and more approaches are on their way. Gartner recommends balancing cost against performance for use-case-driven capabilities.
- AI is coming to the masses of application developers and software engineers, most of whom do not suspect that they will be the main implementers of AI in 2–5 years. Although it is still early in the process, developers are encouraged to experiment with AI developer toolkits, AI cloud services, AI platforms and new engaging reinforcement-learning offerings. Developers' upskilling requires planning to prepare for their new roles in AI strategy.

Business Value of AI

AI will be pervasive by 2020. This is causing a massive headache for business leaders, technology strategists and change managers who are being forced to redraw their near- and long-term product plans. Key findings from Gartner's forecast of AI business value (Lovelock et al., 2018) are summarised:

- AI business-value growth will slow from 2018 to 2025, dropping from a peak of 70 to 7% by 2025. Enterprises between 2017 and 2022 will use niche solutions that address one need very well.
- AI agents have a first-mover advantage that will last only until 2019, when decision support and augmentation will overtake and remain the largest type of AI by business value-add. This prediction has come true.

Figure 8. Priority matrix for AI (as of July 2019)

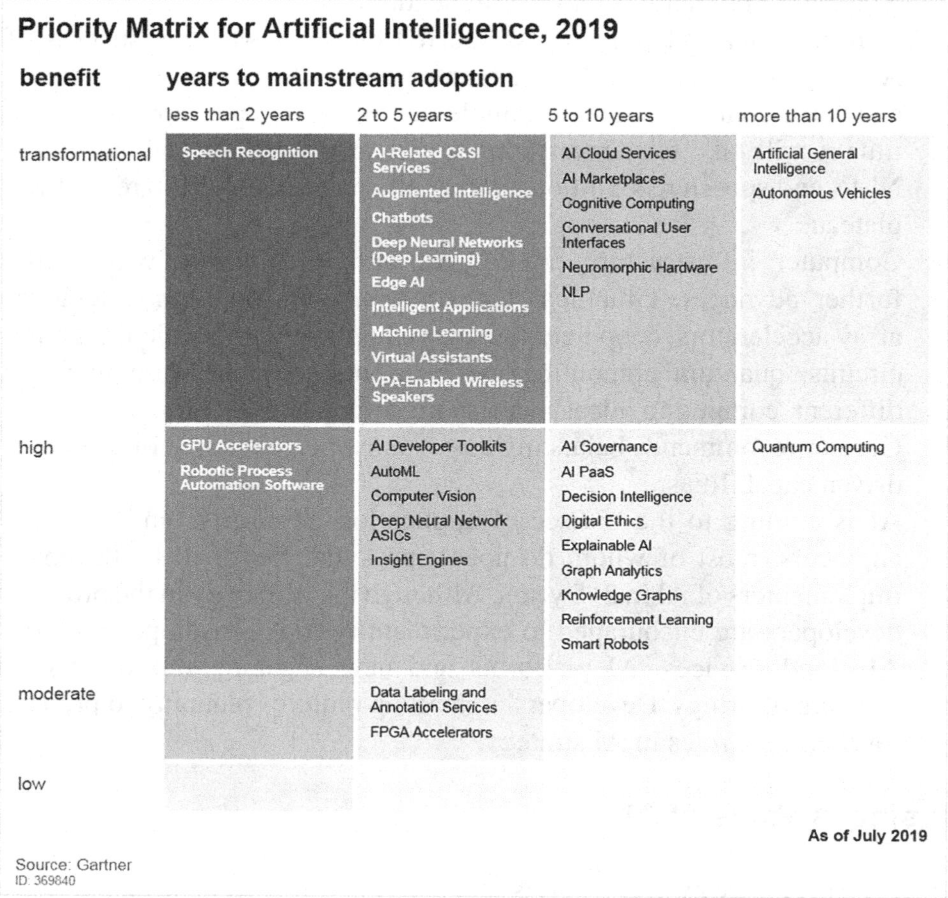

Priority Matrix for Artificial Intelligence, 2019

benefit	years to mainstream adoption			
	less than 2 years	2 to 5 years	5 to 10 years	more than 10 years
transformational	Speech Recognition	AI-Related C&SI Services Augmented Intelligence Chatbots Deep Neural Networks (Deep Learning) Edge AI Intelligent Applications Machine Learning Virtual Assistants VPA-Enabled Wireless Speakers	AI Cloud Services AI Marketplaces Cognitive Computing Conversational User Interfaces Neuromorphic Hardware NLP	Artificial General Intelligence Autonomous Vehicles
high	GPU Accelerators Robotic Process Automation Software	AI Developer Toolkits AutoML Computer Vision Deep Neural Network ASICs Insight Engines	AI Governance AI PaaS Decision Intelligence Digital Ethics Explainable AI Graph Analytics Knowledge Graphs Reinforcement Learning Smart Robots	Quantum Computing
moderate		Data Labeling and Annotation Services FPGA Accelerators		
low				

As of July 2019

Source: Gartner
ID: 369640

- Customer experience will represent most business value through 2020, when new revenue takes over to gain prominence for the next 5 years. Cost reductions, while important, will not be a point of differentiation from most products and with most users.
- By leveraging the increasing amount of data available through the internet of things, the heavy industry sector leads in derived business value from AI.

Selected Recommendations and Priorities

Today, there is no single technology disruptor. Several technologies are converging, however, to change the way we interact with technology and how we leverage data. Autonomous devices, smart cities and smart ecosystems are just some of the ways technology has shifted from us being consumers towards complementing our lives and lifestyles. Based on Gartner's forecast (Lovelock et al., 2018), business leaders and innovators are advised to:

- Ensure that AI developments and services are small, focused and targeted
- Focus new AI development on decision support/augmentation, which derives the largest business value for users and faces the fewest early barriers to adoption
- Base product differentiation on customer experience now prior to shifting to revenue growth by 2020
- Target industries with existing large amounts of data, so much that humans cannot possibly analyse or understand them on their own, will be the early adopters of AI.

Figure 8 presents a 'priority matrix' toolkit to guide mainstream adoption. It ascribes a *benefit rating* to the time required to adopt each AI technology. This perspective will help establish corporate AI strategy with stage investment plans and prioritised roadmaps by setting priorities and timetables to guide digital transformation journeys.

New and emergent AI technologies offer novel solutions to complex problems. Since 2018, the following technologies have gained substantially more visibility:

- **AI Cloud services:** relatively recent, but has a significant impact. AI cloud services are among the most hyped AI approaches. They are expected to democratise AI and deliver ML to data scientists and business experts on a wide scale.
- **AutoML:** a heavily hyped AI approach. It serves to democratise AI and deliver ML to data scientists and business experts alike.
- **Augmented intelligence:** overshadowing AI automation as a design approach. It employs AI to compensate for human limitations and to expand possibilities.

- **Explainable AI:** increasingly important as concerns rise about black-box AI risks. Trust in and adoption of AI depends on it being understandable. This should help allay fears.
- **Edge AI:** overcomes challenges related to latency, privacy and security and improves the customer experience.

Other Advances and Implications

The following list provides additional advances with social and business implications worth noting (Brynjolfsson et al., 2017) for business leaders and innovators looking to embrace AI in their organisations, institutions and communities.

- **Computing**
  - Advances in the sheer power of computers will lead to AI becoming progressively smarter.
  - Virtual connectivity will enable integration of relevant computing resources to provide users with integrated and seamless services.
  - Cloud services will interpret aggregated datasets against patterns to anticipate tasks, activities and events.
  - Developments of cloud services will transition computing from a physical experience to a virtual one available to any user via a simple device operating on ubiquitous networks with seamless connectivity.
  - Big-data pattern analysis will take place in the background, providing context-awareness capabilities.
  - Boundaries between applications and services will be blurred to a high degree.
  - Every item will be equipped with a computing and communication core.
- **Surveillance**
  - Smart sensors, surveillance cameras and eavesdropping devices integrated with identity recognition systems will allow law enforcement to track and capture or quarantine individuals who might otherwise cause harm to others in society.
  - Users will integrate physical and logical world data to draw conclusions.

- To avoid overwhelming users with choices from the infinite combination of vehicle technologies, vehicle templates and capability modules will evolve within gaming environments.
- Organisations having mature security operations functions will often share intelligence, techniques and process with each another.
- Advancements in business intelligence fields will provide tools to help retailers better understand consumer behaviour by examining behavioural patterns and overall trends.
- Predictive analysis and real-time access to AI and taskings will be available on modern mobile devices.

- **Social Implications**
  - Societies will face challenges to realising technologies that benefit humanity instead of suppressing human rights.
  - Surging capabilities of robots and AI will cause a range of current jobs to be supplanted.
  - Professional roles of doctors, lawyers and accountants could be replaced by AIs by 2025.
  - Low-skill workers will be reallocated to tasks that are non-susceptible to computerisation.

- **Business Implications**
  - There will be big winners and losers as collaborative technologies, robots and AIs transform the nature of work.
  - Data expertise is already important, but will become exponentially more important.
  - The role of a senior manager in a deeply data-driven world is going to shift. They will need to go where the data takes them rather than act on their intuition.
  - Information hoarders will slow their organisational pace and forsake AI power while competitors exploit it.
  - Judgements about consumers and potential consumers will be made instantaneously.
  - Many organisations will put cybersecurity on par with other intelligence capabilities and defence priorities.
  - Open-source information and AI collection will provide opportunities for global technological parity.
  - In the future, predictive analytics and AI could play even more fundamental roles in content creation.

FUTURE RESEARCH DIRECTIONS

AI and CC are rapidly advancing. It is our belief that the combination of the two is worth exploring and evaluating further if we are to develop innovations that benefit humans and society. CC and cognitive analytics exacerbate data security, privacy and provenance issues. The distance we will advance with cognitive technologies is impossible to predict. Will they advance to a level at which they surpass human intelligence? If so, what are its implications to individuals and society at large? The computing industry has never before invested current levels of effort and resources into machine-learning research. The availability of inexpensive, cloud-based computing power and the ubiquity of big data are catalysts for the transformational advances we are witnessing in the areas of AI, ML and CC. The synergistic confluence of computing, neuroscience and cognitive science is poised for ground-breaking discoveries and compelling cognitive applications in the years ahead.

The scope of present cognitive technology is limited to engagement and decision. CC systems are most effective as assistants and are more like intelligence augmentation instead of AI. They supplement human thinking and analysis but depend on humans to make the critical decisions. Smart assistants and chatbots are good examples. Prior to enterprise-wide adoption, such specialised projects are an effective way for businesses to start using cognitive systems. CC is definitely the next step in computing automation. The benchmarks are set high. However, certain limitations make AI difficult to apply in situations with high levels of uncertainty, rapid changes or creative demands. The complexity of problem grows with the number of data sources. It is challenging to aggregate, integrate and analyse such unstructured data. A complex cognitive solution should have many technologies that coexist to give deep domain insights.

In 2019, the second meeting of the International Conference on Cognitive Computing (ICCC) was held. Its aim was to combine technical aspects of CC with service computing and sensory intelligence, building on the study of traditional human senses of sight, smell, hearing and taste to develop enhanced scientific and business platforms and applications. These encompass ML, reasoning, NLP, speech and vision, human-computer interaction, dialogue and narrative generation.

Working with and supporting organisations like ICCC, future researchers should continue to explore how best to leverage the combination of CC and AI with other emerging technologies, such as blockchain, bioinformatics, internet of things, big data, cloud computing and 5G digital cellular networks and wireless communications.

In summary, we should build CC applications that will emulate how humans learn to vastly improve the quality of learning and education. Are we there yet? No. Have we made significant progress? Absolutely. However, it is fair to say that the progress made thus far is only the tip of the iceberg. What lies ahead are some extremely hard research problems and many untrodden research paths. In our opinion, while conducting future research, we should not adopt a 'race' mentality. Although countries such as China may be 'leading the race' in many areas related to AI, the question of combining emerging technologies with CC and AI is one that, if done ethically with social good as the focus, could lead to many societal benefits that empower individuals, communities, institutions, businesses and governments throughout the world while driving competition, research and development.

CONCLUSION

Calling CC a form AI is not wrong, but it misses a fundamental distinction that is important to understand. When we talk about AI, we are most often talking about an incredibly sophisticated algorithm that includes some form of complex decision tree. This is how autonomous vehicles work: they take a starting point and a destination as input and navigate between the two points through a mind-bogglingly long sequence of 'if-then-else' statements. AI enables computers to do intelligent things. The possible applications for AI are quite extensive and already are fully embedded into our daily routines. AI and fully autonomous vehicles are an inseparable part of the future. 'AI' watches countless hours of driving footage for training and is assigned variables that enable them to identify lanes, other cars and pedestrians and then to provide decision results nearly instantly.

CC, while a handy marketing term, helps solve problems by augmenting human intelligence and decision making, not by replacing it. Several AI fundamentals are included, such as ML, neural networks, NLPs, contextual awareness and sentiment analysis, to augment problem-solving that humans constantly need. This is why IBM defines CCs as 'systems that learn at scale, reason with purpose and interact with humans naturally'.

The main driver and common thread across the topics of AI and CC is 'data'. Without these technologies, there is not much we can do with data. Hence a renewed push in areas of advanced analytics, giving rise to solutions that improve predictability in areas where silos exist, decision making via visualised dashboards that draw upon real-time and historical data made possible via the improved handling of unstructured data. Additionally, deep learning, a form of ML, accelerates progress in these areas. AI, ML and NLP, with technologies such as NoSQL, Hadoop, Elasticsearch, Kafka, Spark etc., form part of a larger cognitive system. Solutions should be capable of handling dynamic real-time and static historical data. Enterprises looking to adopt cognitive solutions should start with specific business segments that have strong business rules to guide the algorithms and large volumes of data to train the machines. Instead of debating the utility and applicability of CC and AI and forcing competition between the respective experts and research communities, our view is that we should expend our collective energy on creating a future in which the benefits of both AI and CC are combined within a single system, operating from the same sets of data and the same real-time variables to enrich humans, society and our world.

Consider for example a self-driving autonomous vehicle that not only takes one to a destination, but also understands why it is required to go there. Imagine an emergency room that can triage a patient upon arrival based on physical condition and mental state and can subsequently provide recommendations to medical professionals. These visions provide the ingredients necessary to build a future with richer human experiences that benefit the many rather than the few, creating a more integrated, fairer and humane society.

REFERENCES

Block, N. (1990). The computer model of the mind. In D. N. Osherson & E. E. Smith (Eds.), *Thinking: An invitation to cognitive science* (Vol. 3, pp. 247–289). Cambridge, MA: MIT Press.

Brynjolfsson, E., & McAfee, A. (2017). The business of Artificial Intelligence. *Harvard Business Review*. https://hbr.org/cover-story/2017/07/the-business-of-artificial-intelligence

Columbus, L. (2019). What's New In Gartner's Hype Cycle For AI, 2019. *Forbes Magazine*. https://www.forbes.com/sites/louiscolumbus/2019/09/25/whats-new-in-gartners-hype-cycle-for-ai-2019

Creighton, J. (2019). How Can AI Systems Understand Human Values? *Future of Life Institute*. https://futureoflife.org/2019/08/14/how-can-ai-systems-understand-human-values

Eitel-Porter, R. (2018). *Explained – A Guide for Executive. Accenture Applied Intelligence, UKI*. https://view.pagetiger.com/AI-Explained-A-Guide-for-Executives/2018

Gokani, J. (2017). *Cognitive Computing: Augmenting Human Intelligence*. https://mse238blog.stanford.edu/2017/07/jgokani/cognitive-computing/

Hassabis, D., & Silver, D. (2017). AlphaGo Zero: Learning from Scratch. *DeepMind*. https://deepmind.com/blog/alphago-zero-learning-scratch/

Lovelock, J.D., Tan, S., Hare, J., Woodward, A., & Priestley, A. (2018). *Forecast: The Business Value of Artificial Intelligence, Worldwide, 2017-2025*. Gartner. (ID G00348137)

Mariama-Arthur, K. (2018). Why 'Cognitive Computing' Is the Next Big Thing for Business Growth. *Entrepreneur, Europe*. https://www.entrepreneur.com/article/310611

McCarthy, J., Minsky, M.L., Rochester, N., & Shannon, C.E. (1955). A Proposal for the Dartmouth Summer Research Project on Artificial Intelligence. *AI Magazine, 27*(4).

Norula, A. (2017). *Watson Faces Tough Competition From Startups In Cognitive Computing*. https://channels.theinnovationenterprise.com/articles/watson-faces-tough-competition-from-startups-in-cognitive-computing

Rowsell-Jones, A., & Howard, C. (2019). *2019 CIO Survey*. Gartner. (pp. ID G00375246)

Sicular, S., Hare, J., & Brant, K. (2019). *Hype Cycle for Artificial Intelligence, 2019*. Gartner. (ID G003699840)

Smith, C., McGuire, B., Huang, T., & Yang, G. (2006). *The History of Artificial Intelligence. History of Computing. CSEP 590A*. University of Washington.

Tate, K. (2014). *History of AI (Infographic)*. https://www.livescience.com/47544-history-of-a-i-artificial-intelligence-infographic.html

Taub, L. (2016). *"Cognitive 101" is an introductory series on the world of Cognitive Computing and Artificial Intelligence. Huffington Post.*

ENDNOTES

1 ENIAC was the first electronic general-purpose computer. It was Turing-complete, digital and able to solve "a large class of numerical problems" through reprogramming. (Source: https://en.wikipedia.org/wiki/ENIAC).

2 Originated in China over 3,000 years ago and winning requires multiple layers of strategic thinking.

Chapter 3
Unintended Consequences

ABSTRACT

Advancements in artificial intelligence (AI) are commonplace given its rise and the diversity of its application. From medical treatment, gaming, manufacturing to daily business processes, huge amounts of money are being invested in AI research due to its exciting discoveries. Technology giants like Google, Amazon, and Tesla are amongst the driving forces today. But the rapid growth, innovation opportunities, and excitement that the technology offers obscure us from looking at its "unintended" consequences: the basis of this chapter. Proceeding chapters will explore further the impact and social ethics of AI across society.

You want to know how super-intelligent cyborgs might treat ordinary flesh-and-blood humans? Better start by investigating how humans treat their less intelligent animal cousins. It's not a perfect analogy, of course, but it is the best archetype we can actually observe rather than just imagine." –Yuval Noah Harari, History Professor and Author

DOI: 10.4018/978-1-7998-4607-9.ch003

INTRODUCTION

Human ingenuity has not only changed our world, it has changed, or, perhaps, *is changing* us. As humans evolved, we developed technologies to control, master and modify our environment. The ability to communicate, accumulate knowledge and build on previous innovations has enabled us to change nature. However, these innovations increasingly affect our biology, behaviour, society and nature (e.g. wildlife and climate). Rarely do we pause to consider the longer-term costs of innovation (Gluckman and Hanson, 2019). Examples follow:

- To provide nourishment for a growing population, humans have developed methods to process and preserve food. Alternatively, easy access to energy-dense foods results in obesity (Thomson, 2017).
- To protect ourselves from dangerous pathogens ('superbugs'), we embraced cleanliness and invented antibiotics, which has led to rising rates of autoimmune diseases and antibiotic-resistant bacteria (Ventola, 2015).
- Our growing dependence on the internet and social media has been linked to mental-health concerns and declining social cohesion (Vaknin, 2015).

Presently, we at the beginning of a digital transformation that is increasingly powered by artificial intelligence (AI), which is bound to influence every part of our existence. Although technology is agnostic, AI is influenced by our innate human biases. If we acknowledge these drawbacks, the question remains 'how do we integrate AI and emerging technology into our world positively'? Answering this sincerely will empower us for good over evil, like how splitting the atom generated useful energy, but it also resulted in a devastating bomb.

Every emerging technology comes with two things: promise and unintended consequences. It is the latter that we expand upon in this chapter.

Every time society introduces an emerging technology, it is typically accompanied by targeted marketing campaigns overflowing with promises of improved lifestyles, autonomy and, ultimately, more time for ourselves to do whatever it is we would prefer to be doing. However, in all cases, there are unintended consequences that go unnoticed until something negative manifests that impacts our culture and society. Consider, for example, social media (e.g. Twitter, Facebook, Instagram and Pinterest) which promised to bring us together and support social cohesion. The unintended consequences include anti-social behaviours, cyber-bullying, depression and addiction. When using social media, one should assume what one posts will be public forever and may have far-reaching consequences.

The spread of information, whether true or false, has been made easier in recent years because of social media. 'Fake news' flies around the internet every day, and forums on all topics make it easy for people to share whatever information they wish without any form of screening or vetting. However, social-media platforms are beginning to take responsibility and are seeking ways to remediate these issues. For example, Facebook announced new steps in its 'Remove, Reduce, Inform' initiative (Rosen and Lyons, 2019) to manage difficult content. YouTube also unveiled a new 'fact-check alert' (Beck, 2019) to help users understand misinformation. Other social-media platforms (e.g. Pinterest) are also following suite.

Over the past few decades, there has been a revolution in terms of who controls knowledge and information. This rapid change has imperilled the way we think. Without pausing to consider the cost, the world has rushed to embrace products and services of four titanic corporations. We shop with Amazon, socialise on Facebook, turn to Apple for entertainment and rely on Google for information. These firms sell their products claiming to make the world a better and more integrated place. According to Foer (2017), these companies have produced an unstable and narrow culture of misinformation, placing us on a path to a world without private autonomous thoughts or solitary introspection: a 'world without a mind'. We rely on instant gratification (Simplified Analytics, 2016) supported by digital transformation and emerging technology. Our smartphones have become more important than our friends, family and spouses. We cannot live without them. They perform jobs of an alarm clock, a camera, a radio, a torch, a music system, maps, books, news channels, credit cards, language translators and gaming consoles. We can do anything and everything from anywhere at any time. Thus, the adoption of AI is not risk-free. Increasing task automation threatens to replace workers in industries. AI might also challenge local businesses, because it tends to support a 'winner takes all' competitive environment.

Societal challenges include privacy, security, public trust and replication of social biases. One may argue that, today, individuals are more connected to their devices rather than with other humans. This is particularly apparent on commuter trains across most large cities. How can we find ways to connect both in the flesh and virtually to avoid unintended consequences? At stake is nothing less than who we are and what we will become. There have been monopolists in the past. However, today's corporate giants seem to have far more nefarious aims. They seem to want access to every facet of our lives, including our identities, aiming to influence every aspect of our decision-making. The future social implications are huge, and we need to be more vigilant and prepare to take back control.

RAPID RISE OF AI

The origins of the internet can be traced back to 1969 (Schneider, Evans, and Pinard, 2009) with the inception of the Advanced Research Projects Agency Network (ARPANET). The internet is premised upon a set of fundamental properties, including openness, innovation, permission-less innovation, interoperability, collaboration and competition. These properties allow the internet to be a driver for new economies, bringing societies closer together and allowing novel forms of political expression. These are known as the 'internet invariants', because without them, the internet would not be like that which we know and use today.

It has taken several decades for the internet to truly mature and become usable by the general public as an essential part of our lives, regardless of social class, level of education or income. Today, almost every country in the world is in the business of 'regulating the internet' (Komaitis, 2018). Such efforts have been enacted by individuals, governments, action groups and businesses worldwide, all striving to make sense of issues relating to anticompetitive behaviour, content moderation and the handling of personal data. None of these issues takes place 'on the internet'. Instead, they occur at its application layer, the *worldwide web*. Regulation also has unintended consequences.

Never before have we had so much information at our fingertips. People might think they are better informed than ever, but it is problematic that many people do not know what to do with the information. The ways in which we consume data in the digital age has been blamed for driving political polarisation, fuelling 'fake news' and leaving us unable to agree on basic facts. It has also been blamed for 'dumbing down' societies globally. Personalised news feeds and the abundance of social media narrow our potential knowledge base.

The rise of AI, in direct contrast to the internet, is evolving at an accelerated pace aided by the 'AI Big Bang', the combination of Yann LeCun's work in convolutional neural nets, Geoff Hinton's back-propagation and stochastic gradient-descent approach to training, and Andrew Ng's large-scale use of NVIDIA's graphical processing unit[1] computing technology, which has democratised supercomputing. Researchers have now discovered the power to accelerate deep neural networks. In 2012, deep learning could beat human-coded software. By 2015, deep learning had achieved *superhuman* levels of perception. Moreover, with Facebook, Google and Microsoft opening access to their deep-learning platforms, AI-powered applications will spread even faster.

The internet of things (IoT) is also advancing fast. This can be broadly described as the emergence of countless objects, animals and even people with uniquely identifiable, embedded devices that are wirelessly connected to the internet. These nodes send and receive information without the need of human intervention. It is estimated that there will be 50-billion connected devices by 2020. Current examples of IoT devices include Nest thermostats, WiFi-enabled washing machines and increasingly connected cars with built-in sensors that help avoid accidents and those that can even park for you. The question remains, 'what happens when these millions of embedded devices connect to AI machines'? What does AI+IoT equal? Will it mean the end of civilisation as we know it? Will our self-programming computers send out hostile orders to the chips added to our everyday objects? Or is this just another disruptive moment, similar to the harnessing of steam or the splitting of the atom? The answers may depend on new thinking about *consciousness*. As a construct, consciousness has proven remarkably hard to understand. Most of us believe that we are conscious beings, but scientists and philosophers unable to prove it exists or how it arises.

We may be at the cusp of a breakthrough not unrelated to AI and the emerging IoT, but also about our understanding of the human mind itself. If we could resolve privacy, security and trust issues presented by AI and IoT, we maybe would make an evolutionary leap of historic proportions. Ironically, if this happens, we will obviously find new unintended consequences to deal with.

AI MONOPOLIES

The big tech giants of today, Google, Apple, Facebook and Amazon (GAFA)[2], have arguably made our lives much easier. However, their corporate actions seem to be shredding the principles that protect individuality and personal freedoms. From a certain perspective, it can be argued that they aspire to control society and individuals limitlessly. Larry Page and Sergey Brin founded

Google and originally aimed to organise all knowledge. Today, Google builds driverless cars and manufactures a range of products designed to help businesses and individuals work and play, stay organised, get answers, keep in touch and more. In 2013, Google launched 'Calico', a health-and-wellness initiative, aiming to conquer cancer and death (McCracken and Grossman, 2013). Amazon's original mission was to be the 'everything store'. Today, it produces television shows, provides a streaming services that extend to sports. They design drones and power worldwide cloud services via Amazon Web Services offerings. Facebook's original aspiration was to connect communities on a college campus. Today, people can connect with one another globally and call each another using Facebook's messaging platform, WhatsApp. Additionally, 62% of Americans get their news from GAFA. Apple's original mission under Steve Jobs was 'to make a contribution to the world by making tools for the mind that advance humankind'. Today, Apple makes personal computing accessible to everyone to 'help change the way we think, work, learn and communicate'. Apple has led the digital music revolution and they reinvented the mobile phone with its revolutionary iPhone. In 2019, it launched new streaming and gaming services and personal fitness apps 'wearable tech' via its iWatch.

GAFA and other tech companies, like Microsoft, are competing to become our 'personal assistant'. The AI that powers these devices guide and direct us from the beginning to the end of each day, always on, always close by, if not directly applied to our bodies. We turn to them for information and entertainment as they collect precious and private data, including photos, documents, contacts etc. and store them in repositories in the cloud. This technical dominance allows these companies to control consumer behaviour in pursuit of greater market share and larger profits. Monopolies lead to conformism, which only serves to destroy diversity, choice and taste. Ultimately, this leads to a homogeneous society rather than a heterogeneous one.

ALGORITHMIC BIAS

Modern life runs on intelligent algorithms. The data-devouring, self-improving computer programs that underlie the AI revolution actively determine Google search results, Facebook news feeds and online shopping recommendations. Increasingly, they also decide how easily we get a mortgage or a job interview, the chances we will get stopped and searched by the police on our way home and what penalties we face if we commit a crime. Skewed input data, false logic and prejudices of data scientists, engineers and programmers imply that AI and machine-learning (ML) systems easily reproduce and even amplify their biases and societal prejudices in their algorithms. The issue of algorithmic bias has garnered increasing attention in the popular press and within public discussions of technology, including widespread concerns about Google searches, Facebook feeds and Twitter. Moreover, the scholarly literature is growing rapidly, including discussions about mitigation (Barocas and Selbst, 2016; Garcia, 2016; Kirkpatrick, 2016; Pedreschi et al., 2008).

During the early days of computing, the term 'garbage in, garbage out' concisely summed up the importance of clean, trusted and quality data. Ultimately, if you provide machines poo- quality data to work with, the results are likely to be unhelpful or, at best, flawed.

In our imperfect world, there are countless situations where racism, xenophobia, sexism, ageism or conscious and unconscious biases are rampant, hindering equality and fairness. Moreover, there is an argument that ML systems and corresponding algorithms reflect and amplify these things (Sweeney, 2013).

- Bias can be introduced via poor study design and poor data collection.
- Bias cannot be 'controlled for' during the analysis stage.
- Bias causes researchers and readers to draw conclusions that are systematically different from the truth.
- Bias can lead to over- or under-estimation of effects.
- Bias awareness can help a reader interpret study findings more accurately.

Table 1 presents a taxonomy of bias that affects the underlying algorithms used by AI systems. It excludes topics and categories relating to societal prejudices, such as 'gender bias' and 'racial bias'. These are expanded upon in Chapter 8, which explores social implications of AI.

Table 1. Types of bias affecting AI algorithms

Type of Bias	Description
Selection Bias	Refers to data samples taken that do not reflect the subject under investigation. It also occurs when two groups having significant differences are used in the same study. If an algorithm performs analyses the effects of stress at the workplace in comparison to stress at home, two similar datasets should be used for each situation to avoid creating two significantly different results because of group differences. This applies to studies and materials that are included in the research, especially previous studies.
Measurement Bias	Occurs when key information is measured, collected or interpreted inaccurately. Also known as 'information bias' or 'observation bias', it can be further divided into random or non-random misclassification. The latter is divided into subtypes, including 'observer bias' (i.e. that which is introduced by the researcher) and 'recall bias' (i.e. that which introduced by the subject under investigation). Researchers who are measurement-biased may use methods that will influence their outcome or support their initial predictions.
Intervention Bias	Refers to how much the researcher, or other factors, intervene with test data. Many corporate policies have their roots in intervention bias. It makes us likely to introduce unnecessary changes to feel in control of a situation. The best way to correct this type of bias is to examine what scientists call a 'null hypothesis', that is what would happen if we did nothing or if we assume the phenomenon under study was an accident or pure chance. Before making system changes, one should ask 'do we need to do this at all'?
Training Data Bias	Refers to deviations in the training or input data provided to the algorithm. Algorithms are trained and learn for particular uses or tasks (e.g. for the population from which samples are drawn). The input data used, however, can be biased, leading to biased responses for those tasks. Moreover, this type of algorithmic bias is often subtle or hidden, because developers often do not publicly disclose the precise datasets used for training. If we only see the final learned model or its behaviour, we might not even be aware that biased data had influenced the results.
Interpretation Bias	Refers to the misinterpretation of the algorithm's outputs or functions by the user or by the broader AI or ML system. Although this bias can be characterised simply as 'user error', the situation is often more complex. In particular, it represents a mismatch even within the intended context of operation, between the information an algorithm produces and the information requirements of the user or system that uses that output. Moreover, there is widespread potential for this kind of informational mismatch, because developers are rarely able to fully specify the exact semantic content (in all contexts) of their algorithms or models. Systems that take this output as input can thus easily be misdirected by spurious or unreliable features of that information.
Funding Bias	Occurs when a study's outcome is more likely to support the interests of the organisation funding the study. This may be due to the testing methods paid for by 'for-profit' companies, creating an inherent bias towards producing positive outcomes for the company. Products may have gone through internal testing, weeding out ineffective or dangerous products before they get to the external testing stage. When companies pay for research into their products, this conflict of interest is easy to create.
Publication Bias	Occurs when researchers publish only favourable results 'on the basis of the direction or strength of the study findings'. (Dickersin and Min, 1993). Pharmaceutical companies, for example, are notorious for manipulating data in this way to exclude results that support the null hypotheses, sometimes putting the lives of patients at risk.

The different bias types refer to either the researcher, the data or the algorithm. In any case, they are not mutually exclusive, nor is it an exhaustive set, although we believe that it covers most of the possible causes. Importantly, algorithmic bias can arise at every stage of research and during the development–implementation process, from data sampling to measurement and from algorithm design to algorithmic processing. Each entry point for algorithmic bias presents a different set of considerations and safeguard requirements.

We should think about algorithmic bias holistically, including the consumer–human or consumer–machine of all output from the AI or ML system. The *ecosystem* of an algorithm contains many opportunities for bias introduction and compensatory biases, which are geared to minimise the harms (if any) created by the algorithmic biases. The technical research into ML and AI algorithmic bias is still in its infancy (Osoba and Welser, 2017). Algorithm designers make myriad design choices, some of which have far-reaching consequences. Questions of bias and systemic errors in algorithms demand a different kind of skillset, experience and quality-assurance type that ideally measures the situations without onerous regulatory constraints or policing. A more sustainable resolution would require algorithms to adhere more closely to socially defined values. However, this only raises more questions, like 'which socially defined values and who gets to decide'? This is likely to require including values related to free speech, censorship, equitability and other acceptable ethical standards as AI and ML systems become more widespread and embedded across society.

ROBOT COMPANIONS

Wherever there is an unfilled human need, there is a business opportunity that is typically marshalled by marketing campaigns broadcasting new products we never knew we needed. Large-scale social problems, such as the global loneliness epidemic, are driving the demand for robot companions. According to a 2018 survey from The Economist and the Kaiser Family Foundation, more than 2 of 10 adults in the US (22%) and UK (23%) said that they always or often felt lonely, lacking companionship or left out or isolated. Figures like these are ubiquitous in the press recently, with alarming statistics about loneliness now accompanied by equally alarming warnings about how it is stunting our lives and outright killing us. The scourge of loneliness is an issue that we will hear about even more the years to come (Howe, 2019).

Scientists have long known that loneliness is emotionally painful and can lead to psychiatric disorders, such as depression, anxiety, schizophrenia and even hallucinatory deliria. However, only recently have they recognised how destructive it is to the body. In January 2018, Britain installed a 'loneliness minister' (John, 2018) after recognising its serious multibillion-dollar toll on the UK economy. Loneliness is associated with premature death, productivity loss and various health risks. More than a dozen start-ups have developed robot home companions to address this. Although some are struggling, there is little question that the demand for these products exists and is likely to grow with our ageing populations, who need help creating and adhering to schedules, reminders to take medicines and coordinating care. Although most robots are not designed specifically with loneliness in mind, they do provide companionship, which many of the elderly desperately need. The market demand for social robots that satisfy sexual appetites is also on the rise. Although some people might consider 'Tinder' to be morally apprehensive, sex with your own robot is also an option now, and thousands of people are taking advantage. Entrepreneurs have combined advances in materials science, robotics, sensor technology and natural language processing to create *anatomical simulacra* that provide physical pleasure. Moreover, with no regulatory structures in place for these 'sexbots', the effects of this growth industry will inevitably alter social norms.

Noel Sharkey, Emeritus Professor of AI and Robotics at the University of Sheffield and co-founder of the Foundation for Responsible Robotics, said, 'Moving into the future we will see some people using sex robots, but the numbers may still be small. At present use of sex robots and dolls can be considered to be a type of paraphilia – atypical sexual practice – which includes atypical objects, fetishes and voyeurism' (Knapton, 2017). Since 2017, sex-doll brothels have appeared in South Korea, Japan and Spain, raising serious moral, ethical and legal dilemmas, such as 'robotic rape' to the prevention of users developing violent sexual tendencies. Some places have called for a complete ban on child sex dolls. Users can clearly become socially isolated and addicted to machines of this nature, making it even more difficult for them to interact properly with real people. 'If people bond with robots it's very worrying. You are loving an artefact that cannot love you back, and the best they can do is fake it,' said Professor Sharkey.

Understanding social AI as a market maker is critical for company strategists and developers. However, it is equally important to recognise that, for better and worse, the social arrangements we take for granted today are also at stake. The roles people play in their own and others' lives are increasingly mediated by technological third-party actors with greater emotional, linguistic and social sophistication. The implications are both daunting and clear: if part of what makes us human is to connect emotionally with others, and if technology increasingly plays the role of emotional connector, what does it mean to be distinctively 'human'?

ETHICAL ISSUES

AI cannot be made intrinsically ethical more than any other technology just because it is 'intelligent'. There was no 'ethical steam power' or 'ethical electricity'. There were just ethical uses that required norms and regulations. We appear to still be well behind the curve of 'ethical internet,' with abuses outpacing norms and laws. This does not mean we should give up. On the other hand, we should try harder and do a better job.

AI has the potential to do good, and some of it can be quite inspirational and enjoyable. However, the early signs of AI's embeddedness in current technologies (e.g. digital assistants) has highlighted AI's unintended consequences. Ethical behaviour and trust can be built into AI systems by involving those people directly impacted by the proposed solution in the design process, engagement with a diverse range of voices, highest levels of transparency and open and honest fixes when things go wrong, which they inevitably will. There are many people from academia, non-profits, governments and industry who can help shape rules, policies and frameworks to help us develop AI-centric ethical disasters. Until this type of movement is supported by proactive governments, we will remain at risk. We must, therefore, find ways to resolve the issues among those focused on developing and introducing the new technologies. Some of these issues are highlighted next.

Principles

With the increase of AI systems and algorithm-based services, social principles, such as fairness, transparency and accountability (FAT) need to be addressed. Fuelled by *big data*, algorithmic-based AI systems are being adopted to a growing number of contexts and industries. These systems filter, sort, score, recommend, personalise and otherwise shape human experiences, increasingly making or informing our decisions with major impact on access to things like credit, insurance, healthcare, parole, social security and immigration. Although these systems bring myriad benefits, they also contain inherent risks, such as codifying and entrenching biases, reducing accountability and hindering due process. They also increase the information asymmetry among individuals whose data feed the systems being exploited

A mixed approach should be used to address fairness, accountability and transparency by bringing together a diverse community of scholars, experts and advocates from computer science, law, social sciences and humanities (Bellamy et al., 2018). We must evaluate technical solutions with respect to existing societal issues, reflecting upon their benefits and risks, to address pivotal questions about economic incentive structures, unintended consequences, distribution of power and redistribution of wealth to establish a society based on fairness, accountability and transparency upheld by democracy and law.

Diversity

Diversity is a fundamental property of human survival, including that of societies and nations. Recent advances in deep learning has allowed the rapid and automatic assessment of organisational diversity and possible discrimination according to race, sex, age and other parameters. In a pilot study conducted by Diversity.ai (Chekanov et al., 2017), deep-learned predictors of race and sex were applied to the executive management and board member profiles of the 500 largest companies taken from 2016 Forbes Global 2000 List and compared with the predicted ratios to the ratios within each company's country of origin, ranked them by the sex, age and race diversity indices.

The median, the 25th quartile and the 75th quartile for predicted ages were 52, 42 and 52 years, respectively. Females represented 21.2% of the total number of corporate executives photographed. Of the photographed corporate executives, 79.7% were white, 3.6% were black and 16.7% were Asian. Despite the study uncovering a significant under-representations across categories, there were plenty disclaimers presented with the analysis. Ultimately, great care was taken not to accuse any single organisation of neglect or misconduct.

While the use of AI to automatically assess organisational diversity is highly controversial, the study can benefit from a crowd-sourced and -curated effort to improve the quality of the datasets and to automate the process of assessing organisational diversity by developing reporting and recommendation systems for relevant stakeholders. It would be worthwhile to adopt the lessons from a study by Intel in 2016, which explored the opportunities brought about by improving diversity, concluding that 'the tech industry stands to add USD 500B new value to the economy each year' (Intel, Decoding Diversity, 2016).

Tess Posner, CEO at AI4ALL, gave a talk on 'Diversity and Inclusion' where she offered recommendations of a practical approach that could be well-used as part of a crowd-sourced and -curated effort (Chekanov et al., 2017) to help address the AI diversity challenge:

- Test, monitor and audit
- Fairness and ethics standards
- Transparency and explainability
- Diversity and inclusion

Companies like AI4ALL aspire to address diversity and inclusion issues via initiatives covering

- **Diversity:** to provide a richer talent pipeline
- **Education:** to increase awareness and access to AI in poor communities
- **Research:** to advance the understanding of and its application for good for all

Digital Waste and Recycling

Getting rid of accumulating waste has become a major challenge for society. The current solution is mainly centred on garbage either being incinerated or buried in different places, causing harm to the environment and nature. The traditional methods used to process waste not only increases the chances of health hazards to the human workforce but also gives rise to air, water and soil pollution. In this context, AI-powered waste-sorting robots have emerged. These intelligent machines are proficient at multitasking. They are autonomous, scalable and have integrated learning systems that can function tirelessly 24/7. In a research report released by Technavio (Technavio, 2017), the global waste-sorting robot market is expected to grow at a compound annual growth rate[3] of more than 17% by 2021 across markets in several regions worldwide. Apart from this optimism and any future plans of pairing humans and robots, the issue of pollution caused by digitalisation and AI remains. Future environmental legislation running parallel to calls for climate Action (Cooper, 2019) is urgently required. Otherwise the effects of pollution will become increasingly difficult to reverse.

Energy Consumption

As developing nations become more industrialised, energy use is expected to soar as increasing wealth leads to a swelling middle class and the lifestyle trappings that it brings. According to Martin Freer, director of the Birmingham Energy Institute at the University of Birmingham, 'with the growth of the middle class in India and China, there will be an associated demand for air conditioning. The United Nations' Intergovernmental Panel on Climate Change suggests that by the middle of the present century, the demand for cooling will outstrip the demand for heating'. Indeed, it is estimated that, by 2040, the world's energy consumption will have increased by nearly 50% (Leslie, 2017).

The world's scientists agree that we are on a path to disaster that can only be stopped by weaning ourselves off fossil fuels. However, that still leaves us with a problem. How do we ensure the lights stay on? Whatever the solution, we will need to fundamentally move away from the 'power-on-demand' way of consuming energy we have come to expect. We will need to become 'producer-consumers' or 'prosumers'. 'For years, we have consumed energy whenever we like and paid a flat rate for that,' said Julian Leslie, head of electricity network development at the UK's National Grid. 'We will have to start shifting our use of energy to when it is there and available rather than shifting the energy production to match our use' (Leslie, 2017).

The next era of energy consumption will see new smart-grid technology or 'microgrids' of peer-to-peer energy networks that distribute electricity in a small geographic area, usually supplementing, staying connected and continuing to rely on the central power grid while accessing generating units located at or near their point of use that rely on locally available fuels, especially locally available renewable energy resources. Only AI will be able to deliver the active management necessary. Balancing microgrids, negotiating joint actions to enable self-healing networks, demand management and assessing the reliability of production and consumption figures supplied by 'prosumers', to name a few areas, will all require real-time forecasting, monitoring and decision taking. Additionally, the systems running many of those components will need to learn the detailed behaviours of their assigned patch.

Although AI is in its early stages of implementation, it is poised to revolutionise the way we produce, transmit and consume energy. AI also limits the industry's environmental impact at a time when demand is steadily growing, our energy production portfolio is diversifying and we are witnessing the ramifications of fossil fuel consumption on biodiversity, air quality and quality of life (Wolfe, 2017). Until we migrate to a new sustainable AI-enabled approach to energy consumption, we will not achieve a society built on FAT principles.

Social Manipulation and Misinformation

We celebrate the promise of AI as we continue to feel the effects of the unintended consequences of social media. Our growing dependence on the internet and social media has been linked to mental-health concerns and declining social cohesion (Vaknin, 2015). Ironically, we are only at the beginning of a digital transformation that will influence every part of our existence. Our ingenuity has not only changed our world, it has also changed individuals and society.

Speech-driven facial animation is the science behind recent *deep-fake* methods (Vougioukas et al., 2019). Deep-fake techniques use AI and deep-learning neural networks to alter audio and video to pass it off as true and original content. Today, its main limitation is that it only works for well-aligned frontal faces. However, as the technology continues to evolve, deep-fakes are sure to become frighteningly and indistinguishably real. One example viewed many millions of times is a 2008 YouTube clip of Bill Hader in a conversation with David Letterman on his late-night show where Hader's face subtly shifts to that of Tom Cruise as Hader does his impression (Lahoti, 2019). Although it may have interesting applications, many are concerned that the chances of misusing this software are higher with the ability to promote harassment, cyber-bullying and other illegal activities, such as revenge porn, political abuse and fake videos. If we consider the potential harm to our future society, social-media companies will need to proactively develop and implement governance policies, auditing measures and proactive monitoring solutions to protect users from deep-fakes-related misinformation.

There has also been a rise in the circulation of misinformation or fake news on social media. Facebook and Twitter, in particular, have played large roles in its diffusion (Allcott et al., 2018). Worse still is the emergence of AI and intelligent bots that systematically amplify falsehoods at the expense of the truth. Nobody seems to know how to reverse this trend. Despite Facebook and Twitter actively taking steps to make changes to their platforms, there remains much work to do across businesses, institutions and communities to bring about a social-media ecosystem that values and promotes truth above all else. Otherwise, we are in danger of becoming a society built on falsehoods and mistrust that may inadvertently cause deeper emotional health issues, inequalities and discrimination. Surely these are qualities that no individual or community wants to endure.

Dumbing Down

It has become an everyday occurrence to see people of all ages and walks of life constantly staring at screens. Smartphones, tablets, laptops and smart devices have taken precedence over actual human interaction. While shopping in grocery stores and malls, eating in restaurants and even while enjoying a late afternoon stroll in a park, countless people can be found staring at a screen. Is this digital fascination dumbing down the nation? In the UK, London taxi drivers must undergo stringent training to obtain their licence. They must pass a test known as 'The Knowledge', which is among the hardest tests to pass in the world. It has been described as like having an atlas of London implanted into your brain. To become an All-London taxi driver or a 'green-badge holder', one must master no fewer than 320 basic routes, all of the 25,000 streets that are scattered within the basic routes and approximately 20,000 landmarks and places of public interest that are located within a 6-mile radius of Charing Cross. The use of global positioning systems and other satellite navigation systems[4] is prohibited. However, the need to memorise city maps is fast diminishing. Across London, as in many busy cities, ride-sharing services, such as Uber, have disrupted the traditional taxi business. Uber drivers forgo the need to learn 'The Knowledge' and freely use Google Maps (or similar) and follow turn-by-turn instructions to navigate to a customer's destination. The London taxi driver is at risk of extinction, and the practice of memorising city maps will eventually disappear. Inevitably, Uber drivers will eventually find themselves replace by self-driving cars. The basic point here is that emerging technology might be slowly dumbing down society and making us dependent on smart devices. Our fear in the 21st century is that we might be replaced by less knowledgeable or capable humans augmented by machines: a clearly unintended consequence.

Cyber Terrorism

AI is being incorporated into a range of cyber-security products, but the technology can also introduce new threats, according to a report by UK and US experts and researchers from 14 institutions, spanning academia, civil society and industry who engaged in a collaborative project among the University of Oxford's Future of Humanity Institute, the University of Cambridge's Centre for the Study of Existential Risk, the Centre for a New American Security, the Electronic Frontier Foundation and OpenAI. The report, 'The Malicious use of AI' (Brundage et al., 2018), examined the potential security threats from malicious uses of AI technologies and proposed ways to better forecast, prevent and mitigate these threats. 'Because cyber security today is largely labour-constrained, it is ripe with opportunities for automation using AI. Increased use of AI for cyber defence, however, may come with risks,' the report warned. According to the authors, the world is 'at a critical moment in the co-evolution of AI and cyber security and should proactively prepare for the next wave of attacks,' which they predict will be larger in number and scale. Attackers are expected to use AI to learn from others' experiences and to craft attacks that current technical systems and IT professionals are ill-prepared to face. Worth noting are four high-level recommendations from the authors that serve as crucial advice to leaders in businesses, institutions and communities:

- Policymakers should collaborate closely with technical researchers to investigate, prevent and mitigate potential malicious uses of AI.
- Researchers and engineers in AI should take the dual-use nature of their work seriously, allowing misuse-related considerations to influence research priorities and norms.
- Best practices should be identified in research areas for improving and maturing methods that addressing dual-use concerns, such as computer security and AI.
- Leaders should actively seek to expand the range of stakeholders and domain experts involved in the discussions of these challenges.

Ultimately, *collaboration* is the recurring theme.

ECONOMIC RISKS

Most experts expect that AI will have a devastating impact on blue-collar jobs. However, there is mounting concern that Chinese and American AI will have a strong impact on white-collar jobs as well.

Job Displacement and De-skilling

According to Lee (2019), there are clear indications of which jobs will be affected and how soon, which jobs can be enhanced with AI and, most importantly, how we can provide solutions to the profound changes in human history that are coming. Many highly paid skilled jobs (e.g. teachers, doctors, financial and insurance advisers, stockbrokers and management consultants) follow the same basic and repeatable processes that typically involve:

- Gathering data from one or more datasets
- Analysing the data, often supported by a working hypotheses
- Interpreting the results to prove or disprove a working hypothesis
- Determining a recommended course of action, often through a vision or strategy
- Implementing a course of action, often through a roadmap or implementation plan

This scientifically derived method relies heavily on three capabilities:

- the ability to complete early rote tasks quickly and accurately
- experience and judgement in determining a course of action
- savviness for helping clients navigate that course

AI and ML will quickly surpass our abilities with the first two capabilities, and this will shift the skill set required for workers wishing to stay in these careers to focus instead on a much broader set of *thinking* rather than *doing* jobs. (Beck and Libert, 2017). Those who wish to stay relevant in their professions will be required to focus on skills and capabilities that AI has trouble replicating, namely 'soft (human) skills' that require degrees of emotional intelligence effected by understanding, empathising, motivating and interacting with other human beings. After all, it takes a doctor to sit with a patient, understand their life situations (e.g. finances, family and quality of life) and help determine what treatment plan is optimal. Similarly, AI might be able to accelerate diagnoses of complex business problems and recommend actions to improve organisations. However, a human being is still best suited to lead a team into action and navigating political sensitivities while employing the most human of capabilities: creativity, imagination and intelligence.

Decades of research points to emotional intelligence as the critical factor that sets star performers apart from the rest of the pack. Emotional intelligence is the foundation for a host of critical skills; it impacts almost everything we do and say every day (Bradbury, 2017). Emotional intelligence taps into a fundamental element of human behaviour that is distinct from a person's intellect. Presently, there is no known connection between intellect and emotional intelligence. We simply cannot predict emotional intelligence based on how smart someone is. Intelligence is one's ability to learn, and it is the same from adolescents through retirement. Emotional intelligence, on the other hand, can be acquired and improved with practice. Although some people are naturally more emotionally intelligent than others, we can develop higher emotional intelligence over time.

Personality is the final piece of the puzzle. This is what makes us uniquely human. However, like intelligence, personality cannot be used to predict emotional intelligence. Personality is also stable over a lifetime and does not change. Emotional intelligence and personality each cover unique ground and helps define people.

In a world where information will grow more in the next 50 years than in the past 400, where the internet has 1-trillion links, where 300 billion e-mail messages are generated every day and 200 million tweets occur daily (Bradbury, 2017), collective intelligence, emotional intelligence and personality will become differentiators as the adoption of AI and ML continues to rise across businesses. Rather than fight or ignore the progress of AI and ML, it is more advisable to invest in developing one's emotional intelligence. This will help change prepare one's self for the important things in life and ultimately open doors to new possibilities with or without the involvement or use of technology.

Rise of the Gig Economy: Alternative Work Arrangements

It is clear that workers of all classes, nationalities and genders are increasingly turning to alternative work arrangements, including side hustles, freelancing, independent contracting and gigging, to make money in a world of increased automation. According to World Economic Forum (Roy, 2019), the global middle class will play an influential role in how we make money in the future. Today, more than 50% of the world's 7.7-billion people live in middle-class households. The more advanced economies, such as those in Europe and Japan, see their middle-class markets growing by 0.5% each year. Rising economies, namely China and India, are expanding their middle classes at 6% each year. Perhaps most striking, however, will be the maturity of Asia's middle class, which will soon constitute 88% of the world's entire middle class. The implications of these changes mark an inflection point in world history: no longer do the poor make up the majority of the world population. That title now belongs to the middle class, who also provide most of the demand in the global economy. This surprises most people who often think of alternative work arrangements as something that is symptomatic of the working class. Perhaps even more surprising is the fact that automation will replace 11% of the female labour force but only 9% of the male labour force over the next two decades. The explanation is profoundly simple: despite their making up less than half of the global labour force, many jobs often held by women (e.g. administrators, secretaries, cashiers and fast-food workers) are 70% more likely to be replaced by automation. This data contrasts and perhaps even contradicts the narratives circulated by the media that tend to portray technology and robots as overtaking men's work.

In addition to high-risk jobs, high-paying jobs in technology are leaving women behind. Information and communication technology (ICT) specialists are four-times more likely to be male than female, and only 24% of ICT graduates in 2015 were women. An analysis of companies working with open-source software, for example, found that only 15% of their software authors were women. Conversely, women were the majority of university students in 50% of the world's countries at a time when we were experiencing a global labour force shortage of 40-million workers. Considering the changing workforce and the advancement of technology, gender gaps in technology fields should send a signal to leaders. It does not help that men earn higher returns on their digital skills than women. Something needs to change, and it will if we truly commit and invest together (Roy, 2019). As a future society, augmented and powered by AI and intelligent automation, we must:

- Redefine work in the context of a digital and AI-driven economy. What constitutes work in an expanding gig economy? What social protections are in place to keep workers safe, healthy and incentivised?
- Be mindful of changing labour-force demographics and create solutions to support the workforce of the future.
- Act now to proactively retrain the workforce to ensure the right skills, career paths and development opportunities are available to everyone regardless of gender.

- Apply a gender-neutral lens to all decision-making going forward, not just because it is the right thing to do. We should gender-disaggregate the future global economy, and, when we do train and re-skill workers, we must ensure women and girls are not left behind, neither intentionally nor unintentionally.

The Fourth Industrial Revolution has the potential to benefit both male and female workers by creating a society that is FAT and inclusive of everyone.

FUTURE RESEARCH DIRECTIONS

We recommend that future research directions further explore areas such as

- Transparency, privacy and fairness
- Morality and values
- Governance and accountability
- Inclusion and equality

It is our belief that, although AI systems have great potential, they also come with risks. For example, they may malfunction and fail to operate in the ways they were intended. We might also rely on them too heavily in situations that go beyond their abilities, or a technology designed to help society might be repurposed in unethical or harmful ways. It is important that we investigate how these risks might be monitored and mitigated. Additionally, frameworks and policies should be sought that help minimise any potential harm, ideally proactively rather than deal with consequences reactively.

We recommend starting with the belief that AI should be used for socially beneficial purposes and always remain under meaningful human control. Understanding what this means in practice is essential. Finding ways to involve businesses, institutions and communities will be fundamental. Additionally, principles and values built upon transparency, freedom of thought and equality of access will surely help with the prospective challenges ahead. AI systems stand to make societies fairer and more equal. However, we believe different groups will inevitably hold different values, meaning that it will be difficult to agree on universal principles. Similarly, endorsing values held by the majority could lead to discrimination against minorities. Ultimately, we must find answers about how to ensure that the values designed for AI systems reflect society, how we prevent AI systems from causing discrimination and how we integrate inclusive values into AI systems and their underlying algorithms.

The creation and use of powerful new technologies requires effective governance and regulation that ensure they are used safely and with accountability. In the case of AI, new standards and institutions may be needed to oversee its use by individuals, institutions and businesses both domestically and internationally. Like previous waves of technology, AI can contribute to a huge increase in productivity. However, it may also lead to the widespread displacement of jobs which will alter economies in ways that disproportionately affect vulnerable sections of the population. This raises important ethical questions about the kinds of societies and economies we want to build.

CONCLUSION

The lesson of social media and its unintended consequences is not that we should impede progress. Instead, progress is more likely to happen when approached with caution and humility. We are more likely to succeed when we vigilantly anticipate problems. If we concede that 'only experts in AI understand AI', then we will fail to understand that unintended consequences do not yield to experts any more than storms yield to meteorologists. Unintended consequences envelope a much broader range of factors, which, in turn, demand a more inclusive conversation. With the advent of AI, the stakes are even higher. We cannot afford to work it out as we go. Perhaps the most consequential of consequences lie at the intersection of AI and healthcare. Healthcare, not coincidentally, is the area most ridiculed for their slow adoption of AI, and, like our social nature, medicine embodies the same indeterminable mix of good and bad that makes it particularly vulnerable to unintended consequences.

The *human vs. machine* narrative rose to prominence during the industrial revolution when the steam engine and mechanical automation in manufacturing and agriculture began to scale. Now, we have reached the next phase (the Fourth Industrial Revolution) wherein machines threaten the class of people who typical have white-collar jobs, such as the lawyers, doctors and management professionals. Conversely, there are still people in the world who work with their hands and live without clean water, sanitation or modern medicine. Their lives are made difficult from a lack of technology. It is difficult to have a conversation about AI without expanding the discussion into these areas. If

AI is to have positive consequences for human society, we require long-term support in conjunction with focused non-partisan efforts and solidarity among politicians, business leaders and citizens. Additionally, we need all of this without the one-upmanship that typically comes with politics. We must move to a mindset where we can enjoy shared benefits of research and development and technological innovation. Many of these things are essential to resolve, irrespective of the technological innovations that emerge. Arguably, these unintended consequence have a lot to do with what makes us human and the type of society we want. AI and intelligence machines can help make us more human by freeing us to be more creative. However, there is more to being human than creativity. We have qualities that machines will never match; they have a specific task or action to accomplish, whereas humans have purpose. If we stop exploring, dreaming and innovating, we will stop developing and expanding our horizons. We may as well then be machines ourselves.

REFERENCES

Allcott, H., Gentzkow, M., & Yu, C. (2018). Trends in the Diffusion of Misinformation on Social Media. *Stanford University*. https://web.stanford.edu/~gentzkow/research/fake-news-trends.pdf

Barocas, S. (2016). Selbst. A.D. Big Data's disparate impact. *California Law Review, 104*, 671–732.

Beck, L. (2019). *YouTube Added A Fact Checking Alert To Warn Users Against Hoaxes*. https://www.bustle.com/p/youtube-added-a-fact-checking-alert-to-warn-users-against-hoaxes-16822727

Beck, M., & Libert, B. (2017). *The Rise of AI Makes Emotional Intelligence More Important. Harvard Business Review. Reprint H03GC6. HBR.ORG.*

Bellamy, R. K. E., Dey, K., Hind, M., & Hoffman, S. C. (2018). *IBM Research, AI Fairness 360: An Extensible Toolkit For Detecting, Understanding, And Mitigating Unwanted Algorithmic Bias*. https://arxiv.org/pdf/1810.01943.pdf

Bradbury, T. (2017). Emotional intelligence: What it is and why you need it. *World Economic Forum*. https://www.weforum.org/agenda/2017/02/why-you-need-emotional-intelligence

Brundage, M., & Avin, S. (2018). *The Malicious Use of Artificial Intelligence: Forecasting, Prevention, and Mitigation*. https://maliciousaireport.com/

Castillo, M. (2013, September). The Scientific Method: A Need for Something Better? *AJNR. American Journal of Neuroradiology*, *34*(9), 1669–1671. doi:10.3174/ajnr.A3401 PMID:23370475

Chekanov, K., Mamoshina, P., Yampolskiy, R., Timofte, R., Scheibye-Knudsen, M., & Zhavoronkov, A. (2017). *Evaluating race and sex diversity in the world's largest companies using deep neural networks*. https://arxiv.org/ftp/arxiv/papers/1707/1707.02353.pdf

Cooper, R. (2019). European Parliament declares a climate emergency. *Climate Action*. http://www.climateaction.org/news/european-parliament-declares-a-climate-emergency

Danks, D., & London, A. J. (2017). Algorithmic Bias in Autonomous Systems. *Proceedings of the Twenty-Sixth International Joint Conference on Artificial Intelligence, IJCAI-17*, 4691-4697.

Devito, N., & Goldacre, B. (2019). *Catalogue of Bias*. https://catalogofbias.org/biases/publication-bias/

Dickerson, K., & Min, Y.I. (1993). Publication Bias: the problem that won't go away. *Ann N Y Acad Sci 1993, 703135-46*, 146-48.

Ernst, E., Merola, R., & Samaan, D. (2018). *The economics of artificial intelligence: Implications for the future of work*. ILO Future of Work, Research Paper Series, International Labour Organization.

Foer, F. (2017). World Without Mind. Jonathan Cape.

Garcia, M. (2016, Winter). Racist in the machine: The disturbing implications of algorithmic bias. *World Policy Journal*, *33*(4), 111–117. doi:10.1215/07402775-3813015

Gluckman, P., & Hanson, M. (2019). *Ingenious: The Unintended Consequences of Human Innovation*. Harvard University Press. doi:10.2307/j.ctvqc6j28

Gray, J. (2017). The biggest energy challenges facing humanity. *BBC Future*. https://www.bbc.com/future/article/20170313-the-biggest-energy-challenges-facing-humanity

Howe, N. (2019). Millennials And The Loneliness Epidemic. *Forbes*.

John, T. (2018). How the World's First Loneliness Minister Will Tackle 'the Sad Reality of Modern Life'. *Time Magazine*. https://time.com/5248016/tracey-crouch-uk-loneliness-minister/

Kirkpatrick, K. (2016, October). Battling algorithmic bias. *Communications of the ACM*, *59*(10), 16–17. doi:10.1145/2983270

Knapton, S. (2017, Nov. 26). Rise of the 'digisexual' as virtual reality bypasses need for human intimacy. *The Telegraph*.

Komaitis, K. (2018). Splintering the Internet: The Unintended Consequence of Regulation. *Internet Society*. https://www.internetsociety.org/blog/2018/10/splintering-the-internet-the-unintended-consequence-of-regulation/

Lahoti, S. (2019). *Terrifyingly realistic Deep Fake video of Bill Hader transforming into Tom Cruise is going viral on YouTube*. https://hub.packtpub.com/terrifyingly-realistic-deepfake-video-of-bill-hader-transforming-into-tom-cruise-is-going-viral-on-youtube/

McCracken, H., & Grossman, L. (2013). Google vs Death. *Time Magazine*. http://content.time.com/time/magazine/article/0,9171,2152422,00.html

Nice, C. (2017). A Funny Look at the Unintended Consequences of Technology. *TEDTalks*. https://www.ted.com/talks/chuck_nice_a_funny_look_at_the_unintended_consequences_of_technology

Osoba, O. A., & Welser, W. (2017). An intelligence in our image: The Risks Of Bias And Errors. In *Artificial Intelligence*. Rand Corporation.

Pedreschi, D., Ruggieri, S., & Turini, F. (2008). Discrimination-aware data mining. *Proceedings of KDD*. 10.1145/1401890.1401959

Posner, T. (2018). *AI Will Change the World, Who Will Change AI? Why diversity and inclusion matters*. https://www.youtube.com/watch?v=9zony2pjNes&t=307s

Rogers, J., Papadimitriou, I., & Prescott, A. (2018). *V&A Digital Design Weekend Publications*. V&A Publishing/Thames & Hudson.

Rosen, G., & Lyons, T. (2019). *Remove, Reduce, Inform: New Steps to Manage Problematic Content*. https://about.fb.com/news/2019/04/remove-reduce-inform-new-steps/

Roy, K. (2019). How is the Fourth Industrial Revolution changing our economy? *World Economic Forum*. https://www.weforum.org/agenda/2019/11/the-fourth-industrial-revolution-is-redefining-the-economy-as-we-know-it/

Schneider, G., Evans, J., & Pinard, K. (2009). *The Internet – Illustrated*. Cengage Learning.

Simplified Analytics. (2016). *Digital Transformation – Age of Instance Gratification.* https://simplified-analytics.blogspot.com/2016/11/digital-transformation-age-of-instant.html

Sweeney, L. (2013). Discrimination in Online Ad Delivery. *ACM Queue; Tomorrow's Computing Today, 11*(3), 10. doi:10.1145/2460276.2460278

Technavio. (2017). *Global Waste Sorting Robots Market 2017-2021.* Author.

Thomson, C. A. (2017). *Association between Dietary Energy Density and Obesity-Associated Cancer: Results from the Women's Health Initiative. Journal of the Academy of Nutrition and Dietetics.*

Vaknin, S. (2015). *Malignant Self-love: Narcissism Revisited* (10th ed.). Narcissus Publications.

Ventola C. L. (2015). The antibiotic resistance crisis: part 1: causes and threats. *P & T: A Peer-Reviewed Journal for Formulary Management, 40*(4), 277–283.

Vougioukas, K., Petridis, S., & Pantic, M. (2019). *Realistic Speech-Driven Facial Animation with GANs.* https://arxiv.org/pdf/1906.06337.pdf

Wolfe, F. (2017). How Artificial Intelligence Will Revolutionize the Energy Industry. Blog. Special Edition on Artificial Intelligence. *Harvard University.* http://sitn.hms.harvard.edu/flash/2017/artificial-intelligence-will-revolutionize-energy-industry/

ENDNOTES

[1]   Bryan Catanzaro at NVIDIA Research teamed with Andrew Ng's team at Stanford to use them for deep learning. 12 NVIDIA units delivered the deep-learning performance of 2,000 central processing units (Source: https://blogs.nvidia.com/blog/2016/01/12/accelerating-ai-artificial-intelligence-gpus/).

[2]   GAFA is an acronym which stands for 'Google, Apple, Facebook and Amazon'. First used in 2012 in French newspaper 'Le Monde' and later credited to Kabir Chibber's article 'American cultural imperialism has a new name: GAFA,' Quartz, December 1, 2014 (Source: https://qz.com/303947/us-cultural-imperialism-has-a-new-name-gafa/).

[3]   The rate of return that would be required for an investment to grow from its beginning balance to its ending balance, assuming the profits were reinvested at the end of each year of the investment's lifespan (Source: https://www.investopedia.com/terms/c/cagr.asp).

[4]   A system of computers and satellites used in vehicles and other places to help people navigate and determine their location (Source: https://dictionary.cambridge.org/dictionary/english/satnav).

Chapter 4
Robots, Replicants, and Surrogates

ABSTRACT

The human brain is an extraordinary machine. Its ability to process information and adapt to circumstances by reprogramming itself is unparalleled, and it remains the best source of inspiration for recent developments in artificial intelligence. This has given rise to machine learning, intelligent systems, and robotics. Robots and AI might right now still seem the reserve of blockbuster science fiction movies and documentaries, but it's no doubt the world is changing. This chapter explores the origins, attitudes, and perceptions of robotics and the multiple types of robots that exist today. Perhaps most importantly, it focuses on ethical and societal concerns over the question: Are we heading for a brave new world or a science fiction horror-show where AI and robots displace or, perhaps more worryingly, replace humans?

"Replicants are like any other machine - they're either a benefit or a hazard. If they're a benefit, it's not my problem." –Rick Deckard, Blade Runner (1992), A Ridley Scott Film

DOI: 10.4018/978-1-7998-4607-9.ch004

INTRODUCTION

The human brain is an extraordinary machine. Its ability to process information and adapt to circumstances by reprogramming itself is unparalleled, and it remains the best source of inspiration for recent developments in artificial intelligence (AI). This has given rise to machine learning (ML), intelligent systems and robotics. The past few decades have witnessed the increasing role that robots play in society… something that we often take for granted as we forget what they actually do. Many of us still think of robots in the sci-fi humanoid sense and not as self-checkouts or home computers. As such, it never occurs to us that we are entrusting our shopping, work and communications to a robot for improved speed, cost, efficiency and safety. Many cutting-edge technologies are connected with the field of robotics, such as ML and AI, industrial internet of things, man–machine collaboration and autonomous mobile systems.

To most humans, the use of robots is a natural part of our day-to-day activities. They are paving the way to an easier life while enhancing our everyday lifestyles, whether it be by driving us to our destinations, cleaning our houses, providing medical care or producing products we crave more quickly and cheaply. Robots in society have faced criticism by people concerned that they are taking over human jobs. As companies search for faster and more cost-effective ways to do things, they invest in more machinery and fewer people. In cases where safety is the key concern, there is little opposition. However, in other cases, some claim that it leads to people being left unemployed for the sake of profit (Ford, 2016). However, concerns such as these have been here since the original industrial revolution when the Luddites smashed machines that had made manufacturing more efficient. While undoubtedly some jobs will be lost in the short term, historical patterns have shown that machines do not ultimately lead to unemployment. They must be built and maintained; they allow companies to expand and they open up whole new industries and areas.

Intelligent robots are a crucial part of digitalisation of the manufacturing industry (Wilkins, 2019). However, the global manufacturing industry is facing big challenges owing to rapidly changing consumer trends, shortage of resources, shortages of skilled workers, an ageing society and demand for local productions. Given these challenges, innovation and enthusiasm in the robotics market is on the rise.

The International Federation of Robotics (IFR)[1] reported an annual global sales value of USD 16.5B in 2018: a new record. 422,000 units were shipped globally in 2018, an increase of 6% compared to the previous year. IFR forecasted an average growth of 12% per year from 2020 to 2022. Five major industrial robot markets represent 74% of global installations in 2018: China, Japan, Republic of Korea, US and Germany. China remains the world´s largest industrial robot market with a share of 36% of total installations. In 2018, about 154,000 units were installed. This is 1% fewer compared to the previous year, but more than the number of robots installed in Europe and the Americas together. The value of installations reached USD 5.4B, 21% higher than in 2017.

ROBOTICS – A SHORT HISTORY

The history of robotics is intertwined with the histories of technology, science and decades of human progress. Technology used in computing, electricity, pneumatics and hydraulics can all be considered a part of the history of robotics. The word 'robot' itself wasn't created until 1921, when a Czech play by Karel Čapek, R.U.R. (Rosumovi Univerzální Roboti), was first performed. It came from 'robota', which translates to 'forced labour', something that has underpinned the role of robots ever since, that is, until the advance of AI.

There is a long history of dolls or puppets that pretend to be robots but really are not. The UNIMATE is generally recognised as the first industrial robot. It went into service at a General Motors automobile part production plant in 1961. Table 1, which is by no means exhaustive and is based on multiple sources, provides a timeline of major achievements across different nations that have helped robotics to become what it is today.

TYPES OF ROBOTS

There are many definitions of 'robot'. One provided by Mel Siegel, Professor of The Robotics Institute at Carnegie Mellon University, resonates most for me. A robot is a machine that '…senses, thinks, acts and communicates' (Siegel, 2015). The roots of robotics research are in two places: hard automation (the assembly-line machines that do repetitive tasks at high speed with high precision) and AI (the goal of computer scientists to design computers and computer programs that have 'common sense'). The first is the 'act' part of the 'sense, think, act, communicate' paradigm. The second is the 'think' part. Given these roots, we can safely describe robots as programmable machines and systems that are able to typically carry out a series of actions autonomously or semi-autonomously. There are three important factors that constitute a robot:

- Robots interact with the physical world via sensors and actuators
- Robots are programmable
- Robots are usually autonomous or semi-autonomous

Not all robots are autonomous. 'Tele-robots' or 'mobile robots' are entirely controlled by a human operator remotely (e.g. drones). Often, robots are described by prepending adjectives: 'mobile', 'humanoid', 'agricultural', 'bomb-disposal' etc. People naturally understand these with very little ambiguity, which is perhaps the best definition.

Not all robots are 'intelligent', let alone 'artificially intelligent'. Most people assume that a robot must be able to think and make decisions. However, there is no standard definition of 'robot thinking.' Requiring a robot to think suggests that it has some level of AI. Many robots are not artificially intelligent. Until quite recently, all industrial robots could only be programmed to carry out a repetitive series of movements that do not require AI. Non-intelligent robots are quite limited in their functionality. AI algorithms are often necessary to allow the robot to perform more complex tasks. No matter how we define a robot, they require designing, building and programming.

In the subsections below, we first explore types of robots we are most familiar with that are used in manufacturing and industry. We then describe other forms of robots, such as 'replicants' (e.g. androids and humanoids) and 'surrogates' (e.g. sexbots) that are outwardly influenced by ideas and attitudes from fiction and, arguably, human fetishes based on popular television shows such as HBO's 'Westworld' or Hollywood movies, such as 'Ex Machina', 'iRobot' and the 'Terminator' series.

Industrial Robots

An industrial robot commonly refers to a robot arm used in a factory environment for manufacturing applications. Traditional industrial robots can be classified according to different criteria, such as type of movement (degrees of freedom), application (manufacturing process), architecture (serial or parallel) and brand. In 1961 the first industrial robot, Unimate[2], joined

Table 1. Timeline showcasing innovations in robotics

Date	Description of Key Event
1495	Leonardo da Vinci draws designs for first robot.
1727	German philosopher and alchemist Albertus Magnus coins the word "android."
1818	Mary Shelley writes "Frankenstein" – about an artificial life form.
1921	Czech writer Karel Capek introduces the term "robot" in a play called "R.U.R." ("Rossum's Universal Robots").
1941	Isaac Asimov uses the term "robotics" to describe a technology of robots and predicts rise of robot industry.
1961	The first industrial robot called UNIMATE is launched at General Motors .
1963	The first artificial robotic arm called the "RANCHO ARM" is unveiled. Controlled by a computer to help the handicapped.
1968	An octopus like tentacle arm is developed by Marvin Minsky.
1969	Neil Armstrong and his crew land on the moon – supported by robotics and space technology.
1970	SRI International creates "Shakey" – the first robot controlled by AI.
1979	"Stanford Cart" is created – successfully navigates a chair filled room following commands from a computer processing multiple images taken by a TV camera.
1997	A robot beats world chess champion Garry Kasparov.
1999	SONY creates and launches the first robot dog called "AIBO" – able to entertain, communicate and learn.
2000	Honda introduces ASIMO.
2002	The first "Roomba" robot vacuum cleaner is introduced by iRobot.
2004	Seiko Epsom releases the first Micro Flying Robot (μFR) – a helicopter robot which included a camera.
2005	The Battlefield Extraction-Assist Robot (BEAR) developed for use in the extraction of wounded soldiers from the battlefield with no risk to human life.
2006	MIT unveils "Domo" - an experimental robot to interact with humans. Named after the Japanese phrase "domo arigato" (translates as "thank you very much")
2007	"Tico" is a social robot developed by Adele Robots to interact with humans in different environments, primarily in education as a helper for teachers.
2008	"Salvius" (from the word 'salvaged') is the first open source humanoid robot in the US built using recycled materials to reduce the costs of design and construction.
2009	The HRP-4C, nicknamed "Miim", is a feminine-looking humanoid robot created by the a Japanese research facility (AIST).
2010	"TOPIO Dio", manufactured by a Vietnam company, designs a robot to serve in a restaurant or coffee shop or as a cocktail bartender.
2011	"ReWalk" is a commercial bionic walking assistance system that uses powered leg attachments to enable paraplegics to stand upright, walk and climb stairs.
2012	The Hybrid Assistive Limb (also known as "HAL") is a powered exoskeleton suit developed by Japan's Tsukuba University and the robotics company Cyberdyne.
2013	"Nadine" is a female humanoid social robot modelled on Prof. Nadia Magnenat Thalmann. Returns greetings, makes eye contact and remembers conversations.
2014	Harvard researchers unveil "Termite-inspired" biomimetic autonomous robots capable of building complex structures without a central controller.
2015	"FEDOR" is a Russian humanoid robot that replicates movements of a remote operator. Sent a mission to International Space Station (in 2019).
2016	"Sophia" is a high profile social humanoid robot created by Hanson Robotics. She is the first non-human to be awarded a U.N. title and citizenship in Saudi Arabia.
2017	"Atlas" a humanoid robot from Boston Dynamics is capable of doing backflips. Even if it does tumble, it can get back up on its own.
2018	SONY launches a new edition "AIBO"- robot dog – more expressive, responds to voice commands and even learns from its owners developing a unique personality.
2019	Launch of various domestic robots and personal smart devices from Amazon, Google, Facebook, Apple and Samsung.

the assembly line at a General Motors plant to work with heated die-casting machines. Unimate took die castings from machines and performed welding on auto bodies: tasks that were unpleasant for people. Obeying step-by-step commands stored on a magnetic drum, the 4,000-pound arm was versatile enough to perform a variety of tasks.

An industry was then spawned, and a variety of other tasks were also performed by robots, such as loading and unloading machine tools. Unimate industrial robots are among the most widely used in the world. With over 20 years of continued improvement, they are highly reliable and easy to use. More recently, there has been a new qualifier for industrial robots: 'collaborative'. One can collaborate with its human co-workers. Collaborative robots (e.g. 'cobots') are made in such a way that they respect some safety standards so that they cannot hurt a human. Although traditional industrial robots generally need to be fenced off away from human co-workers for safety reasons. Cobots can be used in the same environment as humans and be taught instead of programmed by a human operator.

Over the course of 5 years, the Collaborative Robot market is expected see a revenue compound annual growth rate of 51.4%. Currently, the market size is USD 370M but it is set to touch the USD 4500M mark by 2024. By 2027, the revenue from this sector will be approximately USD 7.5B with a 29% share of the entire industrial robot market[3].

Service Robots

Service robots are different from industrial robots. They automate menial, dangerous, time-consuming or repetitive tasks, thereby releasing human workers to accomplish more intellectual functions. They are semi-autonomous or fully autonomous robots that have some mobility and interact with people, usually in a retail, hospitality, healthcare, warehouse or fulfilment setting (Calderone, 2019).

Domestic service robots typically include devices used for home help, cleaning and gardening. For example, cleaning robots automate routine, dangerous or dirty work with efficiency. Their chores could include disinfecting an area or simply vacuuming a room. Conversely, industrial cleaning robots are used in many different ways, such as glass cleaning for large buildings or mopping, vacuuming or cleaning of industrial sites. There are wall-climbing robots for boiler-wall cleaning. They can also clean, polish and remove paint in vessels and tanks.

Professional service robots are used in a variety of applications at work, in public and in hazardous environments and are more capable, rugged and often more expensive than domestic robots. According to IFR, sales of service robots for professional use had an estimated value of USD 9.2B in 2018. Logistic systems accounted for 40% of the total sales value. Service robots for personal and domestic use had an estimated value of USD 3.7B. More than 12-million robots for domestic tasks make people's everyday life easier (IFR, 2019).

By 2021, the professional service robotic market is predicted to reach USD 37B. Businesses want to automate certain processes for safety, efficiency and productivity (Calderone, 2019). Professional service robots can go where human workers would be in danger. Hence, safety is an important consideration, because robots can handle dangerous jobs while humans focus on intellectual tasks in dangerous situations.

REPLICANTS

Androids are socially intelligent anthropomorphised robots that act as sophisticated tools for humans. While they do not serve sexual or reproductive purposes, Androids like Repliee Q2, Actroid DER, Actroid F and Aiko have been created to assist with a variety of services. Aiko is a female android originally created to assist the elderly with simple tasks and keep them company (Walters, 2014). In each case, the underlying technology includes sophisticated software that elicits responses to physical sensations, like pressure and temperature, for artificial limbs, video recognition and a basic ability to read and converse in dual languages (i.e. English and Japanese). Aiko's face and body are made of silicone that looks and feels like human skin. Actroid F betters Aiko's capabilities by detecting and imitating people's expressions.

Although these advancements are amazing by themselves, they raise difficult questions and dilemmas about how society will distinguish a real human from an android. If we continue further, we realise that we cannot see the internal mechanisms of an android. Thus, we may simply accept that it is a human. This leads us to an important epiphany: a human may be defined from two perspectives. First, one is an organic mechanism and, second, by appearance. The latter has increasingly been the obsession of the 'Gen-Z' population[4] (Weinswig, 2016). Furthermore, rapid progress in artificial human-like organs makes this distinction even more confusing. Artificial humans typically exist as either an android or a geminoid[5]. They can be used to improve the understanding of humans through psychological and cognitive tests. Figure 1 depicts three categories of humanlike robots: (left-to-right) humanoid robot (Robovie II; ATR Intelligent Robotics and Communication Laboratories), android (Repliee Q2; Osaka University and Kokoro Corporation) and geminoid (HI-1; ATR Intelligent Robotics and Communication Laboratories).

Figure 1. Three categories of humanlike robots: (left-to-right) humanoid, android and geminoid

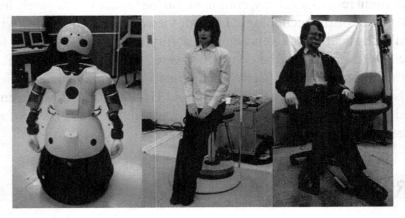

To effectively interact with humans, the success of these androids or geminoids crucially depends on their ability to imitate human appearance and behaviour. Simultaneously, the ideal paradigm is not to create a synthetic human that falls victim to the 'uncanny valley'. Social robots must look and interact in ways that play on people's expectations about what is socially acceptable. Thus, roboticists program and design female robots based on assumptions about gender roles. Doing so, complex notions of gender are reduced to common-sense ideas about how women look, behave and respond.

According to (Sullins, 2011), technology requires ethics, because the design and function of artefacts, including gendered robots, reproduce the values of society while also creating new dynamics among people.

Androids that are gendered to look female are assigned stereotypically feminine characteristics. By reproducing negative stereotypes about women, gendered robots should obey ethics because they communicate values about women to persons who interact with the robots. Aiko, Actroid DER and F, as well as Repliee Q2 are representations of young, thin and attractive oriental women. They have high-pitched, feminine voices and similar movements. Actroid DER has been demoed wearing a tight *Hello Kitty* shirt with a short jean skirt, and Repliee Q2 has been displayed wearing blue and white short leather dress and high-heeled boots. Despite being presented this way, the intended purpose is nonsexual. However, as a result of attributing stereotypically feminine qualities, gender inequalities are replicated, and female androids become sexualised.

Viewers comments attached to YouTube videos of Aiko, Actroid DER and F and Repliee Q2 provide an anecdotal illustration of how someone surfing the web might react. Generally, comments on the female robots rarely focused on the quality of the technology. Instead, viewers were concerned with the android's physical attractiveness or its ability to do stereotypically female tasks. Some examples of the comments were 'make me a sandwich', 'shut up and strip' or 'I'd hit it'. Viewer's comments about the male androids and gynoids videos, such as those of Geminoid HI-1 and Jules, were generally focused on the quality of the technology, realistic features or fear of robots overpowering humans.

SURROGATES

Surrogates or 'sexbots' are physical, interactive manifestations of women used for a sexual purpose. Fanatics hope that, in time and with the right technology, they will be indistinguishable in the way they look, feel and react. This would allow any man to live out needs and fantasies that would be difficult or impossible to actualise with a real woman. Sex robots are anticipated to serve three main applications:

- First, they can be used to assist with therapy or treatment for a diverse array of patients in hospitals or homes, including disabled individuals.
- Second, they could be used to stimulate physical or emotional companionship for individuals in society, not necessarily as part of treatment or therapy.
- Lastly, they could be used for activities that individuals cannot or prefer not to engage in with other people, because they are illegal, dangerous or socially frowned upon. For example, a user that enjoys extremely violent or degrading sex may have difficulty finding human partners with whom to live out such acts. Another example is men who support the sex-trade industry but would prefer to avoid the legal consequences

or social stigma of breaking the law. In this category, sex robots could also have applications in the army or prisons to address the sexual desires of soldiers or convicts.

To men, what is most attractive about sex robots is that 'it can't say no to you,' and the ability, or rather illusion, of sexually controlling or even harming a woman.

The Special Committee on Pornography and Prostitution (Fraser, 1985) defined harm as material that 'represents and nourishes attitudes and activities inimical to the equality of men and women, [which perpetuates] lies about aspects of women's humanity and denies the validity of their aspirations to be treated as full and equal citizens'. Although this definition was created with reference to pornography, it also applies to the harm that sex robots cause women. A user's ability to manipulate sex robots dehumanises women and promotes lies about their sexuality. Sex robots harm women because they desensitise the user and promote the idea that consent is not a necessary part of a sexual interaction.

A glance at magazine newsstands, album covers, music videos and ads show that women are already sexualised and objectified by their environment. Sex robots, by their very design, encourage the idea that women are subordinate to men and are mere instruments for the fulfilment of male fantasies. This type of harm has been explored in the context of pornography and is reproduced in the harm caused by sex robots. Like pornography, the use of sex robots sexualises rape, violence, sexual harassment and prostitution and eroticises dominance and submission. Sex robots further enhance the harms posed by prostitution by presenting them all in one interactive, customised and obedient entity. Sex robots reinforce user's sexist ideas about submission and power through a physically rewarding process. They represent a form of obscenity that is direct, intimate and likely to elicit changes in societal beliefs and attitudes.

Sexuality is socially constructed. Hence, as a society, we have the ability to alter repugnant, abusive and exploitative notions about sexuality and intimacy if we choose to. This should involve dialogue about method, power, class, law and discussions of gender. Sex robots could provide an opportunity to understand and correct violent and demeaning attitudes towards women. If regulated, sex robots could provide a means of researching the roots of sex and intimacy for both genders, de-mystifying female sexuality and addressing the roots of women's oppression. More importantly, input from women's groups, legal practitioners, academics and roboticists is required to canvass applicable solutions and identify the most appropriate methods of regulation.

As a society, we must not let ourselves be blinded by superficial depictions of the 'perfect' intimate partner. Instead, we should seek to apply AI enabled technology in a way that enhances what is valuable, legitimate and liberal without the need to resort to any subjective biases or denigrating either of the male or female (and gender neutral) beings.

HUMANS VS. ROBOTS

Robots can only reach out in ways they have been programmed to do. They can only learn from stimuli they were instructed to pay attention to. It limits them to a small range of experiences that shape their behaviours. There is no meaning in their methods. Babies, on the other hand, are social learners. The real genius of human babies is not simply that they learn from the environment. Other animals can do that. Human babies can understand the people around them and, specifically, interpret their intentions (Beard, 2018). Until recently, scientists tended to think of infants as irrational, illogical and egocentric. In his Principles of Psychology (James, 1957), William James described babies' experience of sensory overload as 'the baby, assailed by eyes, ears, nose, skin and entrails at once, feels it all as one great blooming, buzzing confusion.' This understanding contributed to a mechanistic view of learning and the idea that the sheer repetition of words was what mattered most. We have since learnt this is not true.

Professor Kathy Hirsh–Pasek, an early-childhood development expert at Temple University in Pennsylvania, said 'we arrive ready to interact with other humans and our culture'. Even in utero, babies are learning. At that stage, they pick up sounds. 1-hour-old infants can distinguish their mother's voice from another's. They arrive in the world with a brain primed to learn through sensory stimulation. Human babies can interpret people's intentions, and their brains are specially adapted to learn. We can actively enhance our cognitive development by learning from our environment and social group like babies do (Hirsh-Pasek and Golinkoff, 2016).

According to Hirsh–Pasek, our ability to understand other people arrives around the ninth month, at a moment in a baby's development when they can assess the attention of others by holding or pointing at objects. After 1 year, they can follow another's attention, gazing at, touching or listening to the same thing. At 15 months, they can direct attention. 'Listen to that!

Look over there!' Shared attention is the starting point of conscious human learning. It is why infants do not learn to talk from watching videos, audio recordings or overhearing parental conversations. We have not evolved to do it that way. This is why it matters that we talk to our children. It is also why we cannot learn from robots… yet.

UNCANNY VALLEY

The concept of the uncanny valley originally applied to robots and was first presented by Japanese roboticist Mashiro Mori in a chart shown in Figure 2 (Kageki, 2012). Mori suggested that, as robots looked and behaved more like humans, they became more easily accepted by real humans, up to a point. An example of a function that does not increase continuously is climbing a mountain. The relation between the distance (x) a hiker has travelled towards the summit and the hiker's altitude (y), owing to the intervening hills and valleys. By climbing toward the goal of making robots appear human, our affinity for them increases until we come to a valley, which Mori calls the 'uncanny valley'. The examples outlined below illustrates the uncanny-valley phenomenon.

Figure 2. Representation of the uncanny valley

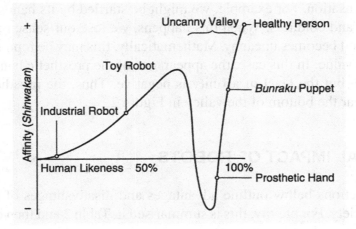

Industrial robots are increasingly recognised as the driving force behind reductions in factory personnel. However, these robots just extend, contract and rotate their arms. They do not look very human and are specifically designed to be functional. From this perspective, the robots must perform functions similar to those of human factory workers. It does not matter whether they resemble humans. Thus, people seldom feel any affinity for them. This is why the industrial robot appears near the start (left side) of Figure 2. In stark contrast, the designer of a robot toy will typically focus more on its appearance rather than its functionality. Although it may be a sturdy and bulky mechanical figure, the robot will start to have a human-looking external form with a face, two arms, two legs and a torso. Children seem to feel deeply attached to these kinds of toy robots. Hence, why the toy robot is shown midway in Figure 2. Creating an artificial human is itself one of the objectives of robotics. Consequently, various efforts are underway to build humanlike robots. For example, a robot's arm may be composed of a metal cylinder with many bolts. However, by covering it with skin and adding a bit of fleshy plumpness, we can achieve a more humanlike appearance. As a result, we naturally respond to it with a heightened sense of affinity.

Recently, owing to great advances in fabric technology, we cannot distinguish at a glance a prosthetic hand from a real one. Some models simulate wrinkles, veins, fingernails and even fingerprints. Though similar to a real hand, the prosthetic hand's colour is pinker, as if it had just come out of the bath. One might say that the prosthetic hand has achieved a degree of resemblance to the human form, perhaps on a par with false teeth. However, when we realise the hand, which at first site looked real, is in fact artificial, we experience an eerie sensation. For example, we might be startled by its handshake and its texture and coldness. When this happens, we lose our sense of affinity, and the hand becomes uncanny. Mathematically, this may be represented by a negative value. In this case, the appearance of the prosthetic hand is quite humanlike, but the level of affinity is negative. Thus, the prosthetic hand appears near the bottom of the valley in Figure 2.

SOCIETAL IMPACT OF ROBOTS

The subsections below outline advantages and disadvantages of robots in human society. For brevity, this is summarised in Table 2 and then expanded upon further with a short narrative.

Table 2. Impact of robots (pros and cons)

Pros	Cons
More efficient production	Some workers displaced – possible structural unemployment
Higher labour productivity and higher wages (and profit)	Creates winners and losers – possible increase in inequality
Cheaper goods increases disposable income of consumers and provides healthy competition among businesses	Automation could lead to increased monopolies of power and control
Avoids repetitive and mundane jobs	Loss of human interaction – dealing with computers leads to lower quality of life
Can improve safety and remove human error	Automated systems can show lack of empathy

Advantages of Robots

Robots can do work that involves boring, monotonous, hazardous and difficult tasks. In this scenario, humans programme robots, involving visualisation, design and planning activities. Robots will do the actual work to make those designs and plans a reality. Robots enable humans to have more leisure time. This may include time for hobbies, time with family and friends and other creative ventures. Ultimately, robots would free-up time for humans and significantly increase our standard of living. Conversely, there are dangerous side effects that imply human laziness, which could result in higher levels of obesity or mental health and psychological issues.

Disadvantages of Robots

Robots are likely to displace blue- and white-collar workers from traditional jobs. Unlike humans, robots can work 24 h/day, 7 days/week without complaint, sickness or vacations. As was the case for previous industrial revolutions and innovations, changes to frameworks involving financial, economic, law and regulatory compliance systems were necessary to enable human societies to flourish, albeit over time. Without the support of governments and businesses, increased automation via robots will lead to inequality and angst among individuals and communities. Ultimately, humans have one of two options:

- We keep our old monetary system and halt the progression of technology from society so that we can keep our traditional jobs, OR

- We can allow AI, robots, automation and intelligent technology to take their course.

It is our belief that the latter is more sensible and will lead to a fairer society. This viewpoint is supported by many people, including the futurist, Jacque Fresco[6], who founded 'The Venus Project', which offers a new holistic socio-economic model used to maximise the quality of life rather than profits. It is based on a *resource-based economy* that seeks to allow technology, robotics and automation to flourish, all for the purpose of enhancing the well-being of all humans without the use of money while also dramatically reducing crime, poverty, hunger, homelessness and many other pressing problems that are common throughout our world today. Fresco believed that 'as AI rapidly develops, machines will be assigned the tasks of complex decision making in industrial, military and governmental affairs. This would not imply a takeover by machines. Instead, it will be a gradual transfer of decision-making processes to machine intelligence as the next phase of social evolution' (Fresco and Meadows, 2002).

Misuse of Robots and Technology

Today, many robots and technology are used to create weapons and other military applications (Parkin, 2015). It is no surprise that so many people fear robots and technologies. It is not the technology and robots that should be feared, however. Rather, it is the people who manage and command the military and related organisations who supply the technology for the purpose of control, killing and destroying humans.

COMMON MISCONCEPTIONS

Perhaps because of the exponential growth of computing and intelligent machines, robots will soon be capable of performing almost any task we can imagine. This trend is increasingly everywhere, such as in assembly lines, bank machines, retail store self-checkout counters and automated customer service agents often supported by online chat bots. In the future, robots will perform all of the dangerous and heavy-duty tasks, such as building city and residential infrastructure. Below is a list of misconceptions commonly attributed with robots:

- **Robots will steal our jobs:** This is threat is perhaps simply a flaw of current outdated economic systems. In the west, our current monetary economic system is built on the premise that corporations will always strive to maximise profit. By hiring more robots and fewer people, in the long run, businesses will greatly save a lot of money while significantly increasing output and productivity. From the perspective of business owners, robots give more 'bang for their buck'. Robots are simply faster, more accurate, more precise and more efficient at performing tasks than any human being. This process is known as 'technological unemployment' (Hellard, 2018). To counteract this, Andy Haldane, Chief Economist of the Bank of England, stated, 'we will need even greater numbers of new jobs to be created in the future. It has not been a feature of the past, but could it possibly be a feature for the future? I believe that it is a much more open question than any previous point, possibly in history'. Eventually, we will need to update and transform our economic systems in ways that encourage and support the integration of robots with humans across our society to enable technological innovation and human evolution.
- **Robots will take away our freedom and fun:** Perhaps the reverse is true. Robots could give us more freedom and opportunities for leisure, because we would spend less time doing mundane, menial and repetitive tasks, and we will spend more time enjoying the things that we want to do. Although this means robots would be doing most of the tasks and labour, humans could still do any of the work themselves if they chose to. Examples include mowing the lawn, vacuuming the house and washing the dishes. This choice is itself a type of freedom that humans can take pleasure in. Without robots, humans will lack choices.
- **Robots will lead to laziness and 'dumbing down':** The response to this builds upon the previous point that humans will have more time for leisure and fun. A direct benefit of robots is the time that an individual would have to spend on work, travel, leisure, hobbies and family, per one's interests. Regarding dumbing down, like any useful technology, to make robots serve us well requires the exercise of good judgement and perhaps new forms of self-discipline and social values that encourage humans to develop other skills that maintain mental and physical agility.
- **Robots are not safe:** Safety is an important consideration in human–robot interactions. Although industrial robots typically operate in

a setting that keeps them apart from people, 'cobots' and 'service' robots are increasingly entering our homes, public spaces and crowded human-inhabited environments. Ironically, humans have entrusted our safety to autonomous cars, yet we give little thought to the fact that they have been largely constructed by robots. Indeed, the car-manufacturing industry is increasingly dependent on and automated by robots. The success of robots in various industries enable humans to achieve and maintain levels of efficiency and effectiveness that we have now become very accustomed to and unable to match on our own. We need to find ways to integrate robots into our lives without increasing safety risks while also ensuring accountability and responsibility without reducing any benefits.

- **Robots will take over and displace humans:** Over the next few decades, it is highly likely that AI and robots will reach and surpass human intelligence. Truly autonomous systems will make their own decisions about what to do things without necessarily consulting humans. How can we trust such systems if we do not know what, and crucially why, these systems will make their decisions? One way to prevent a robot takeover (prevalent in dystopian futures of Hollywood movies) is to give robots only a localised control system instead of a centralised system like 'Skynet' from the 'Terminator' franchise. Additionally, humans who are involved in building and programming robots should do so by observing stringent quality assurance, ethical considerations and failsafe design practices outlined by standards bodies like IEEE Robotics and Automation Society who introduced new standards and principles for AI and autonomous systems that prioritise human well-being (The IEEE Global Initiative, 2016). All future AI, autonomous systems and robot technologies should be aligned to humans in terms of our moral values and ethical principles. They must behave in a way that is beneficial to people beyond reaching functional goals and addressing technical problems. This will allow for an elevated level of trust between humans and AI technologies that encourages positive and fruitful pervasive use in our daily lives. Ultimately, robots should always be created to serve humans and never the other way around.

Replacement of Human Workers

The last misconception outlined above warrants further exploration, given the level of anxiety that exists in society regarding the replacement of human workers. A working paper by published by the National Bureau of Economic Research on the effects of industrial robots on employment and wages in the US between 1990 and 2007 showed that one new robot reduced employment by 5.6 workers. In their recent study, economists Daren Acemoglu of MIT and Pascual Restrepo of Boston University concluded that each additional industrial robot reduced employment in a given commuting area by 3–6 workers while lowered overall wages by 0.25–0.5% (Acemoglu and Restrepo, 2019). An industrial robot is a fully autonomous machine that can be programmed to perform different manual tasks without a human operator or without human supervision. According to the International Federation of Robotics, there are already between 1.5–1.75 million industrial robots in operation, with the automotive industry employing 39% of them (Acemoglu and Restrepo, 2019). 'When robots compete against human labour', wrote Acemoglu and Restrepo, 'we estimate that one additional robot per 1000 workers now reduces aggregate employment to population ratio by 0.34 percentage points and aggregate wages by 0.5%'. However, if the focus is 'only on declines in employment in heavily-robotised manufacturing', and if it presumes that employment losses in other sectors are caused to local demand and will not directly translate into national effects, these effects could be as low as 0.18 percentage points for employment and 0.25% for wages.

A decrease of only 0.25 to 0.5% in employment is already leading the way for doomsday rhetoric, such as in Cain Miller's article in The New York Times, entitled 'Evidence That Robots Are Winning the Race for American Jobs' (Cain Miller, 2017), which painted a grim picture for the 'large numbers of people out of work, with no clear path forward – especially blue-collar men without college degrees'. Robots have affected jobs for both men and women, but the effect on male employment was nearly twice as big. The data does not explain why but Daren Acemoglu viewed that women were more willing than men to take a pay cut to work in a lower-status field. That is one drawback, but it is also true that women's employment is less affected by automation than men, because the lower-earning jobs typically held by women are harder to automate. Otherwise, women who anticipate job losses because of automation are more willing to learn skills that robots are not yet able to duplicate, such as social skills and non-routine interactions. Even if robots begin to replace humans in a variety of tasks, it does not spell doom for human jobs, as many experts suggest. This is because the value of human judgement skills will increase (Acemoglu and Restrepo, 2019).

According to an article by Cynthia Than of Inc. com (Than, 2017), as robots replace lower-skilled jobs held primarily by men, such as those in the automotive industry, men might transition into fields that are currently dominated by women, into occupations that have not yet been able to be fully automated, because they require greater social or emotional sensing. What we might see then is an increase in wages in these particular women's fields as more men enter the profession. An additional benefit to automation is that human workers will develop new cognitive or sensory skills to complement the routine tasks performed by the robot. These 'soft skills', such as adaptability, creativity and the ability to recognise nuanced emotions and respond to them appropriately, are in high demand for a wide range of jobs.

CLOSING THOUGHTS

Now is the right time to decide how we would like robotics and AI to impact our society by steering the EU and other governments towards a balanced legal framework fostering innovation while simultaneously time protecting people's fundamental rights. The number of robots used by businesses to boost their productivity has increased rapidly over the past several years. This is a trend that is most likely to continue. The productivity impact of robots is already comparable to the contribution of steam engines. Additionally, there is evidence that these productivity increases have lifted total labour demand as well as overall wage levels (Bandholz, 2016). These effects, however, are not distributed evenly. As high-skilled and high-wage workers benefit disproportionately, the increased pace of robotisation will further add to already high-income inequality within advanced economies. To enable broader parts of society to reap the benefits of this technological progress, two sets of actions need to be taken. First, we need to rethink our educational system and, second, reallocate the income from owners to workers via a revitalised economic system using tenets of Andrew McAfee's acronym (McAfee, 2015) based on the 'Old McDonald' nursery rhyme: 'E-I-E-I-O':

- **Education:** Focus on skills that technology is not too good at (see above).

- **Infrastructure:** Improve broad infrastructure from roads, airports to networks.
- **Entrepreneurship:** Support young creative businesses, which foster innovation and are a prime source of new jobs.
- **Immigration:** Welcome talented and ambitious people.
- **Original (basic) research:** Support original early-stage research.

It is common to not think about the manufacturing processes behind products we use, and this is often where robots are found. Humans have entrusted our safety to cars, yet we give little thought to the fact that they have been largely constructed by robots. Indeed, the car-manufacturing industry is heavily automated with robots. Due to the success of robots, they are now used extensively for complicated medical procedures and are now filling new military and civilian roles through drone technology. All of these (and many other) industries depend highly on robots in order to achieve and maintain the level of efficiency and effectiveness in which they have now become accustomed to.

Robotics has been criticised as a field that provides technological fixes for social problems (Robertson, 2007). However, it is our view that that merely introducing the notion of culture into robotics discourse and practice does not resolve this issue. Although robotics researchers in Japan have brought attention to culture as part of technological development, their framing of culture in robotics largely has relied on untested and unquestioned cultural assumptions, because robots have yet to be broadly commercialised and adopted by users in ways that will allow them to contribute to their cultural meanings.

Japan accounts for nearly 52% of the world's share of operational robots and leads the post-industrial world in the development of humanoid robots designed and marketed specifically to enhance and augment human society. *Innovation 25*, Prime Minister Abe's visionary blueprint for remaking Japanese society by 2025, has the aim of reversing the declining birth rate and accommodating the rapidly ageing population and emphasises the central role that household robots will play in stabilising core institutions, like the family. In addition to exploring the cultural logic behind the development of autonomous, intelligent, evolutionary humanoid robots, the new bio-and robot technologies are being deployed to deify old or traditional values, such as the patriarchal extended family and socio-political conservatism. In addition to using them to manufacture goods, the aim is to put this new generation of robots to use as cleaners, sales assistants, museum guides, carers for the young and old, television programme presenters and, of particular relevance here, as teachers (Robertson, 2007). This is not a pipedream of robot engineers. Japan and South Korea, for instance, intend to make significant use of humanoid robots within the next decade. However, interest in using robots as teachers, as reflected in the number of publications about them, is increasing around the world (Robertson, 2007).

One concern regarding the mass production and commercial use of robots is about the norms and values that shape a robot's programming, that which gives it social and cultural biases. Programmers are immersed in particular cultures and, unconsciously or otherwise, their cultural norms and values are likely to be reflected in what they have their robot do (Robertson, 2007).

Technocrats from many developed countries, especially those from Japan and South Korea, are preparing for the human–robot co-existence society that they believe will emerge by 2030. Regulators are assuming that, within the next two decades, robots will be capable of adapting to complex, unstructured environments and interacting with humans to assist with the performance of daily life tasks. Unlike heavily regulated industrial robots that toil in isolated settings, the next-generation robots will have relative autonomy, which raises a number of safety concerns (Weng et al., 2009).

It is our belief that Isaac Asimov's 'Three Laws of Robotics' (Asimov, 2013) is not a sufficient foundation for establishing sustainable laws and policies for robot safety that keep up with the accelerating pace of AI and robots. To recap, Isaac Asimov's three laws of robotics comprises the following:

- **The First Law of Robotics:** A robot may not injure a human being or, through inaction, allow a human being to come to harm.
- **The Second Law of Robotics:** A robot must obey the orders given to it by human beings, except where such orders would conflict with the First Law.
- **The Third Law of Robotics:** A robot must protect its own existence as long as such protection does not conflict with the First or Second Laws.

He later introduced a fourth or zeroth law that outranked the others: A robot may not harm humanity, or, by inaction, allow humanity to come to harm.

Since then, Asimov's laws of robotics have become a key part of a science fiction culture that has gradually become mainstream.

These are ultimately based on fiction and need to be revisited and adapted to our modern times. This task is made more difficult as the line between robots and humans is set to become increasingly blurred, according to Osaka

University's Professor, Hiroshi Ishiguro. He predicts a future where robots not only look like humans but are self-conscious (Ishiguro and Nishio, 2007).

Rising inequality and slow productivity gains may be the main economic challenges of the 21st century, and the increased use of robots should affect both of these developments positively as well as negatively. Although empirical literature about the impact of robots is still in its infancy, there is a growing number of studies that support the notion that they will increase productivity, wages and total labour demand. However, they will mostly benefit higher-skilled workers. With an increased use of robots, computers and other machines, the latest round of technological progress now largely comes at the expense of middle- and low-skilled and -wage workers.

And that raises an interesting question: do we need a set of Asimov-like laws to govern the behaviour of robots as they become more advanced?

According to many studies, the productivity impact of robots is already comparable to the contribution of steam engines, yet still lagging behind the impact of information and communications technology (ICT). One must keep in mind that the total value of ICT capital by far has exceeded that of current robot services. Some of the productivity gains from robot densification are shared with workers through higher wages. As robots and machines are capable of taking over a growing number of tasks, humans must focus on their comparative advantages, including non-cognitive skills. Additionally, advanced countries (notably the US) must halt and reverse the trend that the quality of student education is primarily determined by parents' income and wealth, because this unequivocally amplifies the negative inequality spiral. However, even if politicians do adopt the necessary changes to the education system, increased technological progress will most likely continue to lead to growing income inequality, because people have different skills and different financial conditions. Both factors impact the degree to which people can benefit from technological progress. Thus, there is a growing need to reallocate income from rich to poor and/or from owners to workers. One of the most promising solutions to the long-term challenge posed by machines substituting for labour is employee ownership, which allows all workers to earn their income from labour as well as from capital (Bandholz, 2016).

In summary, AI, robotics and intelligent machines offer enormous potential for economic development and societal improvement. However, to truly benefit collectively, we require new frameworks that incorporate new systems for economics, ethics, laws (for fairness, equality and competition), commerce, policies and regulations supported by governments to ensure safety of all citizens across society, regardless of borders, geography, race or wealth. Without this, we are open to factions of our society who will abuse and misuse these powerful and pervasive technologies.

FUTURE RESEARCH DIRECTIONS

It is our belief, that robots are ultimately just an extension of human beings, considering that

- Robots can be automated to do almost any physical and computational task that humans can conceive of.
- Robots would give us more time to do the things we want, and not the things we hate doing.
- Robots and automation is what ultimately is going to set man free.
- Robots would not take over humans and make us their slaves, unless we give them true 'consciousness'.

Giving robots real consciousness (if possible) would be unnecessary and potentially dangerous. However, if we are to believe futurists, such as Ray Kurzweil and Hans Moravec, who argued that machine intelligence could surpass human intelligence this century, perhaps even within the next three decades, we must explore to what extent we need to change (or completely rethink) existing laws and economic, political and commercial systems to create a future that ensures a fairer distribution of wealth and opportunity across society where robots and humans co-exist for the betterment of the human race in ways that protect our collective development and evolution.

CONCLUSION

A study (Šabanović, 2010) based on data collected through participant observation and interviews with robotics researchers in the US and Japan showed that a linear, technologically deterministic view of the interaction between robots and society was dominant. The social impact of robotic technologies derives mostly from their technological capabilities, and the aim is for society to accept and adapt to technological innovations. Social and cultural factors influence the way AI technologies and robots are designed, evaluated and used (and abused). We require a framework to help guide the dynamic interaction between robotics and society that upholds a social values in a world where robots and humans can interact without prejudice or exploitation.

According to Hirsh–Pasek, 'what the machine can't do is be a partner. It isn't social. It's interactive without being adaptive.' For robots to truly replace humans, they will need to develop six critical behaviours of modern learning: collaboration, communication, content, critical thinking, creative innovation and confidence. Deb Roy, an Associate Professor at MIT, discovered that human learning was communal and interactive. For a robot, the acquisition of language is abstract and formulaic. For us, it is embodied, emotive, subjective and quivering with life. The future of intelligence will not be found in our machines, but in the development of our own (human) minds.

The robots of the future may be self-learning, autonomous and smarter than humans. They might express deep emotions but not necessarily *human* emotions. They may be flexible, self-repairing, self-assembling and have a regenerating biological components that decomposes without leaving behind toxic metals. When a robot or intelligent machine learns from experience, there are few guarantees about whether or not it will learn what humans want. Moreover, it might learn something that we humans do not want it to learn. This is perhaps the unspoken *Holy Grail* of many roboticists (and futurists): to create a kind of self-awareness or even create consciousness. Perhaps, for now, we can rest assured that, no matter how advanced robots become, they will not be capable of elaborate thought experiments that led the likes of Einstein or Stephen Hawking to their discoveries and Dostoevsky to fiction or even dream, as with Isaac Asimov's stories Robot Dreams (Asimov, 1986).

REFERENCES

Acemoglu, D., & Restrepo, P. (2019). The Revolution Need Not Be Automated. *Project Syndicate*. https://www.project-syndicate.org/commentary/ai-automation-labor-productivity-by-daron-acemoglu-and-pascual-restrepo-2019-03

Actroid Female Robot. (2006). *Akiba Robot Festival. YouTube video*. Viewer's online comments at https://www.youtube.com/watch?v=WbFFs4DHWys

Asimov, I. (1986). *Robot Dreams*. Byron Preiss Visual Publications, Inc.

Asimov, I. (2013). I, Robot. Harper Voyager.

Bandholz, H. (2016). The Rise of the Machines: Economic and Social consequences of Robotization. Economics Research. *UniCredit Global Themes Series*. https://www.research.unicredit.eu/DocsKey/economics_docs_2016_155340.ashx?M=D&R=37323940

Beard, A. (2018). *Natural Born Learners*. Weidenfeld & Nicolson.

Cain Miller, C. (2017). Evidence That Robots Are Winning the Race for American Jobs. The Upshot. *The New York Times*. https://www.nytimes.com/2017/03/28/upshot/evidence-that-robots-are-winning-the-race-for-american-jobs.html

Calderone, L. (2019). What are Service Robots? *Robotics Tomorrow. Mobile & Service Robots*. https://www.roboticstomorrow.com/article/2019/02/what-are-service-robots/13161

Ford, M. (2016). *Rise of the Robots: Technology and the Threat of a Jobless Future*. Basic Books.

Fraser, P. (1985). *Special Committee on Pornography "Pornography and Prostitution in Canada"*. *Report of the Special Committee on Pornography and Prostitution*. Canadian Government Publishing Centre.

Fresco, J., & Meadows, R. (2002). Engineering a New Vision of Tomorrow. *The Futurist, 36*(1), 33-36. http://www.jacquefresco.info/main/publicity/publicity-print/journals/engineering-a-new-vision-of-tomorrow

Geminoid HI-1. (2006). *YouTube video*. Viewer's online comments at https://www.youtube.com/watch?v=CfL_wZk25TM

Hellard, R. (2018). AI will cause 'technological unemployment'. *ITPro*.

Hirsh-Pasek, K., & Golinkoff, R. M. (2016). *Becoming Brilliant: What Science Tells Us About Raising Successful Children* (1st ed.). APA.

International Federation of Robotics (IFR). (2019). Executive Summary World Robotics 2019 – Industrial and Service Robots. IFR.

Ishiguro, H., & Nishio, S. (2007). Building artificial humans to understand humans. *Journal of the Japanese Society for Artificial Organs*. doi:10.100710047-007-0381-4

James, W. (1957). *The Principles of Psychology: Volume 1*. Dover Publications Inc.

Jules. (2006). *Human or Robot? YouTube video.* Viewer's online comments at https://www.youtube.com/watch?NR=1&feature=fvwp&v=o3jVWwxNHMc

Kageki, N. (2012). An Uncanny Mind: Masahiro Mori on the Uncanny Valley and Beyond. An interview with the Japanese professor who came up with the uncanny valley of robotics. *IEEE Spectrum.* https://spectrum.ieee.org/automaton/robotics/humanoids/an-uncanny-mind-masahiro-mori-on-the-uncanny-valley

McAfee, A. (2015, Mar. 12). Back to Basics with Old McDonald. *Financial Times Blog.*

Parkin, S. (2015). Killer robots: The soldiers that never sleep. *BBC Future. BBC Global News.* https://www.bbc.com/future/article/20150715-killer-robots-the-soldiers-that-never-sleep

Robertson, J. (2007). Robo Sapiens Japanicus: Humanoid robots and the posthuman family. *Critical Asian Studies*, *39*(3), 369–398. doi:10.1080/14672710701527378

Robertson, J. (2010). Gendering Humanoid Robots: Robo-Sexism in Japan. Body & Society -. *Body & Society*, *16*(2), 1–36. doi:10.1177/1357034X10364767

Šabanović, S. (2010). Robots in Society, Society in Robots. *International Journal of Social Robotics*, *2010*(2), 439–450. doi:10.100712369-010-0066-7

Siegel, M. (2015). What is the definition of a robot? *Serious Science.* http://serious-science.org/what-is-the-definition-of-a-robot-3587

Sullins, J. P. (2011). Introduction. *Open Questions in Robo-ethics Philosophy and Technology*, *24*, 233–238.

Than, C. (2017). Why Robots Are Good for Blue-Collar Workers. *Inc.com.* https://www.inc.com/cynthia-than/a-new-study-tells-us-how-many-human-jobs-are-lost-by-one-robot.html

The IEEE Global Initiative. (2016). *Ethically Aligned Design: A Vision For Prioritizing Wellbeing With Artificial Intelligence And Autonomous Systems, Version 1.* IEEE. https://standards.ieee.org/develop/indconn/ec/autonomous_systems.html

Walters, R. (2014). *Technology: Rise of the replicants.* Alphabetic Inc articles in The Financial Times.

Weinswig, D. (2016). *Gen Z: Get Ready for the Most Self-Conscious, Demanding Consumer Segment*. Fung Global Retail and Technology. The Fung Group.

Weng, Y., Chen, C., & Sun, C. (2009). Toward the human-robot co-existence society: On safety intelligence for next generation robots. *International Journal of Social Robotics, 1*(4), 267–282. doi:10.100712369-009-0019-1

Wilkins, J. (2019). Digitalization and innovation driving manufacturing's future. *Control Engineering*. https://www.controleng.com/articles/digitalization-and-innovation-driving-manufacturings-future/

Zlotowski, J., Proudfoot, D., Yogeeswaran, K., & Bartneck, C. (2015). Anthropomorphism: Opportunities and Challenges in Human-Robot Interaction. *International Journal of Social Robotics, 7*(3), 347–360. doi:10.100712369-014-0267-6

ENDNOTES

[1]   International Federation of Robotics (IFR) is a non-profit organisation established in 1987. Members come from the robotics industry, national or international industry associations and research & development institutes across more than 20 countries. The IFR statistical department is the primary global resource for data on robotics. (Source: https://ifr.org/ifr-press-releases/news/robot-investment-reaches-record-16.5-billion-usd)

[2]   Unimate was the very first industrial robot patented in 1954 (granted in 1961) by American inventor, George Devol, and developed with the foresight and business acumen of Joseph Engelberger, the 'Father of Robotics' (Source: https://www.robotics.org/joseph-engelberger/unimate.cfm).

[3]   COBOT INTELLIGENCE INC, CANADA. 'A Detailed Guide To Collaborative Robots Market' (Source: https://cobotintel.com/guide-to-collaborative-robots-market).

[4]   Generation Z (Gen Z), born after 2000, is the first generation not to have known life without technologies and services such as smartphones, iPads, Facebook, Instagram and WhatsApp. Exposure to these technologies and services has influenced this demographic's broader expectations and behaviours (Weinswig, 2016).

[5]   A geminoid is an ultra-realistic android. The latest geminoid Is Incredibly
        Realistic. IEEE Spectrum (Source: https://spectrum.ieee.org/automaton/
        robotics/humanoids/latest-geminoid-is-disturbingly-realistic).

[6]   Jacque Fresco founded 'Sociocyberneering, Inc.', now known as the
        Venus Project, to develop approaches and solutions to major problems
        that face the world today. He died in 2017 and was succeeded by his
        associate Roxanne Meadows (Source: https://www.thevenusproject.com/
        the-venus-project/jacque-fresco/).

Chapter 5
AI in Industry

ABSTRACT

The past two years have seen a tremendous number of changes in the global AI landscape. There has been a stable balance with the US as the unquestioned leader in the global IT market for nearly the past 20 years and by extension the international AI industry as well, which has evolved from the data science and big data analysis sector to become the engine of the 4th industrial revolution, global economic growth, and social progress that it is today. However, when it comes to AI spending, the US is outgunned by China whose government is investing $150 billion to support its goal to become the undisputed global leader in the AI race by 2030. This chapter will offer a broad overview of the UK AI industry and share insights on its present state, near-future, and what can be done in order to optimise the industry's trajectory over the course of the next several years and to maximise the UK's potential to become a global AI leader by 2020. It is not intended to be an exhaustive study and instead demonstrates the forces at work and possible areas for future research.

"What is vital is to make anything about AI explainable, fair, secure and with lineage, meaning that anyone could see very simply see how any application of AI developed and why." –Ginni Rometty, CEO of IBM

DOI: 10.4018/978-1-7998-4607-9.ch005

BACKGROUND

In our world of technology, the mantra 'innovate or die' is more true for organisations than ever, and artificial intelligence (AI) has redefined industries by providing greater personalisation to users, automating processes and disrupting how we work. As with the adoption of cloud computing years ago, the adoption of AI and its speed of deployment varies according to industry. In this chapter, we look at a selection of industries, specifically in the UK, where disruption by AI has already been felt.

As noted in a 2018 Brookings Institution report, 'AI is a technology that is transforming every walk of life. It is a wide-ranging tool that enables people to rethink how we integrate information, analyse data and use the resulting insights to improve decision making' (West, 2019). AI adoption is increasing in nearly all industries, but capabilities vary. To implement AI, organisations must first understand where it can genuinely add value. Even this first step is challenging.

Technological change is never an isolated phenomenon. Its revolution takes place inside a complex ecosystem comprising businesses, governments and societies. To make a country or society fit for this type of innovation-driven competition, the entire ecosystem has to be considered. Automation has driven disruption in the workforce since the Luddite movement against mechanised textile mills in the early 19th century. Although AI is certainly improving and extending the capabilities of such automation, much of its focus is on individual tasks, rather than roles. Still, most of the current AI impetus in the US currently comes from the private sector. America has many of the most innovative technology firms in the world and its talent pool is quite strong. However, when it comes to AI spending, the US has been outgunned by China, whose government has investing USD 150B to support its goal of becoming the undisputed global leader in AI by 2030 (West, 2019).

Over the past two years, several countries have developed national AI strategies, as outlined in Figure 1. In 2017, Canada, Japan, Singapore, China, the UAE and Finland all published national AI strategies. Subsequently, in 2018, Denmark, France, UK, EU, South Korea and India followed suit.

Figure 1. National AI strategies

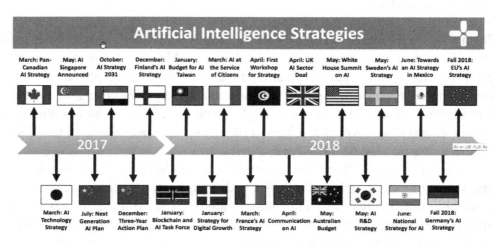

In January 2017, the UK All Party Parliamentary Group (APPG) on Artificial Intelligence was established to explore the impact and the implications of AI. Following recent political developments in the EU, Britain is considering AI a means of neutralising economic risks after Brexit. It has been estimated that AI could add an additional USD 814B (£630B) to the UK economy by 2035, increasing its gross value added from 2.5 to 3.9%. By contrast, to catch up, France's Macron announced USD 1.8B for AI to compete with the US and China. Although China is actively challenging the US as the leader of international AI, the UK is well-positioned to become an international leader in specific niches, including healthcare, marketing, advertising, entertainment and financial technologies. However, there is a clear lack of development in arguably strategically important sectors, such as EdTech and GovTech (i.e. e-governance), which would serve needed societal benefits (Iqbal, 2018).

Given that London is the most advanced financial technological world hub with advanced legal, regulatory and insurance technical sectors, it has an ideal combination of factors needed to become the first to implement the Digital Economy 2.0 around 2022–2024. It is likely to outpace China and the US on this front. The UK might also lead the way in the development of AI ethics, governance and safety frameworks to set the global standard for 'good-trusted AI' by thought-leading international protocols and standards for the prevention of oppression, discrimination and biases resulting from the unethical uses of AI.

INTRODUCTION

AI has become much more than a technological advancement; it is now considered to be the most impactful and growing sector that will affect the future of entire nations. The UK government has proven itself as one of the most proactive and progressive countries in its national AI strategy, making it internationally recognised among the most pragmatic and balanced strategies. Their analysis has established several key contributing factors:

- The UK now has an AI industry of a critical scale in the global economy
- Investment in UK AI businesses has now exceeded USD 5B (£3.8B) overall, and it keeps accelerating
- London is a leading financial global hub
- Scientific prowess and intellectual excellence emanates from AI-savvy UK universities
- UK has a strong reputation for developing ethical traditions related to governance and business

Professor Birgitte Andersen, CEO of Big Innovation Centre, said, 'The UK now has a solid foundation to become a global AI leader, but the government must cement our unique position through investment into AI from all sectors of our economy – science, entrepreneurship, infrastructure, governance, blockchain and skills'. A 2200-page report by Big Innovation Centre and Deep Knowledge Analytics (Iqbal, 2018) placed the UK in the third spot globally for AI, and it foresees it excelling in specific subsectors and areas in the coming years.

The report was the largest industry analysis conducted to date. Its scope as summarised by the infographic in Figure 2 includes 1000 companies, 600 investors, 80 influencers, 35 tech hubs and research institutes and multiple private and government entities that are collectively leading the development of the UK AI-industry. The work behind the report was co-ordinated by Big Innovation Centre with key inputs provided by the APPG, which is a vital source of expertise on the state of AI in the UK. Additionally, inputs from Deep Knowledge Analytics have highlighted advanced studies of deep-tech sectors. An alternate 'industry view' of the report is provided below in Figure 3.

Table 1 describes each of the 11 industry subsectors that will enable AI to thrive in the UK.

An alternate 'AI domain view' of the report is presented below in Figure 4.

Figure 2. AI industry landscape (2018)

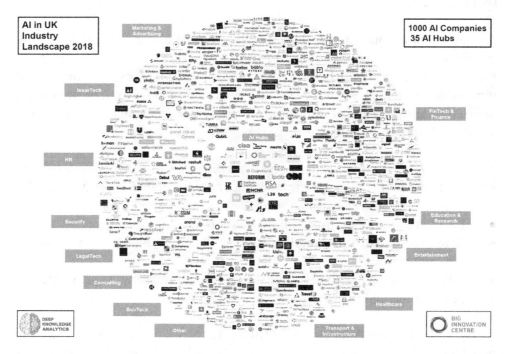

The eight technology domains described above are elaborated further in Table 2.

The remainder of this chapter explores a selection of industry sectors in an attempt to draw attention to specific examples and levels AI adoption and its future social impact. With the exception of manufacturing and retail, we do not explore AI adoption in industries such as banking and finance, telecommunications, insurance, legal, regulatory compliance or HR. In our opinion, these were early adopters that aimed at solving human problems by increasing efficiency across several lines of business. Additionally, they spent significant budgets on powerful computer and graphical processing technologies (MSV, 2017). The following industries have sought to leverage AI to support the following:

Figure 3. Industry subsectors engaged in UK-based AI initiatives

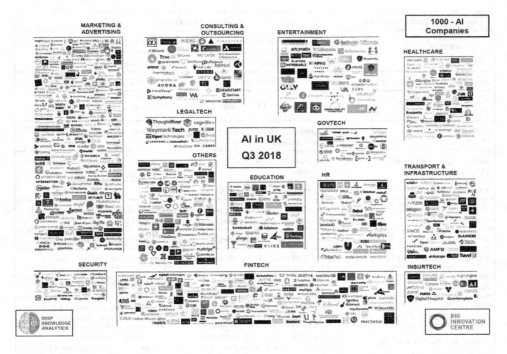

- **Accurate Decision-Making:** Data-driven management decisions at lower cost lead to a different style of advisory, management and organisational models that involve asking the right questions to machines, rather than to human experts. Machines then analyse the data and come up with the recommended results, which can help businesses make better decisions.

- **Automated Customer Support:** Customer-facing systems, such as text chats, voice systems and chatbots can deliver human-like customer service or expert advice experience at reduced costs. Vendors of conversational computing platforms range from the largest (i.e. IBM) and most prominent cloud software development players (i.e. Amazon and Google) to specialised solution providers having development platforms (e.g. Nuance Communications) to niche vendors (e.g. Rulai) that offer unique and powerful capabilities (Koplowitz and Facemire, 2018).

Table 1. Outline of core industry subsectors

Industry (xTech) Subsectors	Description
E-Government (GovTech)	Companies in this section use AI-driven technologies to monitor or conduct various strategic activities. These companies also work with various governmental bodies of UK to help them operate more efficiently.
Transport & Infrastructure	They use AI technologies to enable and accelerate industrial development.
Security (SecurTech)	Companies use AI to improve cyber- and information-security solutions.
Banking & Finance (FinTech)	They use AI technologies to predict, monitor, advise and conduct various financial related services.
Marketing & Advertising (MarTech)	Companies use AI technologies to promote various products and work in sales industries.
Entertainment	AI technologies are applied for entertainment.
Healthcare (& Pharma) (HealthTech)	Companies operating in the healthcare (and pharmaceutical) industry use AI-driven technologies for medical and wellness solutions for people.
Education & Research (EdTech)	Companies use AI technologies in educational or research-related process.
Human Resources (HR) Tech	Companies apply AI for talent searches and human-resource management.
Insurance (InsurTech)	Companies use AI technologies in the insurance industry.
Law and Regulatory Compliance (LegalTech & RegTech)	Companies use AI technology, software and other advanced solutions to provide legal services and analysis and to support regulatory compliance.
Consulting and Outsourcing	Companies engage in research and analysis to support consulting and outsourcing solutions and services for businesses seeking to leverage AI.

- **Fraud Detection:** AI tools learn and monitor behavioural patterns to identify warning signs of fraud to help mitigate and avoid serious incidents. This uses combinations of supervised and unsupervised ML techniques to reduce false positives while also detecting anomalies that may signal more sophisticated forms of online fraud. According to the Association of Certified Fraud Examiners (ACFE) inaugural Anti-fraud Technology Benchmarking Report, businesses are expected to triple their spend on AI and ML to thwart online fraud by 2021. The ACFE study also found that only 13% of businesses currently use AI and ML to detect and deter fraud today (Columbus, 2019).
- **Automated Virtual Assistants:** Automated assistants and planners help users make financial and purchasing decisions via recommendations. These systems are often called robo-advisers and are increasingly being offered across many industries.

Figure 4. AI domains in UK industry

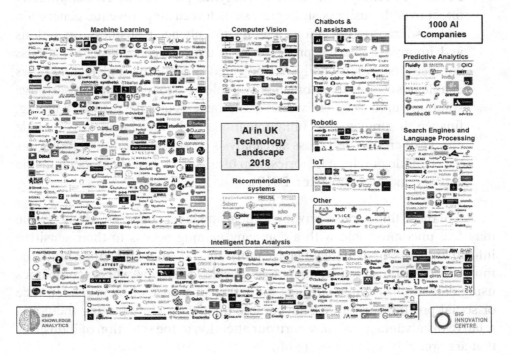

Table 2. AI domains leveraged by industry

Technology Domains	Description
Robotics	Companies building all kind of robots, drones and applying AI.
Computer Vision	Companies in this category are focused on various types of computer vision.
Machine Learning (ML)	Companies use various types of ML algorithms for different purposes.
Intelligent Data Analysis	Companies collect, process and analyse data.
AI Assistants	Companies developing AI-driven assistants, such as chatbots, to automate communications with clients or to help users complete online forms and plan various activities.
Recommender Systems	Companies produce software, which creates a list of recommendations, for example, financial or economic profiles.
Search Engines and Language Processing	Companies use AI-driven search tools, both written and oral.
Internet of Things (IoT)	Companies create AI-driven software applications that help users monitor and maintain hardware devices and sensors.

- **Predictive Analysis:** Predictive analytics powered by AI can directly affect overall business strategies, sales forecasting, revenue generation and resource optimisation, leading to enhanced business operations and improved internal processes that allow organisations to surpass competitors. Additionally, AI-powered algorithms and technologies enable businesses to automatically deploy customised and prescriptive solutions unique to individual customers. Examples across banking, finance, insurance, telecommunications and other businesses include checks of credit worthiness and analysis of a customer digital footprints that include purchase histories, app uses, search histories, social media activity and more (Walker, 2019).

All of these things raise privacy, ethical and legal concerns. Many people may feel uncomfortable with a company gaining access to their sensitive information, even when they behave ethically. The more data they hold, the more that can be stolen by malicious hackers. Perhaps worse, companies using data to discriminate against individuals because of their gender, race or social profile leads to less favourable treatment while putting them at a relative disadvantage. We now turn our attention to the selection of industries that are arguably slow adopters of AI:

- Healthcare and pharmaceuticals (HealthTech)
- Education (EdTech)
- Other selective industries
  - Journalism
  - Automotive
  - Manufacturing
  - Retail

CASE STUDY: HEALTHCARE & PHARMACEUTICALS (HealthTech)

Background

Technologies already familiar to us, including wearable fitness trackers and health-tracking apps, are changing the way we monitor and manage our own health. AI and ML present exciting opportunities to transform healthcare, pharmaceutical and life-science industries to be swifter, more accurate, more efficient with drug discovery, better with genomics, faster with disease identification and diagnoses, and amplified applications of research and development. Compared with other industries, the uptake of AI and emerging technologies in healthcare and pharmaceuticals has been relatively slow. They are among the most heavily regulated and highly competitive industries in the world, and they are faced with unique safety concerns and intellectual-property issues. However, this is gradually changing. For example, the potential of the pharmaceutical centres to reduce costs of drug development is estimated at around USD 2–3B (Hargreaves, 2019). This has led to many consultancies, technology businesses and start-ups converging to offer AI-powered solutions, ranging from smart devices that leverage IoT capabilities, robots, virtual assistants, deep learning and ML to manage complex issues and to respond to data analytics challenges and development. In all cases, 5–10% cost reduction margins could save healthcare and pharmaceuticals industries millions of dollars, leading to lower drug costs for patients. AI and ML will serve in multiple ways (Buvailo, 2018; Faber, 2018; Pearl, 2018):

- **Conducting Repetitive Tasks:** data entry and lab-test analyses, clearing up time to focus on more urgent or complex tasks and to interact with patients.
- **Data Management and Analysis:** pharmaceuticals and healthcare system records analysis to identify errors and inefficiencies.
- **NLP:** helps computers understand and interpret human speech and writing, drastically cutting administrative tasks involving analysis of large volumes of electronic records to provide evaluations, diagnoses and recommendations for patient care and treatment.
- **Medical Consultations:** data analysis of a patient symptoms and medical histories. Positive consequences of the use of AI could include substantial reduction of poor diagnoses and avoidance of incorrect treatments, which may require more holistic solutions.
- **Digital 'robo-nurses':** monitor and follow-up with a patient between doctors and general practitioners. This could lessen hospital visits and reduce the burden on medical and clinical staffs. Thus, the savings could be reinvested and redistributed to other priority areas.
- **Robot-assisted tele-surgery:** specialised procedures are carried out by robot-assisted surgical tools from a remote location. Thus far, commercialised systems have been operated in a same-room cockpit or a nearby control room. A number of hurdles must be overcome for tele-

surgery to become a reality, such as the lag between the operator initiating an action and the remote system actually performing it. However, with improved data transmission speeds supported by 5G cellular networks and advances in surgical robots, there have been reports of successful tele-surgeries in China, India and Spain (Matthews, 2019).

- **Medication Management:** using smart (IoT-type) sensors and mobile applications monitored in real-time by AI to support correct drug dosages and adherence for patients being treated for cancer, schizophrenia and diabetes, it increases the efficiency and safety of treatments.

Open issues regarding regulations and clinical relevance remain, causing both technical companies and potential investors trepidation relating to adoption, compliance and implementation. According to Kuan (2019), following is an outline of some of these obstacles:

- **Updating Regulatory Frameworks:** over the past few years, the US Food and Drug Administration (FDA) has taken incremental steps to update its regulatory framework to keep up with advancing digital transformation. In 2017, the FDA released its Digital Health Innovation Action Plan to provide clarity about the agency's role in advancing safe and effective digital technologies.
- **Achieving FDA Approval:** to account for shifting FDA oversight and approval processes, tech companies must carefully consider how to best design and roll-out products to ensure FDA approval, especially if a product falls under the agency's higher-risk category or if a subsequent update is put at risk following security patches, new features or functionalities.
- **AI is a black box:** apart from regulatory compliance, another challenge to the adoption of AI applications is black-box trust issues. If an incident occurs causing harm to a patient, it should be possible to audit and trace an AI application's decision-making process to identify the root cause of any incident, so that it can be prevented in the future. Perhaps more challenging is that clinicians and physicians are reluctant to trust AI systems, owing, in part, to malpractice-liability risks. Thus, they are less inclined to adopt something that they do not fully understand.

Social Implications

For healthcare and pharmaceutical industries to benefit from the value promised by AI and ML, more must be done across the lifecycle that runs from research and development to commercialisation. This will involve targeted partnerships with an increasingly expanding landscape of tech companies and new outsourcing models to help ease the management of systems and infrastructure technologies while also supporting data analytics, curation and integration practices. Ironically, the implications of this approach will lead to challenges concerning ownership, data privacy and intellectual property disputes (Hargreaves, 2019).

To truly benefit from AI and ML emerging technologies, related industries must find a way to address the tension between the tech mantra of 'move fast and break things' and the principle enshrined in the Hippocratic oath, 'first, do no harm'. In other words, what must we do to allow the science to flourish while keeping patients safe (Ross et al., 2019)? Professionals are central to this debate, not academicians, technologists, politicians and policymakers. Upholding ethics and maintaining public acceptance and trust is the right of all patients. Furthermore, the following areas also require closer support and scrutiny:

- **Education and training:** investment is required to help support educational, training and career development needs of doctors, clinicians and others to accelerate awareness and adoption of data sciences, AI and ML.
- **Data governance:** data used across industries must be certified for accuracy, integrity and quality. For those that meet information handling and governance standards, data should be made more easily available across private and public sectors. In all cases, the government should decide how widely data is shared and with whom. Governing bodies and joint decision-making committees should be established.
- **Modernised regulatory compliance:** emerging technologies are continually disrupting society, which is held back by old-fashioned analogue policies and compliance processes that urgently demand digitalisation. Equally, current approaches to regulatory compliance must be modernised to ensure that AI is introduced safely and to avoid current levels of uncertainty about accountability, responsibility and wider legal implications.

- **Accredited tech companies:** to aid healthcare professionals with the adoption of AI and ML, tech companies should be externally appraised and accredited, much like other regulated and progressive industries, to promote competition and transparency. This will improve confidence in the safety and quality of services being tendered. Moreover, for the post-implementation of products and solutions, tech companies should be rated in terms of product licensing, service performance and post-project performance.
- **Fairness and equity:** AI should be used to reduce, not increase, health inequalities geographically, economically and socially. Care must be taken to ensure AI is used for good, benefitting all members of society.

CASE STUDY: EDUCATION TECHNOLOGY (EdTech)

Background

AI in the education sector has been a disruptive force that has led to educational institutions reacting and adapting their business and teaching models in ways that challenge conventional methods, learning, career development and skill building. EdTech often includes practical application of tech solutions in software development for teaching and learning. This has been extended to emerging technologies, such as AI, virtual reality etc. With so much emphasis on the wider applications of AI, ML and automation, perhaps the question should be 'what is AI not good at'? or perhaps more directly, 'what are humans good at, and what's left for us to do'? Princeton's head of computer science, Jennifer Rexford, stated that AI will change not only *what* teachers teach but *how* they teach. She also reiterated the call for including diversity of thought in developing AI (Kirkland, 2018).

The EdTech market continues to grow at a phenomenal rate, and, according to a study conducted by Technavio, it is predicted to grow by a staggering 45% by 2021. Thousands of businesses are already jockeying for position while teachers and administrators have little time or experience to implement new technology solutions. AI already allows teachers more time and freedom by driving efficiency, personalisation and streamlining administrative tasks to provide better understanding and adaptability. Additionally, AI has been used to enhance language learning, testing knowledge and experiential tutoring and talent acquisition. AI in education can be grouped into five general roles (Bonderud, 2019):

- **Automation:** the simplest application of AI often provides the most immediate benefit. By automating straightforward tasks, such as grading, digital asset management and timetable scheduling, educators can increase the amount of time they spend actively engaging with students.
- **Integration:** AI solutions can integrate with other initiatives, such as smart technologies and IoT-driven solutions, to provide personalised learning for students.
- **Acclimation:** technology is now an integral part of both education and business environments. Most people have access to smartphones and are online almost constantly. AI in schools can help acclimate students to the pace of technological change.
- **Delineation:** students' needs and curricula priorities are constantly shifting, making it difficult for educators to ensure the content that they deliver remains relevant and actionable. AI-driven analytics in education can help spot critical trends and delineate key markers to help teachers design the most effective classroom experience and drive digital transformation.
- **Identification:** data analytics informed by adaptative AI solutions can help identify critical areas for student and teacher performance. Combined with robust security and access controls, AI can help spot and remedy potential problems in their formative stages.

These general roles are being realised through diverse solutions and platforms:

- **EdTech platforms:** support teaching and learning for parents and teachers while supplementing and perhaps improving on traditional learning management systems and online education (Chassignol et al., 2018).
- **Teaching assistants:** support teachers with collaborative lesson planning, peer-to-peer coaching and extended 24×7 support to students outside the classroom.
- **Gamification assistants:** aim to gamify language teaching.
- **Communication software:** helps people non-verbally communicate and learn.

- **Administrative assistants:** automate administrative duties for teachers and academic institutions, including grading exams, assessing homework and providing valuable responses to students.
- **Personalised learning solutions:** allow teachers to offer personalised support to all students. Traditional systems have targeted the middle-range abilities, leaving those who excel (i.e. top 10%) or those who struggle (i.e. bottom 10%) unaided and unable to realise their full potential. Additionally, AI systems help to customise in-class assignments and final exams, ensuring that students get the best possible assistance. Research has shown that instant feedback is one of the keys to successful learning. Via AI-powered apps, students get targeted and customised responses from their teachers. Teachers can then focus efforts on creating smart study guides and flashcards while tailoring their materials to the challenges faced by students.

Looking ahead, we can learn and be inspired by China's rapid progress that has been supported by investments to their education sector, making it the world's largest EdTech market. This includes an ecosystem created through collaboration across education institutions, large technology companies and start-ups (e.g. New Oriental, TAL, Baidu, TenCent, VIPKID and Squirrel AI). According to predictions (HolonIQ, 2019), AI adoption in education will explode over the next 5 years and is expected to reach a global expenditure of USD 6B by 2025. Much of the growth will come from China, followed by the US, together accounting for over half of the global AI education spent.

Social Implications

The increasing use of AI across the education sector raises several ethical questions that centre on data privacy, cybersecurity, bias and the role of AI. Organisations must consider what type of data is being collected, how this information is used and what controls are needed to safeguard privacy. Additionally, administrative jobs are potentially under threat, because AI adoption may impact human staffing.

As new EdTech continues to emerge and mature, cybersecurity remains an important concern that affects the infrastructure and platforms used to host EdTech solutions. Threats range from identity theft, phishing and ransomware attacks. A study found that 32-million educational accounts were compromised in 2017. Test scores, faculty and student information, financial documents and other important credentials were compromised (Kulkarni, 2019).

As discussed, AI systems learn and amplify human biases. This issue must be addressed by raising awareness and keeping humans in the loop while avoiding situations in which competition between humans and computers occurs. As with other industries, AI's role should be to empower human. In education, AI should be used to teach and learn more effectively.

Lastly, and perhaps most importantly, we must remain mindful of two competing approaches to AI adoption in education: AI-led vs. AI-assisted. Our belief is that we should focus on the latter to incorporate emotional and experiential oversight that humans can provide while leveraging all benefits in ways that enhance the overall teaching and learning experience *collaboratively*.

OTHER SELECTIVE INDUSTRIES

Journalism

AI has shaken up present-day journalism. Automated news-writing services and distribution systems, without human supervision, is already a reality. This raises a number of questions.

- What will journalists of the future need to learn?
- Is this new reality likely to improve the working conditions in the industry?
- What do media businesses stand to gain and lose?

Considerable consensus (Christians et al., 2009) about what healthy journalism already exists:

- It must provide a rigorous account of people who are in power and people who wish to be in power in the government, corporations and non-profit sectors.
- It must regard the information needs of all people as legitimate. If anything, it should favour those without property, because those with wealth invariably have the means to get the information they need without trouble.
- It must have a plausible method of separating truth from lies, or at least to prevent liars from being unaccountable and leading nations into catastrophes, such as wars, economic crises and communal discord.

- It must produce a wide range of informed opinions about the most important issues of our times, not only the transitory concerns of the moment, but also the challenges that loom on the horizon. These issues cannot be determined primarily by what people in power are talking about. Journalism must comprise a nation's early warning system, so that problems can be anticipated, studied, debated and addressed before they grow to crises.

The implications of AI for journalism must acknowledge the larger context of the digitisation of media and public life: a transition to apps, algorithms, social media, etc. These things have transformed journalism as an institution, undercutting business models, upending work routines and unleashing a flood of information alternatives. According to (Montal and Reich, 2016), the broadening reliance on algorithms to generate news (e.g. *automated journalism* or *robot journalism*) has significant practical, socio-political, psychological, legal and occupational implications for news organisations, journalists and their audiences. One of its most controversial yet unexplored aspects is the algorithmic authorship. The study detected major discrepancies between the perceptions of authorship and crediting policy, the prevailing attribution regimes and the scholarly literature. To mitigate these discrepancies, a consistent and comprehensive crediting policy needs to be created that sponsors public interest in automated news.

Among the emergent data-centric practices of journalism, none appear to be as potentially disruptive as automated journalism (Carlson, 2015), which characterises algorithmic processes that convert data into narrative news texts with limited to no human intervention beyond the initial programming choices. What emerges is a concern over the future of journalistic labour, the rigid conformity of news compositional forms and the normative foundation of journalistic authority. According to (Meredith, 2014), experienced investigative reporters build up a set of strategies for finding stories, but novice investigative reporters often struggle to find leads. Training and education materials for novice investigators focus on places to look for stories, such as following the money, looking at specific lines in financial filings etc. The complexity of the process is part of the reason that so much investigative journalism is reactive, resulting from tips and whistle-blowers, rather than proactive investigation. Having human values central to news works both ways. It also implies that human bias can permeate algorithms.

Automated news production can be seen as a continuation of the automation that began in newsrooms in the late 1980s with the continuation of data-driven journalism. The goal has always been to break news faster while avoiding rushing. In 2015, the Norwegian News Agency worked on a project to generate automated football news coverage, launched in 2016. With experts in AI, a group of journalists learned new skills as an AI robot was being trained (Albeanu, 2016). 'A large amount of editorial input was needed to help the robot make the right choices. This learning process in the newsroom led to many new ideas about possible areas of automation, from simple news regarding the weather and commodity prices to an ambitious plan to offer fully automated election night services for the local election in Norway next year,' explained Helen Vogt, the former head of innovation at NTB. Vogt has seen her agency benefit from this. 'Automation has helped NTB deliver a much broader news service, reporting on lower-tier matches that we never had the capacity to cover before. This means that all our media customers get the reports they are interested in immediately after the match is over, because the algorithm can work so much faster than humans and is able to produce scores of stories simultaneously, within seconds.'

Will automation put journalists out of work? Instead of seeing automation technologies as adversaries, there are many who propose journalists take the best parts of AI and make them allies to augment (not displace or replace) people. Perhaps more important is the lack of specific legislation on AI in the European Union. There is regulation tailored to the use of algorithms, such as the 'Directive on Markets in Financial Instruments' that addresses automated decisions that use personal data. Better regulations are required to avoid an article being produced automatically that is libellous, regardless of whether it was produced by a machine or a human. The publisher should remain accountable and assume responsibility.

Automotive Industry

For decades, the automotive industry has focused on car building, including design, engineering, manufacturing and retail sales. Automobile manufacturers are faced with a complexity and constantly changing business landscape that is being disrupted by AI and intelligent systems fuelled by an ever-increasing range of models, changing customer requirements, new global mobility players, high investments in electric mobility and new mobility services that make it difficult to remain competitive. Globally declining growth rates, sales figures and margins are forcing every automaker to re-evaluate their business models, internal operating procedures and the shape of their future workforce.

With cars becoming software platforms on wheels and the entertainment centres of the future, consumers are shifting away from assessing a vehicle's driving performance towards reviewing which manufacturer products they can get while obtaining the safest and best in-car experience. With the help of 'Emotion AI' (El Kaliouby, 2017) time spent in cars, even when stuck in traffic, just needs to be enjoyable and productive via computer vision, speech analytics and deep learning. As businesses transform, they will need to constantly ask themselves, 'will this transformational change add value to my customers... or is this an update to simply fulfil an engineers' dream'?

When reflecting on AI in the automotive industry, most people think of self-driving and driverless cars. However, AI can do more. In fact, the value of AI in automotive manufacturing and cloud services will exceed USD 10.73B by 2024 (Eisenberg, 2018). The increasing use of powerful AI techniques promises to revolutionise the driving experiences and mobility strategies that enhance overall driver and passenger experience ranging from personalisation via face and biometrics recognition, non-verbal interaction, hands-free gesture controls, vehicle-to-vehicle communication and more (Atkinson, 2018). According to (Eisenberg, 2018), the most common applications of AI in the automotive industry are:

- **Driving features:** AI powers advanced safety features and enables intelligent shared mobility services between vehicles to improve traffic flow, avoid congestion and report road accidents.
- **Cloud services:** AI-enabled cloud platforms ensure that data are available whenever needed.
- **Automotive insurance:** AI speeds up the process of filing insurance claims, replacing adjusters and enabling do-it-yourself self-service claims while conducting continuous risk profiling to monitor the behaviour of a driver in ways that might affect the claim.
- **Car manufacturing:** AI is increasingly used to assemble more efficient and productive vehicles with collaborative robots that augment humans doing hazardous tasks.
- **Driver monitoring:** AI monitoring solutions use computer vision and deep learning to detect driver behaviour in four areas: driver identification, driver recognition, driver monitoring and infotainment control.

Manufacturing

According to the latest market research report (Research and Markets, 2019), the AI in manufacturing market is expected to reach USD 17.2B by 2025, at a compound annual growth rate of 49.5% from 2018 to 2025. For modern manufacturers, AI is one of the keys to higher output, better product quality, reduced waste and more. It has the potential to transform manufacturing tasks, such as visual inspection, predictive maintenance and assembly to the supply chain, materials and order management to engineering design, manufacturing engineering, shop-floor operations, order fulfilment, logistics and services. Like many other industries, big data goes hand-in-hand with AI for manufacturers that produce enormous data as a result of steep drops in sensor costs, enabling data collection at every stage of production. Some of the common use cases for AI in manufacturing, as developed by McKinsey (Tracy, 2019), are outlined below. All quoted percentages were sourced from the McKinsey analysis.

- **Predictive maintenance:** smart manufacturers use AI systems in conjunction with IoT data to predict and avoid machine failures to minimise disruptions and inconveniences while preventing problems and resolving them quickly. AI-driven predictive maintenance will increase asset productivity by up to 20% and reduce maintenance costs by up to 10%.
- **Yield enhancement:** manufacturers can now use AI systems to decrease scrap rates from defective products and get more value out of the materials that go into the production process. These gains are made possible by using AI systems to identify causes of yield losses that can be avoided via changes to production processes or product designs. The payoffs can be huge.
- **Quality testing:** manufacturers can now use AI to enable quality testing procedures using ML and advanced image recognition systems to automate the visual inspection and fault detection of products and to trigger the automatic ejection of defective products from a production line. These capabilities can increase productivity by up to 50% while increasing defect detection rates by up to 90% compared with processes based on human inspection.
- **Supply-chain optimisation:** in manufacturing, delays, breakdowns or mistakes can lead to significant issues. AI can help manufacturers

better predict the complex interactions between each production unit and automate requests for parts, labour, tools and repairs. An AI-enhanced supply-chain management system can help companies reduce forecasting errors by 20 to 50% to optimise stock replenishment. Likewise, AI can help reduce lost sales caused by stock-outs by up to 65% while reducing inventory by as much as 20–50% in some settings.

- **Research and development:** AI systems can help design and engineering teams collaborate more closely, choose the best materials for a product, identify designs that may be prone to failure and more. With AI, designers can define a problem with goals and constraints while allowing the system come up with dozens or even hundreds of different solutions, some of which might be starkly different from conventional human approaches. Cost reductions of 10–15% and time-to-market improvements of up to 10% are expected.

- **Business support:** in manufacturing, AI can help automate key aspects of labour-intensive support functions using ML and robotic process automation, enabling an increase of 30% in automation rates across functions and up to 90% for some routine service-desk tasks.

- **Collaborative and context-aware robots:** context-aware robots use computer vision and AI to operate alongside humans in shared environments. They use their ability to sense and avoid people and obstructions to carry out assigned tasks, such as finding, picking and moving parts on a manufacturing floor. This will help improve production throughput in labour-intensive settings and increase productivity by to 20% for certain tasks.

Retail

According to an IBM study (Chao et al., 2019), retail will increasingly adopt intelligent automation technologies. This study focused on the convergence of humans and AI and, specifically, how automation could help reduce human error and improve the customer experience. The report surveyed 1,900 retail and consumer-product representatives across 23 countries to determine how AI could revolutionise retail. It found that, when integrating AI into retail, manufacturers must remain transparent and secure to retain customer loyalty, because people are wary of automation and other new technologies. The report identified six ways the retail industry should utilising AI, based on respondents' feedback:

1. Supply-chain planning (85%)
2. Demand forecasting (85%)
3. Customer intelligence (79%)
4. Marketing, advertising and campaign management (75%)
5. Store operations (73%)
6. Pricing and promotion (73%)

Furthermore, according to Tractica, annual global revenue from AI is set to grow from USD 10.1B in 2018 to USD 126B by 2025 (Kirkpatrick and Kaul, 2019). Ultimately, there will be significant opportunities for AI to analyse the massive amounts of data collected by retail companies regarding their customers, their shopping experiences and more. Using this data, AI systems will be used to create online web stores and channels that take customer information and turn it into targeted shopping experiences, online chatbots that answer questions and in-store intelligence to make the experience even more interactive.

IBM's 'Predictive Customer Intelligence' solution provides a great example of how customer information could be leveraged to provide key benefits in the retail sector:

- **Understanding the customer:**
  - Profile customers based on browsing and purchase history.
  - Track propensity to respond to different types of offers.
  - Identify the behaviours that convert browsers to shoppers.
- **Find the right offer:**
  - Increase profits with targeted offers informed by market-basket analysis.
  - Combine the customer profile and history to identify the next likely purchase.
  - Prioritise offers based on expected profit.
- **Find the right channel:**
  - Tailor offers to the point of interaction.
  - Build cross-channel loyalty informed by online activity for use in a physical store.

Companies will be able to create more targeted ads that could differ from store to store. Moreover, these ads will focus on big sellers by region, who needs more marketing and what should be removed from the production line. This further highlights the diverse opportunities and areas that chief marketing officers and sales executives can expand upon to benefit from the introduction of AI.

Future AI-driven applications will be far more extensive than many consumer products and retail companies currently realise. As the AI capability matures, it opens up entirely new ways of doing business that can increase operational agility, improve the quality and speed of decision making and enhance customer experience. Intelligent automation brings with it a new category of risk associated with ethics and machine responsibility. Retail executives, businesses and manufacturers must take steps to avoid creating biases that can generate negative outcomes. Additionally, they should think beyond capitalising on the potential of intelligent automation. This capability is not just about removing human activities from business processes. It should also be about shifting to a culture of speed, agility and innovation while maintaining human involvement across all parts of the supply chain and manufacturing processes.

FUTURE RESEARCH DIRECTIONS

Most research into the impact of AI, such as that carried out by Oxford University researchers Carl Frey and Michael Osborne (Frey and Osborne, 2013), has focused on the negative effects on jobs as they become increasingly automated. Thankfully, albeit slowly, the focus has moved to exploring the benefits and productivity associated with this automation. However, the possible benefits and opportunities of AI go much further. The ability to collect, store and analyse data at scales, speeds and in ways facilitated by AI technologies will allow businesses to improve the quality of products and tailor them to their needs, increasing their value. Across industries, AI will reduce the amount of time that consumers spend doing low-value tasks while reducing friction during the consumption process, leading to increased consumer demand.

Future research should analyse and measure the effects (both positive and negative) to key performance indicators as a result of adopting AI and automation across industries, including but not restricted to:

- Product quality (e.g. consistency)
- Product usability (e.g. consumer utilisation of a product)
- Product functionality (e.g. enhancements as a direct result of AI)

- Productivity gains (e.g. time saved in production, time saved personalising a product)
- Product personalisation (e.g. levels of tailoring by individuals and groups of consumers)

Given AI's potential to cause major upheavals in our way of life and with our societal norms, further research is required to understand the impact of AI technologies and to pre-empt their negative effects. Humanity must be proactive rather than reactive when managing this new industrial revolution. Not only should the technological aspects be investigated, behavioural, societal, policy and governance issues also must be examined. Without this, we will not be able to maximise the benefits of AI-powered advancements for humanity while preventing negative impacts.

CONCLUSION

The exponential advancement in AI, ML, robotics and automation are rapidly transforming industries and societies across the world. The way we work, the way we live and the way we interact with others are expected to be transformed at speeds and scales beyond anything we have observed in human history. This raises inevitable questions about how much AI-powered technologies will impact businesses, consumers and the economy. Although businesses are asking how they can capitalise on the opportunities presented by AI and where their investment should be targeted, leaders need to collectively seek ways to adopt AI in responsible and transparent ways to maintain the confidence of customers, communities and the wider society.

AI will not be adopted across all countries and regions at the same rate. However, there is substantial research that shows that an increasing number of companies now use AI more often than not. The technology appears to be a critical stepping-stone for businesses looking to improve efficiency, reduce costs and embrace greater levels of automation.

A Price–Waterhouse study from 2017 (Cameron et al., 2017) showed that the main contributor to the UK's economic gains between 2017 and 2030 will come from consumer-product enhancements that stimulate consumer demand as a result of AI enabling greater product choices with increased personalisation while driving better affordability over time. The study predicted significant gains by 2030 across all UK regions, as shown in Figure 5.

Figure 5. Positive impact of AI across the UK

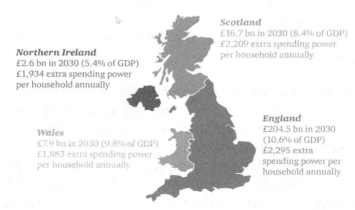

Scotland
£16.7 bn in 2030 (8.4% of GDP)
£2,209 extra spending power
per household annually

Northern Ireland
£2.6 bn in 2030 (5.4% of GDP)
£1,934 extra spending power
per household annually

Wales
£7.9 bn in 2030 (9.8% of GDP)
£1,883 extra spending power
per household annually

England
£204.5 bn in 2030
(10.6% of GDP)
£2,295 extra
spending power per
household annually

The larger total impact on GDP in some UK regions reflects the different trade patterns in each. England, and to some extent Scotland and Wales, have stronger trade links with Europe and the rest of the world. The gains through trade related to AI are likely to put even greater upwards pressure on gross domestic product (GCP) in these countries by 2030.

Key statistics worth noting include:

- UK GDP will be up to 10.3% higher by 2030 as a result of AI. This is the equivalent of an additional £232B, making it one of the biggest commercial opportunities in today's fast-changing economy.
- The impact over the period will come from productivity gains (1.9%), consumption-side product enhancements and new firm entries that stimulate demand (8.4%).
- There will be significant gains across all UK regions, with England, Scotland, Wales and Northern Ireland all seeing an impact from AI by 2030 at least as large as 5% GDP and extra spending power per household of up to £1,800–2,300 a year by 2030.

It will be important to work towards establishing a hybrid workforce in which AI and human beings work side-by-side. The challenge is not just ensuring that we have the right systems in place. It is instead judging what role employees will play in this new model. People should remain responsible for determining their strategic applications of AI while providing challenges and oversight to uphold transparency and trust.

We take an optimistic view on AI, because we prefer to see it as an exciting source of wealth, opportunity and job creation for the future. It will have multi-faceted benefits as long as businesses, employees and governments invest to adopt and adapt.

REFERENCES

Albeanu, C. (2016). *Norwegian News Agency is betting on automation for football coverage*. https://www.journalism.co.uk/news/norwegian-news-agency-is-betting-on-automation-for-football-coverage/s2/a647189/

Atkinson, D. J. (2018). *Automotive Applications of Artificial Intelligence*. Chasis and Safety. Continental.

Bonderud, D. (2019). *Artificial Intelligence, Authentic Impact: How Educational AI is Making the Grade*. EdTech Magazine.

Broussard, M. (2014). Artificial Intelligence For Investigative Reporting. Digital Journalism, 3(6), 814-831.

Broussard, M., Diakopoulos, N., Guzman, A. L., Abebe, R., Dupagne, M., & Chuan, C. (2019). Artificial Intelligence and Journalism. *Journalism & Mass Communication Quarterly*, 96(3), 673–695. doi:10.1177/1077699019859901

Buvailo, A. (2018). *The Why, How And When Of AI In The Pharmaceutical Industry*. Retrieved from https://www.forbes.com/sites/forbestechcouncil/2018/04/24/the-why-how-and-when-of-ai-in-the-pharmaceutical-industry/#14bde55c6d07

Cameron, E., Andrews, J., & Gillham, J. (2017). The economic impact of artificial intelligence on the UK economy. *Price Waterhouse Coopers LLP (PwC)*. https://www.pwc.co.uk//economic-services/assets/ai-uk-report-v2.pdf

Carlson, M. (2014). The Robotic Reporter. Digital Journalism, 3(3), 416-431.

Chao, G., Cheung, J., Haller, K., & Lee, J. (2019). The coming AI revolution in retail and consumer products. *IBM in association with National Retail Federation (NRF)*. https://cdn.nrf.com/sites/default/files/2019-01/The%20coming%20AI%20revolution.pdf

Chassignol, M., Khoroshavin, A., Klimova, A., & Bilyatdinova, A. (2018). Artificial Intelligence Trends in Education: A Narrative Overview. 7th International Young Scientist Conference on Computational Science. *Procedia Computer Science, 136*, 16–24. doi:10.1016/j.procs.2018.08.233

Christians, C. G., Glasser, T. L., Mcquail, D., Nordenstreng, K., & White, R. A. (2009). *Normative Theories of the Media: journalism in democratic societies.* Urbana: University of Illinois Press.

Columbus, L. (2019). AI Is Predicting The Future Of Online Fraud Detection. *Forbes.*

Eisenberg, A. (2018). 5 Ways Artificial Intelligence is Impacting the Automotive Industry. *Ignite.* https://igniteoutsourcing.com/automotive/artificial-intelligence-in-automotive-industry/

El Kaliouby, R. (2017). Driving Your Emotions: How Emotion AI Powers a Safer and More Personalised Car. *Affectiva.* https://blog.affectiva.com/driving-your-emotions-how-emotion-ai-powers-a-safer-and-more-personalized-car

Faber, K. (2018). *How Artificial Intelligence is Transforming Personalized Medicine.* Retrieved from https://www.innovationmanagement.se/2018/06/21/how-artificial-intelligence-is-transforming-personalized-medicine/

Frey, C. B., & Osborne, M. A. (2013). *The future of employment: how susceptible are jobs to computerisation?* UK Department of Engineering Science, University of Oxford.

Hargreaves, B. (2019). Pharma companies slow to adopt AI will be 'left behind'. *William Reed Business Media Ltd.* https://www.outsourcing-pharma.com/Article/2019/12/11/IQVIA-on-the-adoption-of-AI-and-machine-learning

Holon, I. Q. (2019). *2019 Artificial Intelligence & Global Education Report.* https://www.holoniq.com/wp-content/uploads/2019/05/HolonIQ-Extract-AI-and-Global-Education-May-2019.pdf

Iqbal, R. (2018). Artificial Intelligence Industry Landscape Overview Q3/2018. *Big Innovation Centre.* https://www.dka.global/ai-in-uk-report

Kirkland, R. (2018). *The role of education in AI (and vice versa).* https://www.mckinsey.com/featured-insights/artificial-intelligence/the-role-of-education-in-ai-and-vice-versa

Kirkpatrick, K., & Kaul, A. (2019). *Artificial Intelligence Market Forecasts. Research Report.* Tractica.

Koplowitz, R., & Facemire, M. (2018). The Forrester New Wave. *Conversational Computing Platforms, Q2,* 2018.

Kuan, R. (2019). Adopting AI in Health Care Will Be Slow and Difficult. *HBR.* https://hbr.org/2019/10/adopting-ai-in-health-care-will-be-slow-and-difficult

Kulkarni, A. (2019). AI in Education: Where is It Now and What is the Future? *Lexalytics Blog.* https://www.lexalytics.com/lexablog/ai-in-education-present-future-ethics

Matthews, K. (2019). How better data, 5G, and surgical robots will improve healthcare. *Robot Report.* https://www.therobotreport.com/better-data-advancing-healthcare-robotics/

Montal, T., & Reich, Z. (2016). I, Robot. You, Journalist. Who is the Author? Digital Journalism, 5(7), 829-849.

MSV. (2017). *The Era Of Artificial Intelligence, GPUs Are The New CPUs.* Forbes.

Pearl, R. (2018). *Artificial Intelligence In Healthcare: Separating Reality From Hype.* Retrieved from https://www.forbes.com/sites/robertpearl/2018/03/13/artificial-intelligence-in-healthcare/#5eb249e51d75

Research and Markets. (2019). *Artificial Intelligence in Manufacturing Market by Offering (Hardware, Software, and Services), Technology (Machine Learning, Computer Vision, Context-Aware Computing, and NLP), Application, Industry, and Geography - Global Forecast to 2025.* Markets and Markets.

Ross, J., Webb, C., & Rahman, F. (2019). *Artificial Intelligence in Healthcare.* Academy of Medical Royal Colleges.

Tracy, S. (2019). *Artificial Intelligence is Transforming Manufacturing.* CIO Magazine. IDG Communications, Inc.

Walker, J. (2019). *Artificial Intelligence Applications for Lending and Loan Management.* https://emerj.com/ai-sector-overviews/artificial-intelligence-applications-lending-loan-management/

West, D. M. (2019). Trump's executive order on artificial intelligence is a drop in the bucket compared to the $150 billion China's spending on AI. *The Brookings Institution.* http://assets.businessinsider.com/china-150-billion-program-dwarfs-trumps-executive-order-on-ai-2019-2

Chapter 6
AI in Emerging Markets

ABSTRACT

In this chapter, the authors explore the effects of artificial intelligence (AI) disruption in emerging markets (EM) – countries that are harnessing technology much faster and more enthusiastically than many of their developed-market compatriots. Dubbed the Fourth Industrial Revolution (4IR), AI technologies are disrupting at speeds that have no historical precedent. With the potential economic benefits of AI already clear, governments in many EM countries— including China, South Korea, Russia, Hungary, Poland, the UAE, and Saudi Arabia—are pursuing policies that will help leapfrog developed markets. However, there are risks including concerns that a potential global recession may slow the rapid growth that the likes of China and other EM countries have enjoyed thus far. Additionally, there are key challenges relating to social, ethical, and legal frameworks as well as a need for security policies.

"If AI is to be a boon and not a global burden, its benefits will need to be shared" –Lee Kai-fu, chairman of Sinovation Ventures

DOI: 10.4018/978-1-7998-4607-9.ch006

INTRODUCTION

What Are Emerging Markets (EM)?

'EM' was coined in 1981 by Antoine van Agtmael[1] who had decades of experience successfully anticipating and acting on global EM trends. The International Monetary Fund classified[2] the world into advanced and developing economies on the basis of:

- per capita income level (i.e. how much citizens of a country earn)
- export diversification (i.e. how diverse a country's exports are)
- degree of integration into the global financial system (i.e. a country's level of financial sophistication)

Reclassification only happens when a significant change occurs or the case for change in terms of the three criteria above becomes overwhelming. The Morgan Stanley Capital International (MSCI) EMs Index[3], launched in 1988, is another type of classification used for EM countries. Reviewed quarterly, it reflects changes in the underlying equity markets. EM countries are economies that are moving toward becoming what are known as *developed markets*. These countries are crucial to driving global economic growth. Examples of advanced markets include the US and Western Europe, including the UK. Examples of developing economies include countries across the Asia–Pacific region and Latin America. They have lower levels of liquidity, less established markets and lower levels of per-capita income.

Although there are many EMs worldwide, the four largest are Brazil, Russia, India and China (BRIC), as depicted in Figure 1. Many investors believe that these markets are relatively stable and may eventually replace the G7 as the world's next superpowers. This makes them essential for any international investor's portfolio (Kuepper, 2019). The BRIC economies differ greatly from each other in many ways:

- **Brazil:** nothing short of an economic miracle over the past decade. In fact, the country is now the second-largest producer of iron ore in the world and produces more ethanol than Asia and Europe combined.

- **Russia:** a leading exporter of oil and natural gas to Europe. It has benefitted from the secular growth of commodities and continues to expand.
- **India:** its demographic dividend and significant farm output (second in the world) creates an economy that investors regularly add to their portfolios.
- **China:** the third-largest economy after the US and the European Union by measure of GDP and is the biggest exporter in the world.

Figure 1. Gross domestic product (GDP) per capita in the main industrialised and EM countries (2019)

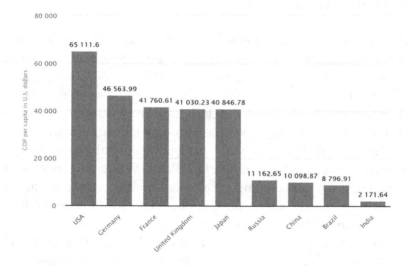

It is expected to surpass the US in the coming years. However, the country's communist government and related controversies presents key risks.

Why Are EMs Important?

EMs are attractive, because they tend to grow faster than their developed counterparts, and they attract global investors. As an EM country becomes more industrialised, it will spend heavily on infrastructure and other areas that encourage foreign investment, leading to rapid growth and expansion in liquidity and capital. This leads to a myriad of benefits, such as increased jobs in industries like manufacturing, which then leads to greater numbers of exports. Again, China is a prime example. Historically, its economy was mostly based on agriculture. However, this has changed to one based on manufacturing and is changing the world and global economics as we know it. Robust growth and development can eventually lead to developing economies overtaking those that are considered to be more advanced. A good example is India, who overtook the UK in terms of GDP at the end of 2016, aided by uncertainty over BREXIT.

Recently, EMs have experienced volatile performance, driven by changes in monetary policy, increasing political uncertainty and deteriorating conditions for international trade. According to Morning Star (Gard, 2019), 2019 was a mixed year for EM investors, with countries like Brazil and Russia posting outsized returns, while India and others underperformed. The strong US dollar, trade worries and China's sagging growth had ripple effects across the developing world. Political and currency crises in Chile, Argentina and Turkey have damaged investor sentiment.

Artificial Intelligence (AI) in EMs

AI is the broadest description of the technological process that is capable of automated decision making. Within AI is *machine learning* (ML) wherein machines can identify patterns in vast amounts of data to help draw conclusions and learn from these. This translates to huge opportunities resulting from increased innovation and productivity. Recent reports by McKinsey and Price–Waterhouse have predicted that AI could incrementally contribute 14–16% or over USD 13T to current global economic output, a productivity growth of 1.2% between now and 2030 via a combination of labour automation and innovations in products and services.

In EM countries, AI offers opportunities to drastically accelerate improved infrastructure and services that will lower costs and barriers to business entry and deliver innovative business models that can leapfrog traditional solutions and benefit underserved individuals and communities. With technology-based solutions becoming increasingly important to economic development, the goals of ending poverty and boosting shared prosperity have become at least partially dependent on harnessing the power of AI. Although EMs are already using basic AI technologies to solve critical development challenges, much more can be done and private-sector solutions will be critical to scaling the new business models. All of these solutions require innovative approaches to expand opportunities and mitigate risks associated with this new technology.

Let us fast-forward to the age of *artificial general intelligence* and perhaps *artificial super intelligence*, when human intelligence will be superseded. What do we expect to happen to EMs or even developed economies? 21st century historian Yuval Noah Harari predicted national and international borders being re-defined not around people but rather data colonies. We can also imagine a future in which 'the really big struggle will be against (human) irrelevance, with an unprecedented inequality not just between classes, but also between countries' (Harari et al., 2020). This dystopian future can be avoided if developed and EM countries unite to jointly address the technological challenges facing society *without* destroying nationalism and collectively upholding the same universal rules internationally in an effort to avoid digital dictatorships and uphold human rights.

Why Is AI Gaining Momentum?

When considering recent developments in mobile telephony and banking, similar growth dynamics could occur with AI. Data derived from smartphone digital transactions are key enablers for AI development. AI is facilitating financial inclusion by developing algorithms that derive value from vast amounts of untapped data sources accessible through smartphones, allowing services to be offered to people not currently served by financial institutions.

With the rise of 5G, the speed and bandwidth becoming available will allow huge amounts of data to be transmitted, received and interconnected to multiple devices that can intercommunicate. When AI is layered on top, this will allow further rapid and insightful services and smarter decision making.

Early progress in basic ML algorithm, the limitations of legacy technologies and a growing mass of technology users have enabled EMs to implement basic AI solutions, such as credit scoring and targeted advertising. Ant Financial in East Asia, M-Shwari in East Africa, M-Kajy in Madagascar and MoMo Kash in Cote d'Ivoire are early examples of AI delivering financial services to the poorest people. M-Shwari uses ML to predict the probability of defaulting borrowers, which allowed it to deliver small loans to 21 million Kenyans by the end of 2017 (Strusani and Houngbonon, 2019).

Improved business productivity stemming from automation of core business processes and human capital development can significantly lower production costs. This, in turn, can lead to increased access to credit... a critical advantage that AI technologies are already delivering. This further reduces overall business costs and increases the level of competition within markets and industries. AI solutions can also help overcome lacking infrastructure and large information asymmetries in EMs by supporting product innovation in the form of new business models while leapfrogging solutions tailored to serve previously unserved and underserved populations. Nonetheless, if EM countries cannot compete in the future global economy, they will be left behind to follow a downward spiral economically. To harness the potential of new business models, new ways of delivering services and shifting sources of competitiveness, EM countries must implement innovative approaches to expand AI's opportunities and to mitigate risks. AI-enabled productivity growth directly raises output and employment indirectly through increased consumption.

EM countries often lack the data necessary to fine-tune development interventions. AI's ability to tackle unstructured data, such as text, images and audio, will be useful for extracting the information needed to improve development outcomes. For instance, an experiment in rural India relied on textual transcriptions of village assemblies to identify the topics discussed and how the flow of conversation varied with the gender and status of the speakers, thereby shedding light on the functions of these deliberative bodies. This has become an important aspect of political accountability (Parthasarathy et al., 2017). Other experiments included the use of ML on value-added tax data in India to better target firms for audits and to predict travel-demand patterns after hurricanes (McKenzie, 2018) and to determine where food insecurities will occur to help target aid interventions (Knippenberg et al., 2018).

Although there currently seem to be few cases where AI and ML have been used for interventions like these, the promise lies in using AI and ML for individualised and dynamic scenarios that could be subsequently scaled to help the poor and underserved navigate through bureaucracies.

Frontier Leapfrogging

It used to take decades for a technological breakthrough to spread across countries. Diffusion and adoption were slow, and there were considerable barriers. The process is different now. Mobile phones, for example, reached billions of people in less than 20 years. Today, nearly 70% of the world's population uses mobile phones not only to communicate, but to also read news, check weather, make payments, sell products and more. These devices have become an indispensable feature of modern existence, regardless of where we live or what they do for a living. The internet is another technological advance that more than half the world's people use every day. These are great examples of enabling technologies used by communities and societies to bypass or leapfrog the linear path of progress. Frontier technologies open new windows of opportunity for communities and countries to catch up and accelerate development (Zhenmin, 2018).

AI presents one of the greatest examples of frontier technologies. As AI-powered technologies continue to mature and become more widespread throughout society, they will ultimately lead to the rise of interrelated and interdependent technologies that will fundamentally transform the world. Advances in one will foster breakthroughs in others. In the case of AI, smarter and more efficient robots and automation processes will pave the way for innovations, such as autonomous vehicles. Additionally, AI is making it easier to diagnose diseases and is propelling breakthroughs in genetic technology. Many of these frontier technologies are fortunately within the reach of billions of people.

Unlike our experiences with previous breakthroughs, communities and societies will be able to adapt and adopt frontier technologies with relatively low upfront costs. We will not require massive capital investments to replicate an algorithm or to make it work in a new economic or social setting. Technology built in one corner of the world can be easily transported to another often by clicking a button. Portability, replicability and affordability are the essence of many frontier technologies. They can create an even playing fields for all countries (Zhenmin, 2018).

Although there is no guarantee that frontier technologies, such as AI, will serve society's needs, if we do not put the right policies and institutions in place, the opportunities will potentially cause more harm than good. For example, AI and robots are feared to eliminate millions of jobs without replacing them with new ones. The creators and owners of such machines will likely become more prosperous at the expense of millions of people. The displacement of jobs by robots could also foreclose manufacturing and industrialisation opportunities in many EM countries. With advances in AI-powered technologies, we are likely to experience higher levels of wage and income inequalities, unless appropriate countermeasures, including strengthened social protection, are put in place. Nevertheless, these fears come with an important silver lining. If we manage to harness AI-powered technologies and make them accessible and available to the people who need them most, particularly those in EM countries, there is a strong chance that they will achieve positive sustainable development outcomes. So, how can we ensure that EM countries will benefit from AI-powered technologies without paying a huge price to access them? First and foremost, EM countries must build necessary human capital. In parallel, the enabling infrastructure should also be built. If EM countries still lack basic water, sanitation and electricity, we cannot expect them to take advantage of digital and AI capabilities. This is where governments play an important role.. However, *action is required now* to avoid missing the window of opportunity.

SOCIAL IMPLICATIONS

Consumer Satisfaction

According to a survey[4] by the Confederation of British Industry, consumer satisfaction levels of goods and services from EMs have been in clear decline (Figure 2) compared with satisfaction in European markets (Figure 3).

With the UK on course to kickstart its BREXIT agenda (31 Jan, 2020), the effects on EM countries will likely be most felt in the financial markets and trade and investment channels. According to Velthuijsen et al. (2016), the short- to medium-term effects of BREXIT on EMs is likely to be mixed. Countries that have extensive trade relations with UK and EU will be affected most. The longer-term outlook will, of course, hinge on the final outcome of the negotiations between the UK and the EU and between the UK and individual EMs.

However, the cost of imports from the UK is expected to decline for EM countries as the British Pound loses value. However, this is likely to be offset by price hikes by UK exporters to compensate for higher import prices. Additionally, good trade deals agreed upon between the UK and EU will

Figure 2. Satisfaction levels of UK businesses with links to EM countries between 2011 and 2013
Source: https://www.statista.com/statistics/323491/businesses-satisfied-with-links-to-emerging-markets-in-the-united-kingdom-uk/

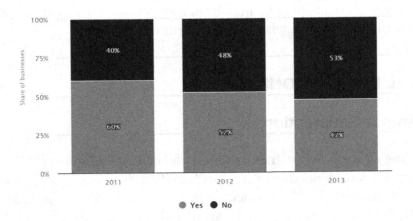

Figure 3. Satisfaction levels of UK businesses with links to EU countries between 2011 and 2013
Source: https://www.statista.com/statistics/323472/businesses-satisfied-with-links-to-eu-market-in-the-united-kingdom-uk/

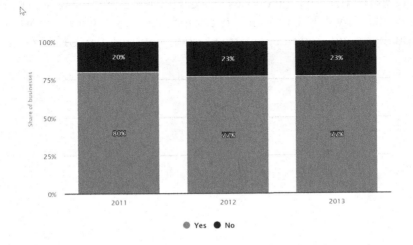

create benefits globally. To benefit, EM countries will need to exercise fiscal discipline and use BREXIT to take advantage of opportunities to financially diversify their trade of products.

Impact on Jobs

A rewarding, secure and well-paying job is fundamental to happiness and a foundation of social cohesion. According to the World Happiness Report, 'One of the most robust findings in the economics of happiness is that unemployment is destructive to people's wellbeing'. Perhaps unsurprisingly, media attention has focused on the negative impact of AI on EM countries, particularly the resulting job losses. Although there are many inevitable disruptive effects of AI, its opportunities should not be under-estimated. How an EM country manages these disruptive influences goes hand-in-hand with how the positive benefits of AI are harnessed.

Creating and expanding markets can help create jobs and raise consumption to the benefit of the wider economy. For instance, online marketplaces that rely on AI solutions across Africa are expected to create around 3-million jobs by 2025 by expanding the supply of goods and services, making assets more productive and unlocking new demand in remote locations by helping boost consumer spending. Digital technologies will make it easier for women to enter the workforce and, equitably, build their own businesses. There are four basic business models for such digital platforms:

- **B2C:** business-to-consumer
- **B2B:** business-to-business
- **C2C:** consumer-to-consumer
- **C2B:** consumer-to-business

Platforms, such as Jumia, Konga.com and Takealot.com can serve as both B2C and B2B marketplaces. Classified-ad sites, OLX and Avito are C2C platforms. South Africa's Thundafund, a crowdfunding platform for entrepreneurs, is an example of a C2B marketplace (Dupoux et al., 2019). In Africa, the economic activity generated by online marketplaces can boost employment and incomes in several ways. It can create entirely new jobs, stimulate skills development programmes and increase demand for goods and services in locations currently beyond the reach of conventional retail networks. It can also bring new people into the formal workforce, including women and youth, who, in some countries, have been excluded. Digital illiteracy among

African consumers and vendors presents a number of obstacles to growth in online commerce. However, a growing number of public-private initiatives increasingly offer training programmes to address the digital talent shortage.

Apart from the challenges of AI, *human* challenges exist: corruption, tax evasion, money laundering and the lack of functioning institutions. These are what Harvard Business School calls *institutional voids*, wherein dilapidated or non-existent infrastructure highlights formidable challenges. If these challenges can be managed (by humans), then the potential for AI is limitless. China offers a good example. It is estimated that AI will boost China's GDP by 26% by 2030, compared with 14% in the US (Rao and Verweij, 2017).

Growing Inequality

In 2017, Thomas Piketty and a working group released the first edition of the World Inequality Report, the most comprehensive ever report on world inequality. The research included analysis of more than 175-million data points on inequality. Piketty stated, 'for the first time ever, this report examines how global growth has been shared among individuals in the entire world since the 1980s, with a particular focus on emerging countries where inequality data had previously been sparse or non-existent' (Piketty, 2017).

The primary research indicated that income inequality increased in nearly all world regions in recent decades, although at different speeds. Since 1980, income inequality has increased rapidly in North America, China, India and Russia, while growing moderately in Europe. However, there are exceptions to this pattern. In the Middle East, sub-Saharan Africa and Brazil, income inequality has remained relatively stable, but at extremely high levels. Key insights worth highlighting include:

- On a global scale, since 1980 the richest 1% captured twice as much as the poorest 50% of the world's population. In other terms, 27% of all new income generated worldwide was captured by the richest 1%, while the poorest 50% of the world's population captured only 13%. These figures are brought into sharp contrast, considering the top 1% currently represents 75-million individuals, whereas the bottom 50% represents 3.7 billion. The population in between, largely comprising lower- and middle-income earners in North America and Europe, who have experienced sluggish or even zero income growth rates.
- Since 1980, there have been large shifts in the ownership of capital. Understanding who owns this capital is crucial in determining

inequality. Net private capital, the assets of individuals minus their debts, has risen enormously in recent decades. Conversely, net public capital–the assets of governments minus their debts, has declined in nearly all countries since the 1980s owing to large scale privatisations and rising public debts. Public capital is now approaching or below zero in rich countries. As a result of this exceptional situation, it becomes extremely challenging for governments to invest in education, healthcare or environmental protection.

- Wealth inequality among individuals also increased sharply since 1980. Significant increases in top wealth share have been experienced in China and Russia following their transitions from communism to more capitalist economies. The top-1% wealth share doubled in both China and Russia between 1995 and 2015, from 15 to 30% and from 22 to 43%, respectively.
- Global income and wealth inequality will steadily rise if countries continue to follow the same trajectory they have been on since 1980, despite strong growth in EMs. By 2050, the share of global wealth held by the world's 0.1% richest (7.5-million individuals) will be equal to that of the middle class (3-billion individuals).
- However, rising global inequality is not inevitable in the future, and limiting it will have tremendous impacts on global poverty eradication. If all countries follow the same inequality trend as Europe since 1980, the incomes of the bottom half of the world population could rise from €3,100 in 2017 to €9,100 in 2050. Alternatively, if countries were to follow the US trend, the incomes of the bottom 50% would rise to just €4,500 by 2050.

According to Revenga and Dooley (2019), rising inequality could be tackled by a threefold approach. First, we must reduce inequality of opportunity and any inter-generational transmission. Second, new policies are needed to correct the failures of the labour market to provide decent employment and earning prospects. Third, progressive taxation and spending is critical in ways that complement, not substitute, new policies that include drivers to address inequality transparently and measurably.

Sustainability

The global recovery since the 2008 financial crisis and improvement in commodity prices have provided favourable external conditions for many

EM countries. In an environment of zero-return for investment-grade debt, many investors have preferred to take high-quality EM risk over low-quality high-yield risk in developed markets. Today, many EM countries have emancipated themselves from the troubles of the past, but not without sacrifices and compromises. Many have suffered from poor governance and weak institutions. Governments operated via deficit spending, high public debts and gaping current account deficits are examples. Corporations also exploit their positions with flawed business practices and corruption, hampering long-term growth (Blanc-Adams, 2018).

Brazil is an EM that is coming out of one of its deepest recessions with remarkable growth. In the third quarter of 2017, GDP growth of +1.4% showed the strongest gain in nearly 4 years. This was expected to accelerate to over 4% in 2019 on the basis of a supportive electoral outcomes. The turnaround in the economy was accompanied by a drop-in inflation from a peak of over 10% in 2016 to less than 3% in 2017, enabling Brazil's central bank to cut rates, fuelling a consumption-led recovery and enabling businesses to lift investments (Blanc-Adams, 2018). Brazilian politics have been troubled but are also improving. After years of stasis, positive reforms have helped streamline the economy, the most distinctive being implementation of spending limits, the removal of loan subsidies and the launch of a new privatisation programme.

The emancipation we are seeing in EM countries is part of a wider global economic, ecological and social progress that is driving both developed and EM countries and will likely be a durable and permanent source of growth and prosperity. Improved corporate governance and sustainable sourcing of goods/inputs are examples of this new longer-term mentality. These may cost more money in the short term, but the long term pays off with consumers, voters and investors. Similarly, with many EM countries fighting off corruption, corporates can now make environmentally conscious investments and engage in positive communication and engagement with customers. If more businesses are able to proactively respond to challenges, as with Brazil's experience, and contribute to innovation and growth, the economies in developed and EMs are likely to be more sustainable with higher degrees of GDP growth.

International Trade

According to Joshua Meltzer of the Brookings Institution, the development of AI will affect international trade in a number of ways (Meltzer, 2018). One is the macroeconomic impacts of AI and the related trade effects. For instance, should AI increase productivity growth, it will increase economic growth and provide new opportunities for international trade. Current global rates of productivity growth are low, and there are various suggested causes. One reason is that it takes time for an economy to incorporate and make effective use of new technologies, particularly complex ones like AI and its economy-wide impacts. This process requires time to build a large enough capital stock to have an aggregate effect and for the complimentary investments needed to take full advantage of AI investments, including access to skilled people and business practices. Systems using AI to match or surpass human-level performance in more and more domains leads to rapid advances and increasing stock prices. Measured productivity growth, however, has declined by half over the past decade, and real income has stagnated. This could be attributed to:

- False hopes
- Mismeasurement
- Redistribution
- Implementation lags

The lags have been the biggest contributor to the paradox, perhaps because AI implementations, especially those based on ML, have not yet been tangibly realised at scale. Moreover, as with other general-purpose technologies, their full effects and potential will not be realised until the technology moves from being *producer focused* to *consumer focused*, such as when there are stable, affordable and scalable products in the marketplace that consumers can readily implement and easily benefit from.

AI is already having an impact on the development and management of global value chains (GVC). AI can be used to improve predictions of future trends, including changes in consumer demand, and better manage risk along the supply chain. By allowing business to better manage complex and dispersed production units, such tools improve the overall efficiency of GVCs. For example, businesses can use AI to improve warehouse management, demand prediction and improve the accuracy of just-in-time manufacturing and delivery. Robotics can increase productivity and efficiency in packing and inventory inspection. Furthermore, development of GVCs will be affected by the broader trends toward using AI to develop smart manufacturing. For instance, Industry 4.0 is based on sensors, the internet of things and cyber-physical systems that connect machines, material, supplies and customers. This incorporates the capacities at the factory level of predictive machines and self-maintenance, complete communications between companies along the supply chain and the ability to manufacture according to customer specifications, even in small or single batches. Such developments could strengthen GVCs and give rise to improved international trade.

RISE OF CHINA

According to Kai-Fu Lee, former CEO of Google China, ranked by Forbes as #1 among the leaders of China's AI revolution, AI is reshaping the world, and we need to start thinking now about how to address these gigantic changes (Lee, 2019). AI is already presenting new economic opportunities and new problems of governance for both the US and China. Lee believes China will be the next tech-innovation superpower and suggests that China has already caught up with the US at an astonishingly rapid and unexpected pace. China has shifted from a population in 1982 where a third were under the age of 15 to one in which half are middle aged. To drive its GDP forward, it will be less capital intensive and more focused on productivity improvements. Doing so will require more AI-derived business strategies. For those EMs where populations are still younger than those on average in developed markets, there is a correlation to adoption rates of new technology.

China provides a window into seeing how EMs cope with the challenges. China is now an economic powerhouse that is integrated into the global economy. According to the Ministry of Industry and Information Technology of China, China's internet sector had a revenue growth of 22.9% in the first half of 2018, substantially outpacing the growth of the overall economy, which grew at 6.9% in 2017. In the AI sector, China was home to 592 AI firms in 2017, accounting for 23.3% of the total number of AI firms worldwide. Broadband infrastructure development, the backbone of AI development, has laid the foundation for China's new digital economy. By 2018, broadband network coverage in China will include all urban areas and 90% of the countryside. Investment in rural broadband, for instance, has led to e-commerce sales opportunities for farmers and village enterprises. 5G, the next-generation mobile internet technology, will facilitate further AI deployment for businesses and cities. According to Deloitte, China has built 350,000 new cell sites since 2015, outspending the US in 5G infrastructure by USD 24B.

Like other EMs, China faces a talent gap in AI and related technologies. Educators are teaming with firms to provide new courses. The government is also pitching in to support digital literacy and entrepreneurship. Beijing has issued numerous directives to promote vocational education, e-learning, mass entrepreneurship, makerspace development and entrepreneurship education in universities. For instance, the Ministry of Education is co-developing public hubs and training centres for industrial robotics at 115 higher education vocational institutes across China in collaboration with major robotics companies.

The rapid expansion of AI-powered services, such as online shopping and food delivery, also rely on hard-working, low-wage migrant workers, such as delivery people and parcel sorters, who earn as low as USD 300 per month in China. According to the National Bureau of Statistics of China, in 2016, 65% of migrant workers in China had not signed formal labour contracts with their employers, depriving them of training opportunities and making them vulnerable to labour abuse. Although automation can improve occupational health and safety by delegating dangerous work to machines, they also pose risks of wage cut and layoffs, especially for older workers who command higher wages but require training to work with newer and smarter machines. The lack of bargaining power may trap workers in informal and temporary contracts instead of moving them up to more value-added and stable positions. The new jobs and training opportunities will be no panacea. For instance, AI algorithms rely on massive, accurately labelled training datasets, such as pictures, voices and videos, to improve their accuracy. Machines are still unable to complete tasks, such as image classification. Thus, companies increasingly outsource such time-consuming tasks to students and trainees in the EMs, spending one-half to one-tenth of what it costs to hire workers in the US. In China, a team of fewer than 100 workers and vocational school students at a small data processing company can label 60,000 images in 1 week. Yet, with future improvements in areas, such as unsupervised learning, these foot soldiers for AI development may soon find their training and work experience obsolete. To nurture home-grown technology entrepreneurs, Alibaba has teamed with UNCTAD[5] to train 1,000 entrepreneurs from developing countries, including 200 from Africa.

Participation of emerging economy stakeholders would be vital to such a global partnership. Although each emerging economy has its unique political, legal and cultural contexts, space exists for the global community to shape broad principles that contribute to inclusive development. Such a 'glocalisation' approach is possible when the regime not only includes policymakers and private firms, but also creates greater roles and voices for educators and researchers, technologists, entrepreneurs, trade unions and other public interest groups. Ultimately, the success of AI innovation rests upon a future where growth benefits can be shared among all people.

In other EMs, there are examples of micro-level implementations of AI across all sectors. For example, healthcare companies in Korea are using AI to sift through millions of datasets related to dissertations and clinical test data. In Russia, the oil and gas sector is looking to AI to reduce the costs of seismic surveys. Semiconductor makers in Taiwan look to benefit from the rise of autonomous driving that AI makes possible, because of the estimated increase in demand for memory chips and processors to handle the data required for self-driving cars to work. In recent decades, China and India have presented the world with two different models on how EMs can climb the development ladder.

- **China model:** the nation leveraged its large population and low costs to build a base of blue-collar manufacturing. The country then steadily worked its way up the value chain by producing better and more technology-intensive goods.
- **India model:** they combined a large English-speaking population with low costs to become a hub for outsourcing of low-end, white-collar jobs in fields such as software testing and business process outsourcing. If successful, these relatively low-skilled jobs can be slowly upgraded to more advanced white-collar industries.
- **Both models:** based on a country's cost advantages in the performance of repetitive, non-social and largely uncreative work for both manual labour in factories or cognitive labour in call centres.

Unfortunately for EMs, AI thrives at performing precisely the above types of work. Without a cost incentive to locate in developing countries, corporations will bring many of these functions back to the countries where they are based. This would leave EMs unable to grasp the bottom rungs of the development ladder. The resultant large pool of young and relatively unskilled workers that once formed their greatest comparative advantage will become a terrible liability. Increasing desperation in the developing world will occur in stark contrast to the massive accumulation of wealth among the AI superpowers. AI runs on data, and that dependence leads to a self-perpetuating cycle of consolidation in industries: the more data you have, the better your product, and, the better your product, the more users you gain. Furthermore, the more users you gain, the more data you have. Simultaneously, developing countries will have to carve out their own niches within the AI landscape. Factory robots can work anywhere in the world. A microlending algorithm developed using the credit reports of American consumers would be useless in an agricultural country like Ethiopia, where borrowers do not have credit cards or traditional mortgages. To capitalise, governments must fund the AI education of their best and brightest students with the goal of building local companies that employ the technologies. Maths and engineering prodigies should be discovered early, trained vigorously and sent to top global universities to study AI.

Neither of these tasks will be easy. Fostering a million small businesses is far more difficult than building a hundred mega-factories. Paying for top students to study abroad is also a daunting task for countries still dealing with malnutrition. However, if developing countries can strike a balance, AI can offer them an invaluable new opportunity: the chance to improve livelihoods and grow an economy without having to suffer exploitative sweatshops or environmental degradations.

Potential Risks

Figure 4. EM and developing economies: inflation rates from 2014 to 2024

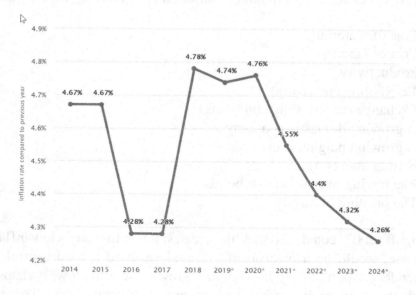

Figure 4 shows the average inflation rates of EMs from 2014 to 2018, with projections to 2024. In 2018, the average inflation rate in EMs amounted to about 4.78%, compared with the previous year (Plecher, 2019).

Inflation is a function of the supply and demand for money. Not everything inflates at the same rate, however. More money usually causes more spending and increased demand. Production then rises with the product prices. High inflation is often associated with lower growth and financial crises (IMF 2001; Mishkin, 2008). Rising price levels are further linked to weaker investor confidence, undercut incentives to save and eroded financial and public sector balance sheets. Moreover, the damage of high inflation can fall disproportionately on the poor, because poorer households are more reliant on wage incomes, have less access to interest-bearing accounts and are unlikely to have significant holdings of financial or real assets apart from cash. For these reasons, low and stable inflation has been associated with better growth and development outcomes, financial stability and poverty reduction.

Extremely low inflation, on the other hand, such as that which has prevailed in many advanced economies over the past decade, can also be problematic. It can make it difficult for central banks to lower real short-term interest rates sufficiently to provide the requisite stimulus to demand, given the lower bounds on nominal interest rates. It can also tip into deflation, a sustained decline in prices, which can exacerbate recessionary tendencies (Blanchard et al., 2010; Arteta et al., 2018). In reality, inflation is affected by several things[6]:

- Cost of materials
- Cost of labour
- Productivity
- Tax (falling and rising)
- Exchange rates (falling and rising)
- A growing domestic economy
- A growing neighbouring economy
- Falling interest rates
- The buying of government bonds
- The printing of money

Rogoff (2003) concluded that 'the greatest threat to today's low inflation, of course, would be a reversal of the modern trend toward central bank independence, particularly if economic growth were to slow, perhaps due to reductions in globalisation and economic liberalisation'. The rising protectionist sentiment of recent years and reform fatigue in some economies could slow the pace of globalisation and structural policy improvements.

FUTURE RESEARCH DIRECTIONS

It is our belief that, if EMs adopt an AI-first approach, it will give rise to critical improvements that will positively basic services, including finance, education and health. Moreover, rather than mimicking mature economies, if AI is used to help redefine how the infrastructures of these economies work, it could lead to market-innovations that ultimately accelerate the progress of EMs. Nevertheless, challenges remain that are areas for future research. Examples include the cost of implementing AI in daily life. The technology may offer tremendous potential, but it must also be commercially viable. Another example is data security. Questions related to privacy and data protection will not abate anytime soon, and they must be answered. Given that AI has transformative potential, there are challenges we must confront if it is to fulfil its potential to help emerging economies:

- Implementing strategies to augment human intelligence requires us to appreciate our shortcomings. We must believe that using AI will fundamentally make us better at what we are passionate about. The AI will not always be correct. Factors, such as human bias, will continue to creep into programming algorithms, and agreeing on a code of ethics for machine decision-making will be difficult. However, humans are not always right either. Embracing AI is a cultural shift that needs to be managed conscientiously.
- Most AI technologies are typically developed in wealthy markets rather than EMs. There are many reasons for this. The systems require billions of dollars of investment and highly specialised skills that are more often found in the US and Europe. It means that AI systems are not yet the general-purpose machines that can easily be deployed across the world. The need for AI to focus more on developing economies is particularly evident in healthcare. Developing economies carry most of the global disease burden. However, the top killers in Africa are not of deep concern to the US or Europe.

To truly democratise AI and make it available to EMs, we must focus on transitioning from product development to consumer demand to opens marketplaces that encourage consumers to invest and to use proven and working AI solutions that can be bought, implemented and applied to the day-to-day lives of citizens across EM countries. Some of the key challenges and areas for future work include:

- **Codes of Conduct:** AI systems require good quality data to learn and better handle increasingly complex tasks. EM Countries need to establish codes of conduct to:
  ○ Ensure businesses get a good deal on partnerships with AI technology companies
  ○ Work with accredited suppliers to develop AI technology that are fit-for-purpose
  ○ Establish clear guidelines to drive data privacy and data protection practices
  ○ Adopt regulated data management practices to drive compliance and standards
- **Democratising AI:** if the cost of entry to AI is prohibitive, adoption will be restricted. Lowering the barrier for businesses to develop commercial applications is critical for an AI marketplace to be established in EM countries. This will unlock opportunities for data scientists to develop algorithms, solve business problems and potentially monetise their work, while businesses can work with these experts to meet the challenges they could not meet on their own.
- **Early Adoption:** AI early adopters are those that will gain the greatest competitive advantage from AI. Early adopters are already leveraging AI, ML and automation to provide highly personalised web experiences at scale.
- **Sustainable AI:** EM countries must consider ways to sustain the development, production and distribution of AI-powered technologies at scale by considering:
  ○ The assembly and accumulation of data and insights
  ○ Relevant business applications of ML and deep learning
  ○ The activation of AI applications across businesses and institutions
- **Ethics/Privacy/Fairness:** governments should establish policies and protocols that incentivise businesses and institutions in EM countries to leverage AI that is socially beneficial and increasingly touches society as a whole in a wide range of fields, including healthcare, security, energy, transportation, manufacturing and entertainment in ways that are fair to all citizens especially those who are poor and underserved.

There is a lack of systematic approaches, and the entire thought-leadership around the impact of AI in developing markets is left to the private sector. AI is based on the ingestion and processing of data, and the data for emerging economies is not yet on the radar of the creators of today's AI. It should be a priority of companies, countries and international bodies to increase their focus on developing AI systems that are suited to driving systemic transformation in emerging economies. Our current approach needs to change. If it does, the societal and commercial impact could potentially rise beyond our imagination.

CONCLUSION

The promise of AI has many advocates and opponents who respectively hold optimistic and pessimistic views (Brynjolfsson et al., 2017). Typically, the optimists tend to be technologists and venture capitalists; the pessimists tend to be economists, sociologists, statisticians and government officials. There is often little interaction between the two. Each talks over the other rather than engaging in dialogue with an open mind.

The differences between EMs and more developed economies in terms of infrastructure and services could prove to be a positive advantage, because AI can provide the opportunity to redefine how economies can work more efficiently without simply replicating long-standing processes and infrastructure from developed economies.

When we listen to the optimists, we are convinced that breakthroughs in AI and ML will be real and significant. Conversely, when we speak with the pessimists, we are convinced that productivity growth has slowed down recently and the gains realised have been are unevenly distributed, leaving many people with stagnating incomes, declining metrics of health and wellbeing and good cause for concern. Individuals are growingly uncertain about the future, and many of the businesses that once enjoyed significant market share (e.g. Kodak, Xerox, Yahoo and Blackberry) have fallen on harder times. These points of view are symptomatic of the current state of the global economy, which needs to be transformed to fully realise the potential of AI and automation.

Many of the human jobs that AI will replace, such as credit scoring, language translation or managing a stock portfolio, are currently regarded as skilled. They have limited human competition and are well-paid. Equally, many of the jobs that AI cannot yet replace, like cleaning, gardening or cooking, are relatively unskilled and are low-paid. On the flipside, why invest in costly AI systems when it is so much more cost effective to hire low-paid humans to do the same job? This is something that occurs regularly in EM countries. Although this may not be ethical, it is a business model well exploited by technology companies like Amazon. AI-based innovations are costly, difficult to measure and take time to implement. This can, at least initially, depress productivity as it is currently measured. Entrepreneurs, tech leaders and consumers will find powerful new applications for machines that can learn how to recognise objects, understand human language, speak, make accurate predictions, solve problems and interact with the world with increasing dexterity and mobility.

Although it may not be equally crucial, another major driving force for the location of research and development (R&D) in emerging economies has been the cost-related factor, particularly in the case of outsourcing. The total costs in Ems, such as India and China, are much less than those in industrialised countries, mainly because of lower-wages. Generally, wage costs account for the largest proportion of total R&D activities. Often, in EMs, the advantages of lower-wages are usually eroded by higher material, communications and other costs. For instance, some of the inputs may not be available locally and may need to be imported under special conditions, and this adds to cost. Similarly, the lack of infrastructure facilities may require businesses to invest in captive facilities, adding to the total costs. For example, shortages of power would require investing in backup facilities, or poor communication lines would require investing in a communication network.

Another primary driving force for location of R&D in emerging economies, particularly in Brazil and China, has been the need to be in proximity to regional markets. Part of the reason for this is that R&D units in these countries are closely linked to their own and/or customers' production units located in the region. R&D performed in these units is also mainly that of product design and engineering. Local R&D personnel in emerging economies are more sensitive to local and regional market needs to come up with better-suited products. Simply adapting products developed in industrialised countries does not seem to bring much success in EMs. Consumer affluence in emerging economies is growing fairly rapidly, placing greater demands on companies catering to such markets. Consumers in EMs demand products having the same high functionality and quality as those sold in the industrialised world, but at lower prices. 'Emerging products for EMs' is their motto. If a company wants to prosper in these large markets, their business strategies should focus on making profits by selling volumes rather than earning higher profit margins on low volumes. For instance, Nokia designed and developed low-cost mobile phones in India and exported several millions of these phones to Africa and other developing regions.

Realising the benefits of AI is not automatic. It will require effort, leadership and entrepreneurship to develop. Individuals, organisations and societies will need to adapt and change the way they do things. The winners will be those most willing to adapt to the lowest adjustment costs. This will be partly a matter of good fortune. However, with the right strategies and leadership by governments, institutions and businesses, it is something that we can all prepare for collectively for shared benefit.

The initial uses of AI in EM countries has been at the micro level, solving small specific problems in a defined industry in a local region. As AI and ML advances and there is a higher supply of proven and affordable AI services and solutions, we expect to see more complex issues being targeted and resolved. Only then can AI positively impact the everyday lives of citizens in EM countries, not just in disaster intervention, education, health care and agriculture, but also in mitigating poverty, malnutrition and pollution. On their own, citizens and local businesses cannot be successful without the aid and leadership of non-governmental organisations and government agencies that must partake with a strong sense of trust, integrity and community-service to create a snowball effect that helps drive AI adoption. Additionally, non-profit and for-profit organisations (including start-ups) will need to engage in a holistic and humanitarian approaches to enable AI-ready societies. Localised services and solutions that can subsequently be scaled and shared among neighbouring regions and countries including to further enhance productivity and increase GDP across EM countries. To promote an AI-ready society, EM countries must integrate human intelligence with machine intelligence so they can successfully co-exist while reinforcing the roles of people to drive growth. Additionally, NGOs and governments need to

- **Encourage AI-enabled regulation:** update and create adaptive, self-improving laws to close the gaps between the pace of technological change and the pace of regulatory response
- **Advocate an AI code of ethics:** ethical debates should be supplemented by tangible standards and best practices in the development and use of intelligent machines
- **Redistribution the benefits of AI:** policy makers should highlight how AI can result in tangible benefits and proactively address any potential or perceived downsides

For AI to the game changer we expect, transforming businesses, people's lives and society as a whole is required. For this, we must

- Create the right environment for existing and new businesses to innovate and make the most of the product, productivity and wage benefits that this technology can bring.
- Look at how to obtain the right talent technology and access to data to make the most of this opportunity. To meet this challenge, we must be even more innovative in the ways we develop technology skills in EM countries, perhaps supported by talent from developed-markets.
- Promote 'responsible AI' solutions and services that every part of society can benefit from.

Future AI-ready societies must include producers, consumers and policymakers on a national and international basis to ensure the principles of inclusive growth, sustainable development and human-centric values for both developed and developing economies. Such an interdisciplinary and collaborative approach would produce optimal solutions and efforts that foster comprehensive environments for trustworthy AI.

REFERENCES

Arteta, C., Kose, M. A., Stocker, M., & Taskin, T. (2018). Implications of Negative Interest Rate Policies: An Early Assessment. *Pacific Economic Review*, *23*(1), 8–26. doi:10.1111/1468-0106.12249

Blanc-Adams, C. (2018). Emerging Markets and Sustainability – Enrich not Exploit. *J. Stern & Co. LLP*. https://www.jsternco.com/wp-content/uploads/2020/01/Emerging-Markets-and-Sustainability-Enrich-not-Exploit.pdf

Blanchard, O. J., Dell'Ariccia, G., & Mauro, P. (2010). Rethinking Macroeconomic Policy. *Journal of Money, Credit and Banking*, *42*(s1), 199–215. doi:10.1111/j.1538-4616.2010.00334.x

Brynjolfsson, E., Rock, D., & Syverson, C. (2017). *Artificial Intelligence and the Modern Productivity Paradox: A Clash of Expectations and Statistics*. NBER Working Paper No. 24001, p.10. https://www.nber.org/papers/w24001.pdf

Dupoux, P., Ivers, L., Dannouni, A., Sqalli, Z., & Ngambeket, G. (2019). How Online Marketplaces Can Power Employment in Africa. *Boston Consulting Group (BCG)*. https://www.bcg.com/publications/2019/how-online-marketplaces-can-power-employment-africa.aspx

Gard, J. (2020). What Next for Emerging Markets? *Morning Star. Fund Research and Highlights*. https://www.morningstar.co.U.K./U.K./news/198438/what-next-for-emerging-markets.aspx

Harari, Y. N., Rutte, M., & Gadiesh, O. (2020). How to Survive the 21st Century. Davos 2020. *World Economic Forum*. https://youtu.be/eOsKFOrW5h8

Knippenberg, E., Jensen, N., & Constas, M. (2018). *Resilience, Shocks, and the Dynamics of Food Insecurity: Evidence from Malawi*. Working Paper. https://static1.squarespace.com/static/59c807a890bade1b5925f72e/t/5a9ef2b253450a57bf5f6a7c/1520366270740/Resilience%2C+Shocks+and+the+Dynamics+of+Food+Insecurity+%28JMP%29.pdf

Kuepper, J. (2019). The Four Largest Emerging Markets. *The Balance*. https://www.thebalance.com/the-four-largest-emerging-markets-1979060

McKenzie, D. (2018). How can machine learning and artificial intelligence be used in development interventions and impact evaluations? *Worldbank Blogs*. https://blogs.worldbank.org/impactevaluations/how-can-machine-learning-and-artificial-intelligence-be-used-development-interventions-and-impact

Meltzer, J. (2018). The impact of artificial intelligence on international trade. *Brookings Institution*. https://www.brookings.edu/research/the-impact-of-artificial-intelligence-on-international-trade/

Parthasarathy, R., Rao, V., & Palaniswamy, N. (2017). *Deliberative Inequality: A Text-as-Data Study of Tamil Nadu's Village Assemblies*. World Bank Group Policy Research, Working Paper WPS 8119. http://documents.worldbank.org/curated/en/582551498568606865/Deliberative-inequality-a-text-as-data-study-of-Tamil-Nadus-village-assemblies

Piketty, T. (2017). Growing inequality in emerging markets becoming entrenched feature of economic growth. *Namibia Economist*. https://economist.com.na/31428/columns/growing-inequality-in-emerging-markets-becoming-entrenched-feature-of-economic-growth/

Plecher, H. (2019). Inflation rate in emerging market and developing countries 2024. *Statistica*. https://www.statista.com/statistics/805547/inflation-rate-in-the-emerging-market-and-developing-economies/

Rao, A. S., & Verweij, G. (2017). Sizing the Prize: What's the Real Value of AI for Your Business and How Can You Capitalize? *PwC*. https://www.pwc.com/gx/en/issues/analytics/assets/pwc-ai-analysis-sizing-the-prize-report.pdf

Revenga, A., & Dooley, M. (2019). Is inequality really on the rise? *Brookings*. https://www.brookings.edu/blog/future-development/2019/05/28/is-inequality-really-on-the-rise/

Strusani, D., & Houngbonon, G. V. (2019). The Role of Artificial Intelligence in Supporting Development in Emerging Markets. EMCompass, No. 69. *International Finance Corporation*. https://openknowledge.worldbank.org/handle/10986/32365

Velthuijsen, W., Yalcin, H., & Yildirim, B. (2016). Brexit Monitor. The Impact on Emerging Markets: Risks vs Opportunities. *PricewaterhouseCoopers B.V. PwC*. https://www.pwc.nl/nl/brexit/documents/pwc-brexit-monitor-opkomende-markten.pdf

Zhenmin, L. (2018). Frontier Technologies: A Window of Opportunity for Leapfrogging! UN Chronicle, 55(3-4).

ENDNOTES

[1] Antoine van Agtmael is on the President's Council on International Activities at Yale University, the Advisory Council of Johns–Hopkins University's Paul H. Nitze School of Advanced International Studies, and a member of the Council on Foreign Relations (Source: https://fpgroup.foreignpolicy.com/people/antoine-van-agtmael).

[2] IMF FAQ (Source: https://www.imf.org/external/pubs/ft/weo/faq.htm#q4b).

[3] MSCI Emerging Markets Index (Source: https://www.msci.com/emerging-markets).

[4] Survey results published by Statista Research Department, Aug 15, 2019.

[5] UNCTAD stands for United Nations Conference on Trade and Development. It is a permanent intergovernmental body established by the UN General Assembly in 1964. Headquartered in Geneva, Switzerland, it serves the citizens of the 195 countries (Source: https://unctad.org/en/Pages/aboutus.aspx).

[6] YouTube video: What is inflation? (Source: https://www.youtube.com/watch?v=UMAELCrJxt0).

Chapter 7
Ethics of AI

ABSTRACT

While the 'AI ethics' debate has been raging for some time, there are legitimate questions about employing AI and automation that are explored in this chapter. AI ethics isn't just about doing the right thing or making the best AI systems possible, it's also about who wields power and how AI affects the balance of power in everything it touches across society including businesses, institutions, and governments – ultimately, affecting the privacy and human rights of all individuals globally. AI must be developed with an understanding of who humans are collectively and in groups (anthropology and sociology), as well as who we are individually (psychology), and how our individual brains work (cognitive science), in tandem with current thinking on global cultural ethics and corresponding philosophies and laws. One thing is clear, without ethics, all visions of AI's future will have little impact.

"It's not artificial intelligence I'm worried about, it's human stupidity." –Neil Jacobstein, Chair of the AI and Robotics track at Singularity University

INTRODUCTION

Artificial intelligence (AI) is a key technology that will profoundly change our economic, political and social structures in the future. Equally important is a

DOI: 10.4018/978-1-7998-4607-9.ch007

widely held belief that AI represents one of the great human rights challenges of the 21st century (Elsayed–Ali, 2019). Although the *AI ethics* debate has been raging for some time, there are legitimate questions about employing AI and automation. It is not just about doing the right thing or making the best AI systems possible, it is also about who wields power and how AI affects the balance of power in everything it touches across societies, businesses, institutions and governments. Ultimately, AI affects the privacy and human rights of all individuals globally.

It is important to pause here and reflect on our individuality: humans across the globe are *different*. Hence, AI algorithms and automated processes will not work equally effectively worldwide, because different regions have different cultural models of what constitutes sociability and ethics. The values, morals and ethical choices that each individual makes on a daily basis are rooted in their cultural framework and sense of sociability. On their own, cultures, legal standards and regulatory frameworks will not get us out of the predicament we find ourselves in regarding AI. For that, we not only need tech developers to read some moral philosophy, we also need politicians, business leaders, community activists and citizens to do the same. Presently, we appear to be dancing around the edges of the issue. We treat tech design and development as if it is inevitable. Thus, we reactively minimise risks after the fact rather than look more deeply at the values, goals and moral commitments being built into the technologies.

AI must be developed with an understanding of who humans are collectively and in groups (e.g. anthropology and sociology), who we are individually (i.e. psychology) and how our individual brains work (cognitive science) with current thinking on global cultural ethics and corresponding philosophies and laws. What it means to be human can vary depending upon not just who and where we are, but also *when* we are, and how we see ourselves at any given time. When crafting ethical guidelines for AI, we must consider ethics in all forms, particularly accounting for the cultural constructs that differ between regions and groups of people in time and space.

The ethics that are informing AI and automated digital technology are essentially biased. Many of the proposals for ethics in AI that have been developed by computer scientists, engineers, politicians and other powerful entities are flawed. They neglect much of the world's many cultures and states of being and they lack the diversity in education, culture, ethnicity and gender found in today's complex world. For example, a search of the Organisation for

Economic and Co-operation and Development (OECD)[1] AI ethics guidelines document revealed no mention of the word 'culture' but many references to 'human'. Therein lays one of the problems with standards, and with the bias of the committees who are creating them. An assumption is being made of what being 'human' means, and the assumption that the meaning is the same for everyone (Applin, 2019).

Although there is a growing body of research and proposals from known scholars, civil societies, international organisations and governments need to collaborate further to accelerate our understanding of how existing legislative and regulatory frameworks can be applied to address AI ethics while also creating practices to continuously review, amend and monitor policies to allow for experimentation and adoption. This will require policy expertise, education and capacity-building across government policymaking departments, regulatory agencies, industry and civil society.

ETHICS – A DEFINITION

The term 'ethics' is derived from the Greek word 'ethos'[2], which can mean *custom*, *habit*, *character* or *disposition*. At its simplest, ethics is a system of moral principles, and it affect how people make decisions and lead their lives, helping to balance what is good for individuals and society. We subscribe to The Ethics Centre[3] definition, 'ethics is the process of questioning, discovering and defending our values, principles and purpose.'

- **Values** tell us what is good. They are the things we strive for, desire and seek to protect.
- **Principles** tell us was is right. They outline how we may or may not achieve our values.
- **Purpose** is the reason for being. It gives life to your values and principles.

These ethical concepts have been derived from religions, philosophies and cultures, and they infuse debate on topics that affect individuals and society like abortion, human rights and professional conduct.

WHAT IS THE PURPOSE OF ETHICS?

For ethics to be useful and practical, rather than simply moral principles, they need to affect the way human beings behave. However, human beings often behave irrationally. They follow their *gut instinct*, even when their consciousness suggests a different course of action. Whenever we make a choice, it is always possible for us make a different one. The Danish philosopher, Soren Kierkegaard, captured this dilemma when he described standing on the edge of a cliff. The only thing that prevents us from falling into the void is our choice to do otherwise.

Ethics is only possible, because we can act against our nature based on our conscience. It stops us from simply describing what is likely to happen and allows us to make judgements about what should happen. Of all the ways we might act, which is the best? Of all the possibilities, which one should we bring into reality? Those are questions ethics seeks to answer.

WHY ETHICS IN AI?

AI will bring about capabilities to tackle issues from environmental disasters to financial crises, from crime, terrorism and war, to famine, poverty, ignorance, inequality and poor living standards. However, AI is not without its problems. To ensure AI can do good, we first have to understand the risks. The potential problems that come with AI include a lack of transparency about what goes into the algorithms. Being able to explain what constitutes an AI is therefore critical. This is why ethics in AI is an important matter. However, when exploring the subject, it quickly becomes clear that it has more to do with ethics that affect humans and society rather than AI technologies and intelligent systems. Many ethical questions revolve around what will happen when we replace humans with AI or enhance humans with AI. This worry is also held by Paula Boddington, Oxford academic and author of 'Towards a Code of Ethics for AI' (Boddington, 2017). AI itself is an umbrella term that encompasses a diverse set of technologies. Hence, 'AI ethics' raises a wide array of questions, dilemmas and challenges that need to be explored thoroughly. For example, in the event that AI replaces blue- and white-collar jobs, what happens to the people facing redundancy? This raises ethical issues, because it affects people's well-being and employment. Machinery increasingly involves AI. Autopilots include AI capabilities and autonomous self-driving vehicles are set to rise with companies like Tesla. These innovations are calling for ethics to be built into AI devices that are increasingly making decisions on our behalf. The classic *trolley problem* (Thomson, 1985) from philosophy has been translated into a scenario where an autonomous vehicle is faced with an accident that might harm human beings. If autonomous vehicle comes to a decision where it is going to have to crash one way or the other, or kill the driver or someone else, what sort of ethics could be programmed to resolve that? These examples show that certain decisions that would be acceptable for a human being would not necessarily be tolerated when taken by AI. Earlier this year, a team of scientists designed a way to put the decision into the hands of the human passenger. The 'ethical knob' would switch a car's setting from 'full altruist' to 'full egoist', with the middle setting being impartial.

AI engineers and design teams too-often fail to discern the ethical decisions that are implicit in technical work and design choices, or alternatively, they treat ethical decision-making as just another form of technical problem solving. Ethical issues can all too easily be rendered invisible or inappropriately reduced or, worse, simplified (IEEE, 2016). After all, we are only human. The risk remains that we may misuse or underuse AI. This is why 'AI ethics' must be considered.

CATEGORIES OF ETHICS

While we have already provided a definition of ethics. Nonetheless, it is important to break down its true meaning. Like AI, ethics has several categories and branches, each with their own meaning and significance. Figure 1 provides a useful visual summary of the types of ethics and where ethics of AI fits. Each category has a place in the functionality of a society.

Metaethics

This category is essentially focused on our definitions of 'right' and 'wrong'. We will not elaborate on this, because the other categories are more compelling in the context of AI.

Figure 1. A mind-map highlighting ethics categories derived from philosophy

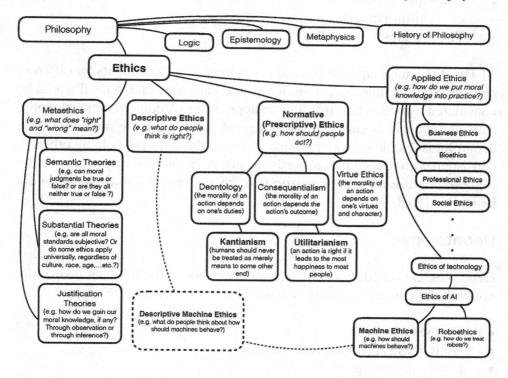

Descriptive Ethics

Before we proceed, it is important to understand the different ethics categories as depicted in Figure 1.

Normative Ethics

Also known as prescriptive ethics, the field of normative ethics comprises various theories that specify what bases upon which the morality of an action should be judged. Every action involves three main elements: the action itself, the agent performing the action and the outcome of this action. When reasoning about what action one should take in a situation, these three elements become relevant. The main approaches to normative ethics focus on one or more of these three elements.

- Deontology
  - Kantianism

- Consequentialism
  ◦ Utilitarianism
- Virtue ethics

The three major approaches can result in similar judgements for different reasons. For example, an action that would help someone in need would be considered a good action by all three approaches. A consequentialist would consider it good, because it brings a good outcome to the one in need. A deontologist would consider it good, because the action of helping others is consistent with one's duties towards society. A virtue ethicist would consider it good, because a virtuous person with character traits of kindness would be inclined to do it.

Deontology

Deontological (or 'duty-based') ethics are concerned with what people do, not with the consequences of their actions.

- Do the right thing
- Do it because it is the right thing to do
- Do not do wrong things
- Avoid wrong things because they are wrong

Deontologists live in a universe of moral rules, such as

- It is wrong to kill innocent people
- It is wrong to steal
- It is wrong to tell lies
- It is right to keep promises

Someone who follows duty-based ethics should do the right thing, even if that produces more harm (or less good) than doing the wrong thing. People have a duty to do the right thing, even if it produces a bad result.

Kantianism (or 'Kantian' Ethics)

These are based upon the writings of the German idealist philosopher, Immanuel Kant, who believed that it was possible to develop a consistent moral system by using reason. In Kantianism, there are two questions that we must ask ourselves whenever we decide to act:

- Can I rationally expect that everyone will act as I propose to act? If the answer is 'no,' we must not perform the action.
- Does my action respect the goals of human beings rather than merely using them for my own purposes? Again, if the answer is 'no', then we must not perform the action.

Consequentialism

Consequentialism is based on two principles:

- Whether an act is right or wrong depends only on the results of that act
- The more good consequences an act produces, the better or more right that act

This gives us guidance when faced with a moral dilemma:

- A person should choose the action that maximises good consequences

Then, it gives this general guidance on how to live:

- People should live to maximise good consequences

Utilitarianism

Utilitarianism argues that an action is morally permissible if it results in maximising the happiness or well-being and minimising the pain of the majority. This is the main paradigm of consequentialism. It focuses on the consequences of an action, and, in the broader sense, reduces morally relevant factors to outcomes, which it reduces to a single value: 'utility' (hence the name). Although this can make it seem simple and shallow, classic utilitarianism underlies various complex claims about the moral rightness of an act.

Virtue Ethics

This focuses on the agents and their inherent virtues and moral character. It looks at the virtue or moral character of the agent carrying out an action, rather than ethical duties and rules or the consequences of particular actions. Virtue ethics not only deals with the rightness or wrongness of individual actions, it provides guidance about the sort of characteristics and behaviours a good person will seek to achieve.

Applied Ethics

There are five sub-categories:

- Business ethics
- Bioethics
- Professional ethics
- Social ethics
- Ethics of technology
  - Ethics of AI
    - Machine Ethics
    - Roboethics

Business Ethics

Business ethics is the behaviour that a business adheres to in its daily dealings with the world. The ethics of a particular business can be diverse. They apply not only to how the business interacts with the world at large, but also to their one-on-one dealings with a single customer, both non-profit and for-profit. However, this is not just about codes of conduct. More importantly, it is also about corporate social responsibility, the act of *whistleblowing* and managing *group-think*, which, according to social psychologist, Irving Janis, is 'a deterioration of mental efficiency, reality testing and moral judgement that results from in-group pressures' (Janis, 1982). Thus, ethics fly out the window!

Bioethics

Bioethics is the application of ethics to the field of medicine and healthcare. Today, it is multi-disciplinary blend of philosophy, theology, history and law with medicine, nursing, health policy and the medical humanities. Furthermore, the field of bioethics now encompasses a full range of concerns, from difficult private decisions made in clinical settings to controversies surrounding stem-cell research, to implications of reproductive technologies, to broader concerns such as international human subject research, to public policy in healthcare and to the allocation of scarce resources.

As AI systems take on expanded roles of healthcare, from research to medical diagnostics and even with treatment, the increasing use of AI is forcing nurses, doctors and researchers to ask, 'how do longstanding principles of medical ethics apply in this new world of technological innovation'? The answers (Fenech, 2018) gives rise to several use cases for which a number of ethical, social and political challenges are raised:

- What effect will AI have on human relationships in health and care?
- How is the use, storage and sharing of medical data impacted by AI?
- What are the implications of issues around algorithmic transparency and explainability on health?
- Will these technologies help eradicate or exacerbate existing health inequalities?
- What is the difference between an algorithmic decision and a human decision?
- What do patients and members of the public want from AI and related technologies?
- How should these technologies be regulated?
- Just because these technologies could enable access to new information, should we always use them?
- What makes algorithms and the entities that create them trustworthy?
- What are the implications of collaboration between public and private sector organisations in the development of these tools?

Furthermore, as AI-driven personalisation becomes an increasing feature of healthcare, the solidarity of all healthcare practitioners, as outlined by Nuffield Council on Bioethics, will need to be redefined and re-evaluated to 'uphold the collective commitment to carry costs (e.g. financial, social and emotional) to assist others' (Prainsack and Buyx, 2011).

Professional Ethics

This is defined as professionally accepted standards of personal and business behaviours, values and guiding principles. Codes of professional ethics are often established by professional organisations to help guide members in performing their job functions according to sound and consistent ethical principles.

The purpose of professional ethics is to protect and guide practitioners and to maintain public trust in the profession. These are underpinned by core principles:

- Competence, honesty and integrity
- Independent professional judgement
- Due care and diligence
- Equality and respect
- Professional behaviour

Social Ethics

Social ethics include the collection of values and behaviours of a given culture or group of people. Hence, they vary greatly from culture to culture and are based around ethical choices and values that society deems acceptable. The welfare of society as a whole is put ahead of the interests of any individual, and this helps to ensure that everyone is kept accountable by each other.

Ethics of Technology

We should consider technology ethics in two contexts. One depends on whether or not the pace of technological innovation is benefiting humans, and the other depends on whether we should empowering some people while stifling others. As long as there is technological progress, technology ethics is not going to disappear. In fact, questions surrounding technology and ethics will only grow in importance. Technology ethics includes issues arising from AI, cybersecurity, information technology, biotechnology and other emerging fields. We will focus on the first of these: AI.

Ethics of AI

AI is a field of technology that people are exploring to make better sense of humanity and our world to make better choices. AI has a fundamentally ethical aspect. However, just because something is more efficient does not mean that it is morally better. However, efficiency is often a dramatic benefit to humanity. Many organisations are exploring AI with the assumption that is not necessarily the best for everyone. They are looking for something good, whether it is making sense of large datasets or improving advertising.

However, is that ultimately the best use for the technology? Could we perhaps apply it instead to social issues, such as the best way to structure an economy or the best way to promote human flourishing? There are lots of good uses of AI, but are we really aiming towards good uses, or are we aiming towards cheaper goods?

Machine Ethics

Machine ethics (i.e. machine morality, computational morality and computational ethics) is concerned with the moral behaviour of AI systems. As the role of AI in decision-making expands in everyday matters, such as self-driving cars, ethical considerations are inevitable. Computer scientists and engineers must examine the possibilities for machine ethics, because, knowingly or not, they have already engaged or will soon engage in some of the same. We have a limited understanding of what a proper ethical theory is. Not only do people disagree on the subject, but individuals also have conflicting ethical intuitions and beliefs. Programming a computer to be ethical is much more difficult than programming a computer to play world-champion chess: an accomplishment that took 40 years. Chess is a simple domain with well-defined legal moves. Ethics operates in a complex domain with some ill-defined legal moves (Moor, 2006).

Roboethics

Robots are increasingly helping humankind in scientific, humanitarian and ecological enterprises, useful for safeguarding our planet and its inhabitants. Hence, scientists, engineers and stakeholders are being forced to carefully analyse new rules, regulations and practices to ensure safe and ethical applications of robots in society. In the next 20 years, we expect to see autonomous vehicles, aircraft, robots, devices, swarms and software, all of which will (and must) be able to make their own decisions without human intervention. Thus, it will become increasingly important to develop and build robots that can behave ethically. Consequently, many areas of robotics will be impacted, especially those where robots interact with humans, ranging from elder care and medical robotics to robots for various search and rescue missions including military robots to all kinds of service and entertainment robots. Although military robots make the headlines, owing to questions about 'whether and when autonomous robots should be allowed to use lethal force', 'whether they should be allowed to make those decisions autonomously' etc., the impact of other types of robots (e.g. social) has become an increasingly important topic as well.

The term 'roboethics' was introduced by Veruggio (Veruggio, 2005) and was officially proposed during the First International Symposium on Roboethics 2004. It included debates about questions such as: 'can a robot do good and evil' and 'can robots be dangerous for humankind'? During the symposium, participants from leading international institutions signed the 'World Robot Declaration', which stated that

- Next-generation robots will be partners that coexist with human beings
- Next-generation robots will assist human beings both physically and psychologically
- Next-generation robots will contribute to the realisation of a safe and peaceful society

During the same year, the IEEE Robotics and Automation Society established a Technical Committee on roboethics, to provide a framework for handling ethical implications of robotics research by promoting the discussion among researchers, philosophers and ethicists while supporting the establishment of shared tools for managing ethical issues in this context. The fields of application of roboethics (Veruggio, 2005) include:

- **Economy:** Technological change continually disrupts employment patterns. Machines have already replaced people in a variety of jobs. This can only increase as machines become more intelligent.
- **Effects on society:** What is it going to happen when these smart robots become our servants and house stewards and when our lives will depend on them? Technological addiction to robots can be more dangerous and disrupting than to television, the internet and video games.
- **Healthcare:** Medical ethics involve issues concerning the progress of surgery through robotics and possible shifts in focus from patients to technology. Bio-robotics, designing and applying robotic prosthesis and hybrid bionic systems is going to face bioethical problems.
- **Lack of access:** Excessive or incorrect patenting of intelligent machines may reduce commercial competition and make robotic products too expensive for most to benefit.

- **Deliberate abuse/terrorism:** Robots will have a dramatic effect on how wars are fought. If we no longer need to worry about human life, war would be far less costly.
- **Law:** The entitlement of responsibility for actions or non-actions done by robots.

CURRENT AI-ETHICS INITIATIVES

Over the past few years, a number of prominent individuals, institutions, government agencies and non-profit organisations have been established to champion the need for AI ethics for the benefit of society. There are too many to name, but below are some examples worth noting.

Academic Organisations

Notable examples include universities with dedicated centres, such as the Digital Ethics Lab[4] at Oxford University, the Leverhulme Centre for the Future of Intelligence[5] at Cambridge and the One-Hundred Year Study on AI[6] (i.e. AI100) at Stanford University.

Projects and Special Interest Groups

Projects are explicitly engaged in exploring ethical considerations (e.g. OpenAI[7], a research laboratory based in San Francisco, California that aims to provide open source AI code). Another includes the Machine Intelligence Research Institute[8], which aims to ensure smarter-than-human AI has a positive impact.

Professional Bodies

Notable examples include IEEE's Standards Association Global Initiative for Ethical Considerations in the Design of Autonomous Systems (IEEE, 2016) and the Engineering and Physical Sciences Research Council[9] (EPSRC), which is the UK's main agency for funding research (~ £800M per year) in engineering and the physical sciences.

Corporations

The Partnership on AI[10] was set up to benefit people working in collaboration with Amazon, Microsoft, Facebook, Google, DeepMind and IBM.

Government Agencies

There are many governments across the US, UK and Europe that have departments specifically set up to develop policies and regulations for AI, robotics and automated systems. Other notable initiatives include AI4People[11], the first global forum in Europe on the social impact of AI; the European Consultation on AI, which engages EU citizens on the debate for AI ethics and governance; the European Commission, which got 25 EU member states to sign a 'Declaration on Co-operation on AI'[12].

Non-Profit Organisations

The Future of Life Institute, based in the US, has a programme of grants funded by Elon Musk and the Open Philanthropy project, given to 35 projects working on different questions related to the issue of developing beneficial AI. There are many more initiatives that involve scientists, academics, engineers, lawyers, policy-makers, politicians, civil society and business representatives. All are necessary to understand the nature of post-AI societies and the values that should underpin the design, regulation and use of AI in these societies.

WHO IS RESPONSIBLE FOR AI?

While reflecting on the questions raised when exploring the ethics of AI, perhaps a more important question we should ask ourselves is, 'are AI and autonomous systems responsible for their own actions?' In the human world, the negligence of a professional can lead not only to financial loss on the part of their client but also to stress and anxiety, sometimes to the extent of causing depression and other psychiatric injuries. Many claimants think that they should be awarded compensation not only for their financial losses and psychiatric injuries, but also for their frustrations and distresses. According to Mills and Reeve[13], professionals, particularly lawyers and their insurers may be alarmed at the suggestion that damages for distress could be recovered by a claimant in a wider class of cases.

The late British politician, Tony Benn, had many memorable quotes during his 50-year parliamentary career. Perhaps his most famous was his 'five questions for people of power' (Palmer, 2014):

- What power have you got?
- Where did you get it from?
- In whose interests do you use it?
- To whom are you accountable?
- How do we get rid of you?

According to Benn, 'anyone who cannot answer the last of those questions does not live in a democratic system'. Remarkably, these questions can easily be adapted to AI systems. As AI has more and more power invested in it by human beings, often by companies who do not ask enough questions of themselves or their vendors, problems of responsibility will likely increase. Is power in the hands of the people who create the AI, or is it in the hands of the user or consumer? Where do responsibility and accountability lie, and how do we change that if it goes wrong? These are areas where we are floundering. As AI continues to mature and increasingly proliferates our society and affects individuals, communities, businesses and institutions everywhere, we need clear answers to these questions.

Responsibility

When a human is substituted by an AI system, we should be able to determine who holds the power. To whom is the AI accountable, and, crucially, how we can stop (or even nullify) them. Furthermore, 'who is responsible'? There are three potential answers: the developer, the trainer or the operator. Depending on the root cause of the negligence or error, we should be able to hold one of these three accountable (Van Amerongen, 2017).

- **The creator of the algorithm:** The algorithm that underpins an AI system may include errors or unintended bias introduced by its creator. Some of these errors may only manifest after some time. The creator of the algorithm is responsible for any damage caused by AI system owing to a poor and defective product. This is analogous to a car (or indeed any product) manufacturer who we would hold responsible for any product failures.

- **The supplier of data:** With an AI system, testing is where all the work done on data gathering and preparation can be seen to have succeeded or otherwise. Training data are put through the algorithms and compared against expected results. The arc through testing and evaluation is especially emphasised when developing AI systems, and this critical juncture is also the reason why AI generally requires more iterations before it is ready for use in production. If the data supplied is inadequate because it is unrepresentative (i.e. biased), inaccurate or not properly curated, this will lead to problems during testing. In this scenario, we hold the supplier of the data accountable for any issues.
- **The person operating the AI:** Before an AI system can be deployed into production for consumers, it requires judgement calls about its feasibility, applicability and readiness. This is typically done by operators and testers. If AI system produces results which are less than 99% accurate, and it is therefore deemed to be ineffective, then we would hold the operator responsible.

Liability

Can an AI system be held criminally liable for its actions? Criminal liability usually requires action and mental intent. Thus, one the following three scenarios could apply to AI systems (Kingston, 2018):

- **Perpetrator via another:** applies when an offence has been committed by a mentally deficient person or animal who is therefore deemed to be innocent. However, anybody that instructed the mentally deficient entity can be held criminally liable, such as a dog owner who instructed the animal to attack another individual. Ultimately, the person who instructs the AI system, either the user or the programmer, is likely to be found liable.
- **Natural or probable consequence:** occurs when the ordinary actions of an AI system might be used inappropriately to perform a criminal act. A real-life example is the case of a robot in a Japanese motorcycle factory. The robot erroneously identified an employee as a threat to its mission and smashed the surprised worker into a machine, killing him instantly. Then, it resumed its duties (Weng, 2009). Liability would fall

on anyone who might have foreseen the product being used the way it was: the programmer, the vendor or the service provider.

- **Direct liability:** this requires both an action and an intent. An action is straightforward to prove if the AI system takes an action that results in a criminal act or fails to take any action when there is a duty to act. The intent is much harder to prove but is still relevant. If a self-driving car is breaking the speed limit on the road it is on, this is a strict liability offence, and the AI system will be assigned the criminal liability. The owner may not be liable and less likely to be blamed unless the instructions that came with the self-driving car spelt out limitations of the system and the possible consequences of misuse in unusual detail.

In summary, the legal liability of AI systems depends on at least three factors:

- Whether the AI is a product or a service.
- Whether the AI knew that a course of action could lead to an offence. It seems unlikely that AI systems would contravene laws that require knowledge that a criminal act is likely to be committed.
- Whether the limitations of AI systems were communicated to the purchaser. Because AI systems have both general and specific limitations, legal cases of such issues may well be based on the specific wording of any warnings about such limitations.

Figure 2. Framework for the ethics of data and AI

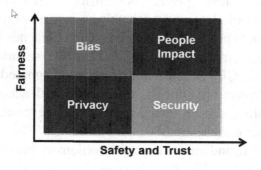

FRAMEWORKS FOR ETHICS

Any business that develops, markets and sells AI systems needs to do so ethically. Therefore, a framework for ethics that brings together AI, data and people is needed guide leaders and executives. Figure 2 presents such a framework for consideration, as adapted from the Josh Bersin Academy, which primarily focuses on human-resource topics, talent management and learning solutions.

AI, data ethics and trust have topped the tech thought–leadership agenda in recent months. This framework focuses on two dimensions: fairness and safety+trust. When we look at these two dimensions, we find that there are four sub-components.

- **Privacy:** The first ethical issue to consider is privacy. When an employee joins a company, he or she consents to collection and use of their data. However, employers do not have the right to expose this data, share it or link it with personally identifiable information. In the UK and Europe, under GDPR rules, organisations are obligated to remove and obfuscate an employee's personal data if asked to. Additionally, the GDPR and privacy rules deal with issues of disclosure and protection. Ultimately, companies must ensure that employees have been trained on privacy rules and procedures to uphold GDPR compliance. The GDPR is technologically neutral. In theory it does not matter whether personal data is being processed by an algorithm or being delivered as part of a service. GDPR applies. However, when technology is doing the processing (AI, ML, voice recognition, driverless cars etc.), the principles of data ethics should be engaged.
- **Security:** The sister of privacy is security. Security covers the storage and protection of data and such things as password and encryption policies that help prevent misuse of data and breaches involving sharing data with third parties. In the UK and Europe, security considerations are part of the GDPR rules and include designated personnel, such as a Data Protection Officer, responsible and accountable for data protection. Fines can be levied up to 2% of revenue if a company is found to lapse in these areas.
- **Bias:** The third and most difficult problem is bias. Every predictive analytics system will come prepared with bias built in. We must remember that all algorithmic systems are based on existing data. If

the existing data is biased, the predictions and recommendations will also be biased. This is a very difficult problem to solve, and many organisations and vendors are working on it.

- **People impact:** The final dimension is arguably the most important. This is about the intent in capturing data and how it might impact people. According to GDPR rules, companies are not allowed to capture data just to see what it might tell them. If employees believe they are being monitored for the wrong reasons, they have a right to due process. Companies should ask, 'why are we implementing this particular analytics or AI tool'? 'will it help people'? or 'is it being used for monitoring or any other surreptitious reason'?

Figure 3. Summary of AI ethics (FATE)

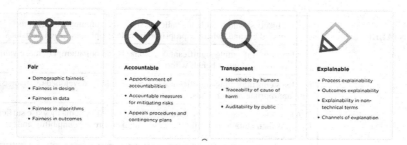

AI ETHICS GUIDELINES

Given the framework above, it is no surprise that tech and data ethics have become popular. In addition to frameworks, guidelines are also required to comprehensively support organisations to create values and goals that are aligned to AI ethics. AI ethics guidelines are summarised in Figure 3 (denoted by the acronym 'FATE'):

Table 1 expands on each of the AI ethics guidelines summarised above. This is supplemented by second table which provides further resources to help fast track company leaders and executives wanting to get started with establishing their own AI ethics frameworks. These AI ethics guidelines

Table 1. AI ethics guidelines

Dimension	Guidelines
FAIR	1. Consideration should be given to whether the data ingested is representative of the affected population.
	2. Consideration should be given to whether decision-making processes introduce bias.
	3. Significant decisions informed by the use of AI should be fair.
	4. AI operator organisations should consider whether their AI systems are accessible and usable in a fair manner across user groups.
	5. Consideration should be given to the effect of diversity on the development and deployment processes.
ACCOUNTABLE	1. Accountability for the outcomes of an AI system should not lie with the system itself.
	2. Positive efforts should be made to identify and mitigate any significant risks inherent in the AI systems designed.
	3. AI systems informing critical decisions should be subject to appropriate external audit.
	4. AI subjects should be able to challenge significant automated decisions concerning them and, where appropriate, be able to opt out of such decisions.
	5. AI systems informing significant decisions should not attempt to make value judgements on people's behalf without prior consent.
	6. AI systems informing significant decisions should be developed by diverse teams with appropriate backgrounds.
	7. AI operator organisations should understand the AI systems they use sufficiently to assess their suitability for the use case and to ensure accountability and transparency.
TRANSPARENT	1. Traceability should be considered for significant decisions, especially those that have the potential to result in loss, harm or damage.
	2. People should be informed of the extent of their interaction with AI systems.
EXPLAINABLE	1. AI operator organisations could consider providing affected AI subjects with a high-level explanation of how their AI system works.
	2. AI operator organisations should consider providing affected AI subjects with a means to request explanations for specific significant decisions, to the extent possible given the state of present research and the choice of model.
	3. In the case that such explanations are available, they should be easily and quickly accessible, free of charge and user-friendly.

match those offered by Microsoft, who has several internal working groups dedicated to AI ethics, including those of fairness, accountability, transparency and ethics in AI (FATE). The group comprises nine researchers working on collaborative research projects that address complex social implications of AI, ML, data science, large-scale experimentation and increasing automation. Microsoft also has an advisory board AI ethics and the effects in engineering and research (Aether), which reports to senior leadership (Todd, 2019).

Table 2. AI ethics guidelines (extended)

Resource	Reference	Description
Future of Life Institute	Asilomar AI Principles https:// futureoflife. org/ai-principles	Developed in conjunction with the 2017 Asilomar conference, this list of principles has been universally cited as a reference point by all other AI ethics frameworks and standards introduced since it was published. Signed by more than 1,200 AI and robotics researchers and over 2,500 other technical luminaries, including the likes of Stephen Hawking, Elon Musk and Ray Kurzweil, it offers a simple list of foundational principles that should guide business leaders, governmental policy-makers and technologists as we move forward with AI advancement.
IAPP	Building Ethics into Privacy Frameworks for Big Data and AI https://iapp. org/resources/ article/ building-ethics-into-privacy-frameworks-for-big-data-and-ai/	Not a framework itself, per se, this handy document is nevertheless a must-read for enterprise executives trying to get their arms around AI ethics issues. It offers a concise explanation of the ethical concerns at play in applied uses of AI and big data, as well as the consequences of ignoring these issues. It then offers a condensed run-down of the tools available to organisations seeking to not only develop internal frameworks but to operationalise data ethics policies. It guides AI ethics leaders in considering industry-specific concerns, organisational nuances and even departmental differences in creating a framework that is as flexible as it is holistic. According to the IAPP report: 'various data ethics frameworks should have common features to ensure a uniformly high ethical standard of data practices. However, these frameworks will be most effective if they are flexible enough to be tailored for each specific company and organisation, adjusting for a company's size, resources, subject matter area and impact on data subjects.'
IEEE	The IEEE Global Initiative on Autonomous Systems https:// ethicsinaction. ieee.org/#read	Since 2016, IEEE has been taking the lead on organising discourse among technical thinkers, business leaders and public policy experts about the ethical design of autonomous and intelligent systems. As part of this work, The IEEE Global Initiative on Ethics of Autonomous and Intelligent Systems published Ethically Aligned Design, a veritable bible for addressing 'values and attentions as well as implementations' of these systems. This nearly 300-page digital volume offers a ton of value to executives embarking on the journey of developing an internal framework. In addition, The IEEE Global Initiative spearheads work on IEEE P7000 Standards Working Groups, which offers standards guidance processes for addressing ethical concerns during system design, data privacy, algorithmic bias and other hot topics in AI ethics.
The Public Voice	Universal Guidelines for AI https://epic. org/2018/10/ breaking--universal-guideline. html	Introduced in October 2018, these guidelines were written to be 'incorporated into ethical standards, adopted in national law and international agreements, and built into the design of systems.' It is a human rights-driven document with an emphasis on transparency, fairness from bias, data accuracy and quality and an obligation by government to curtail secret profiling or scoring of citizens. 'Our concern is with those systems that impact the rights of people,' write its creators. 'Above all else, these systems should do no harm.'
EU Council of Europe	Guidelines on AI and Data Protection https:// ec.europa.eu/ digital-single-market/en/ news/ethics-guidelines-trustworthy-ai	Drafted by an independent group of AI ethics advisers and tweaked using more than 500 comments during a five-month feedback period, this is one of the most recent and comprehensive public frameworks on AI ethics to date. This is not an official policy document or regulation by the European Commission, but instead a set of suggestions meant to guide public discourse on what trustworthy AI looks like. These guidelines are intended to help AI designers and users choose systems that are lawful, ethical and robust, with seven system tenets at the heart of what it takes to create trustworthy AI: • Human agency and oversight: Including fundamental rights, human agency and human oversight • Technical robustness and safety: Including resilience to attack and security, fall-back plan and general safety, accuracy, reliability and reproducibility • Privacy and data governance: Including respect for privacy, quality and integrity of data and access to data • Transparency: Including traceability, explainability and communication • Diversity, non-discrimination and fairness: Including the avoidance of unfair bias, accessibility and universal design and stakeholder participation • Societal and environmental well-being: Including sustainability and environmental friendliness, social impact, society and democracy • Accountability: Including auditability, minimisation and reporting of negative impact, trade-offs and redress.

Table 2 presents five more resources to help leaders and executives establish their own guidelines.

In conclusion, the ICO also has AI on its radar. In the ICO's Technology Strategy for 2018–2020, AI is one of their top-three priorities. This is why in March 2019, the ICO launched a programme to build a framework for auditing AI. They have since published an overview of the framework that aims to look at both governance and accountability and AI specific risk areas (see Figure 3).

- Fairness and transparency in profiling
- Accuracy
- Automated decision-making models
- Security
- Data minimisation
- Exercise of data subject rights

Although the ICO is clearly looking at AI from the GDPR compliance perspective, they are not the only organisation working on data ethics approaches. The UK government has created the Centre for Data Ethics and Innovation to anticipate both 'the opportunities and the risks posed by data-driven technology'. Their 2019–2020 work programme is set to look at:

- Personalised and targeted messaging via online services
- Algorithm bias
- Identifying the highest priority opportunities and risks
- Respond to existing 'live' issues

The outcome of this work will be two-fold. A strategy document will essentially identify issues and how they will be dealt with. They will outline how AI and technology can make the world a better place. What is certain is that governments, regulators and policy-makers are currently playing catch-up, whether to mitigate bad impacts or to create conditions needed to amplify and spread the benefits of the good.

FUTURE RESEARCH DIRECTIONS

AI will become increasingly sophisticated. Advanced AI could help to solve major problems in domains, such as medicine and healthcare, energy usage, food supply and transportation. Many thinkers predict the emergence of an artificial general intelligence or a superintelligence, whereby the intellect of AI greatly exceeds the cognitive performance of humans in all domains. However, a real concern is that AI is predominantly developed by privately-owned companies. The most significant players are Google, Facebook, Amazon, Microsoft, IBM, Baidu, Tencent and Alibaba. Except for the last two, they are all members of the *Partnership on AI*, an industry group that pledges to use AI safely and follow a set of rules.

Perhaps it is no surprise that governments and societies have struggled to keep pace with AI's rapid technological transformation. This incredible speed of change has created huge opportunities and societal benefits, but also great risks that are not yet fully understood nor mitigated. Such problems include unfair decisions made by algorithms in domains like criminal justice and mortgage lending, massive data breaches and privacy violations and potentially huge job losses and displacement. There is even a risk of arms races and proliferation of lethal autonomous weapons. Finally, authoritarian regimes could use surveillance, disinformation and lie-detection technologies to repress and control populations.

There is a similarly growing consensus that the development of AI cannot be left to technologists and private companies alone. Governments and societies must agree upon how AI should develop, what role it should play and whether restrictions should be imposed. Future research should focus on ethical, policy and regulatory questions, perhaps with study and investigations of 'Asilomar AI Principles' linked with AI, such as:

- What are the most serious ethical and societal risks associated with AI?
- Do we need new regulations, laws or institutions to govern AI?
- What are the EU and other governments currently doing?
- How can we ensure that policies and regulations do not hamper innovation and progress?
- Can humans and AI coexist in harmony?

Additionally, it is our belief that we lack a unified understanding of what safe and beneficial AI means, given that every society on account of cultural differences and values may have competing definitions. Stuart Russell, a professor of computer science and Director of the Centre for Intelligent Systems and Smith–Zadeh Chair in Engineering at UC Berkeley, suggested that we focus on provably beneficial AI systems. To work out the objectives that AI should be built upon, we require philosophers, not necessarily data scientists and engineers. Thus, a crucial part of developing the necessary grammar of AI will lie in developing new utopias and dystopias, learning from them and strengthening the oversight of AI. These are not completely academic debates. They will happen in newspaper columns, Twitter discussions and in Hollywood movies. In some ways, this type of broad discussion will enable the democratisation of AI. The crucial insight is that not every problem, not even a technological one like AI, always needs a technological answer. 'The solution to this problem', as Russell rightly concluded, 'seems to be cultural.'

CONCLUSION

As AI supercharges businesses, governments and societies, executives and stakeholders are under the spotlight to ensure that AI is used responsibly beyond complying with the spirit and letter of applicable laws, codes of conduct and principles. Ethical debates are well underway about what is right and wrong when it comes to high-stakes AI technologies, such as autonomous weapons and surveillance systems. There has been an outpouring of concern and scepticism regarding how we can imbue AI systems with human ethical judgement, when moral values frequently vary by culture and can be difficult to code in software.

Numerous instances of AI bias, discrimination and privacy violations have already appeared in the news, leaving leaders rightly concerned about how to ensure that nothing bad happens as they deploy their AI systems. Within businesses, leaders and executives should help the workforce build and use AI systems responsibly by focussing on key areas (Burkhardt, et al., 2019), as summarised below:

- **Data acquisition:** data is the fuel of AI. The more data used to train AI systems, the more accurate and insightful the predictions. Taking shortcuts and caving in to pressure to get products/services out the door to customers would be inappropriate. At all times, questions about ethics should be front and centre to ensure customers and society benefit.
- **Dataset suitability:** ensuring data is representative and reflects the subjects being analysed is critical. Measures must be taken to avoid any form of social, racial or gender bias. Questions should be asked about how datasets have been sampled, and real-world scenarios should be

brainstormed where possible to anticipate and uncover preventable issues.

- **AI-output fairness:** Alongside dataset suitability, context is also important to avoid historic human biases and poor judgement to be applied. New definitions and metrics that encourage fairness-by-design should be promoted, which could include hardening and adjusting existing data management and governance practices.

- **Regulatory compliance and engagement:** Leaders should direct their organisation from compliance to co-creation practices to ensure that data-science, regulatory and legal teams combine to define, monitor and record clear compliance metrics for AI initiatives.

- **AI-model explainability:** to engender trust among employees, customers and society, business should ensure that they can explain the algorithms and models that underpin AI systems. Ultimately they will move away from black-box or opaque models and embrace practices that are part of the maturing field of explainable AI.

Figure 4. Explainable AI (XAI)

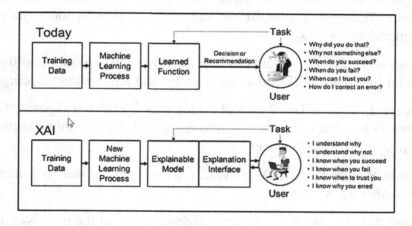

In the UK, ICO is preparing guidance[14] that tells organisations how to communicate explanations to people in a form they will understand. Companies could be fined if they fail to explain decisions made by AI: up to 4% of a company's global turnover. Figure 4 presents an infographic that summarises the value of explainable AI (Bersin, 2019).

Businesses, institutions and governments should provide tools and training on topics, such as fairness, to encourage employees and citizens to learn about the ways that bias can crop up in training data and help them master techniques to identify and mitigate them. Without these types of support mechanisms, business is likely to fall short and increase the liability of poorly designed or damaging AI systems. Whether algorithms wind up working for the benefit of humanity will depend on a system of oversight that we do not yet fully possess. Without ethics, all visions of AI's future will have little impact.

REFERENCES

Applin, S. A. (2019). Everyone's talking about ethics in AI. Here's what they're missing. *Fast Company*. https://www.fastcompany.com/90356295/the-rush-toward-ethical-ai-is-leaving-many-of-us-behind

Awad, E. (2017). Moral Machine: Perception of Moral Judgment Made by Machines. *Massachusetts Institute of Technology*. http://moralmachine.mit.edu/

Bersin, J. (2019). *People Analytics and AI in the Workplace: Four Dimensions of Trust*. https://joshbersin.com/2019/05/the-ethics-of-ai-and-people-analytics-four-dimensions-of-trust/

Boddington, P. (2017). Towards a Code of Ethics for Artificial Intelligence (Artificial Intelligence: Foundations, Theory, and Algorithms). Springer.

Bossmann, J. (2016). Top 9 ethical issues in artificial intelligence. *World Economic Forum*. https://www.weforum.org/agenda/2016/10/top-10-ethical-issues-in-artificial-intelligence/

Burkhardt, R., Hohn, N., & Wigley, C. (2019). *Leading your organization to responsible AI*. McKinsey.

Elsayed-Ali, S. (2019). AI and human rights: taking on the real risks of AI. *Element AI*. https://www.elementai.com/news/2019/ai-and-human-rights-taking-on-the-real-risks-of-ai

Fenech, M., Strukelj, N., & Buston, O. (2018). Ethical, Social, And Political Challenges Of Artificial Intelligence In Health. The Wellcome Trust. *Future Advocacy*. https://wellcome.ac.uk/sites/default/files/ai-in-health-ethical-social-political-challenges.pdf

IEEE. (2016). *Ethically Aligned Design*. The IEEE Global Initiative for Ethical Considerations in Artificial Intelligence and Autonomous Systems. Version 1. Section 1. Page 37. https://standards.ieee.org/develop/indconn/ec/autonomous_systems.html

Janis, I. (1982). Group Think. Houghton Mifflin.

Kingston, J. (2018). Artificial Intelligence and Legal Liability. *Cornell University*. https://arxiv.org/ftp/arxiv/papers/1802/1802.07782.pdf

Moor, J. H. (2006). The Nature, Importance, and Difficulty of Machine Ethics. *IEEE Computer Society*. http://www.psy.vanderbilt.edu/courses/hon182/The_Nature_Importance_and_Difficulty_of_Machine_Ethics.pdf

Palmer, E. (2014). Tony Benn Dead: \'Five Questions on Power\' and Other Memorable Quotes. *International Business Times*. https://www.ibtimes.co.uk/tony-benn-dead-five-questions-power-other-memorable-quotes-1440277

Prainsack, B., & Buyx, A. (2011). Solidarity: reflections on an emerging concept in bioethics. *Nuffield Council on Bioethics*. https://nuffieldbioethics.org/wp-content/uploads/2014/07/Solidarity_report_FINAL.pdf

Thomson, J. J. (1985). The trolley problem. *The Yale Law Journal*, *94*(6), 1395–1415. doi:10.2307/796133

Todd, D. (2019). Microsoft Reconsidering AI Ethics Review Plan. *Forbes*. https://www.forbes.com/sites/deborahtodd/2019/06/24/microsoft-reconsidering-ai-ethics-review-plan/

Van Amerongen, R. (2017). *Who is responsible when Artificial Intelligence fails?* https://www.linkedin.com/pulse/who-responsibility-when-artificial-intelligence-amerongen/

Veruggio, G. (2005). The Birth of Roboethics. Scuola di Robotica. *ICRA 2005, IEEE International Conference on Robotics and Automation Workshop on Robo-Ethics*. http://www.roboethics.org/icra2005/veruggio.pdf

Weng, Y.-H., Chen, C.-H., & Sun, C.-T. (2009). Towards the Human-Robot Co-Existence Society: On Safety Intelligence for Next Generation Robots, 1. *International Journal of Social Robotics*, *267*(4), 273. doi:10.100712369-009-0019-1

ENDNOTES

1   Organisation for Economic Co-operation and Development (OECD), is an intergovernmental organisation that represents 37 countries for economic concerns and world trade (Source: www.oecd.org).

2   Definition of 'ethos' (Source: https://www.dictionary.com/browse/ethos).

3   The Ethics Centre is a not-for-profit organisation which strives to bring ethics to the centre of personal and professional lives (Source: https://ethics.org.au/why-were-here/what-is-ethics/).

4   Digital Ethics Lab (Source: https://digitalethicslab.oii.ox.ac.uk/).

5   Leverhulme Centre for the Future of Intelligence (Source: http://lcfi.ac.uk).

6   AI100 (Source: https://ai100.stanford.edu/).

7   Open AI (Source: https://openai.com/).

8   MIRI (Source: https://intelligence.org/).

9   EPSRC, part of UK Research and Innovation (Source: https://epsrc.ukri.org/).

10   The Partnership on AI (Source: https://www.partnershiponai.org/).

11   AI For People (Source: http://ai4people.com/).

12   EU Commission (Source: https://ec.europa.eu/digital-single-market/en/news/eu-member-states-sign-cooperate-artificial-intelligence).

13   Mills and Reeve, a UK based law firm (Source: https://www.mills-reeve.com/).

14   The ICO, in conjunction with the Alan Turing Institute, is developing 'Explaining AI decisions guidance', and it is expected to take effect in 2020 (Source: https://www.newscientist.com/article/2225186-companies-could-be-fined-if-they-fail-to-explain-decisions-made-by-ai/#ixzz69vkRYryL).

Chapter 8
Social Implications of AI

ABSTRACT

'Social implications' generally refers to anything that affects an individual, a community, and wider society. The social implications of artificial intelligence (AI) is an immensely important field of study since AI technology will steadily continue to permeate other technologies and, inevitably, our society as a whole. Many of the social implications of this technological process are non-obvious and surprising. We should ask ourselves, What type of society do we want and what role will AI play to influence and shape lives? Will people simply become consumers served by intelligent systems that respond to our every whim? Are we reaching a tipping point between convenience and dependency? How will AI affect social issues relating to housing, finance, privacy, poverty, and so on? Do we want a society where machines are supplementing (or augmenting) humans or perhaps even substituting humans? It is important to be as clear as possible about likely social implications of AI if it truly helps benefit individuals and society.

"Artificial intelligence will reach human levels by around 2029. Follow that out further to, say, 2045, we will have multiplied the intelligence, the human biological machine intelligence of our civilization a billion-fold." –Ray Kurzweil, Futurist and Inventor

DOI: 10.4018/978-1-7998-4607-9.ch008

BACKGROUND

Social implications generally refer to anything that affects an individual, a community or wider society. The social implications of artificial intelligence (AI) is an immensely important field of study, because AI technology is expected to steadily continue to permeate other technologies and, inevitably, our society as a whole. Although AI stands to bring about great societal benefits, it will certainly have its downside, as summed by the words of Ray Kurzweil, a futurist and creator of optical recognition technology who once said 'fire cooks our food and also can burn down your house'. Similarly, the problem of 'AI washing' threatens to overinflate expectations for the technology, undermining public trust and triggering a backlash (Waddell, 2019). The tech sector's 'fake-it-till-you-make-it' attitude plays into this problem. If AI is to truly be a force for good, it must have the capacity to develop from experience with people and learn from success and failures in social settings. Without self- and social-awareness, professional codes of ethics and increased levels of social and moral responsibility, society will never truly enjoy the benefits of AI (Whitby, 2003). Given that humans tend to use any notion of non-human agency as a convenient curtain behind which to hide their own culpability (Whitby, 1988), this may well serve the parts of society who would rather block the positive application of AI to protect their own self-interests, personal agendas and, most of all, economic and political power. With this in mind, we should ask ourselves 'what type of society do we want'? Will people simply become consumers served by intelligent systems that respond to our every whim? Are we headed for a society of abundance (Blumenthal, 2011), which, despite requiring a co-operative culture (Linde and Neuvonen, 2017), is instead fast approaching a tipping point between convenience and dependency? Will society ultimately become a fusion of human, machine and information systems (e.g. *trans-humanism*) that forges a new level of co-existence and interdependence between technology and humankind (Yoshiyuki et al., 2014)? Trying to prevent or opt out of advancements in AI is a misguided and futile strategy.

AI FOR SOCIAL GOOD

To analyse potential applications for social good, the McKinsey Global Institute (Chui et al., 2018) conducted a study in which they compiled a library of circa 160 AI social-impact use cases (see Figure 1) that could potentially help hundreds of millions of people in both advanced and emerging markets (EM).

Figure 1. AI spans many distinct social domains

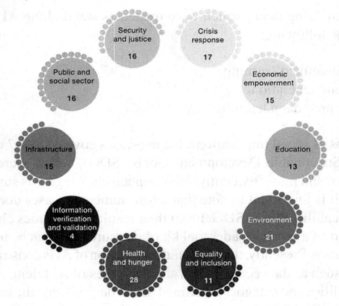

Artificial intelligence (AI) has broad potential across a range of social domains.

AI use cases per domain, number

Security and justice — 16
Crisis response — 17
Economic empowerment — 15
Education — 13
Environment — 21
Equality and inclusion — 11
Health and hunger — 28
Information verification and validation — 4
Infrastructure — 15
Public and social sector — 16

Note: Our library of about 160 use cases is not comprehensive and will continue to evolve. This listing of the number of cases per domain should thus not be read as exhaustive.

McKinsey&Company | **Source:** McKinsey Global Institute analysis

The study looked at domains of social good where AI could be applied and the most pertinent types of AI capabilities, as well as the bottlenecks and risks that must be overcome and mitigated if AI is to scale up and realise its full potential for social impact. It was divided into five sections:

1. Mapping AI use cases to domains of social good
2. AI capabilities that can be used for social good
3. Overcoming bottlenecks, especially around data and talent
4. Risks to be managed

5.   Scaling up the use of AI for social good

Eighteen AI capabilities were identified that could be used to benefit society. 14 fell into three major categories:

- computer vision
- natural-language processing
- speech and audio processing

The remaining three, which were treated as stand-alone AI capabilities, include the following:

- reinforcement learning
- content generation
- structured deep learning

In terms of social implications, the use-cases covered all 17 of the United Nations' Sustainable Development Goals (SDG), which were among the best-known and most frequently cited societal challenges, as summarised by Figure 2. It is important to note that a low number of cases does not reflect AI's applicability to that SDG. From their results, it becomes clear that AI is merely part of a much broader tool kit of measures that can be used to tackle societal issues. Presently, the value and application of AI is constrained mainly by issues such as data accessibility and shortages of AI talent. Additionally, the capabilities and categories outlined above demonstrate the breadth, depth and complexity of AI.

The heat map shown in Figure 3 demonstrates clear patterns when AI capabilities are mapped to domains that directly affect society. The patterns highlight the growing maturity and application of AI across several distinct domains used for social good and the betterment of society. However, in terms of the business value of AI, the truth is that most companies lack clarity about where or how they can use it. Companies must first reckon the dearth of skills required for training the technology or face the daunting task of modernising their data management platforms via digital transformation programmes. Those that think they can 'set it and forget it', which may be tempting for a solution that seemingly stacks neatly into a 'tech stack' environment, will not create the outcomes they need. It is one thing to be foiled by a smart speaker (e.g. Amazon's Alexa) in one's kitchen or living room that politely persists when it does not understand a question. It is quite

Figure 2. Many AI use cases support high profile societal challenges

Many artificial-intelligence (AI) use cases support the most frequently cited societal challenges.

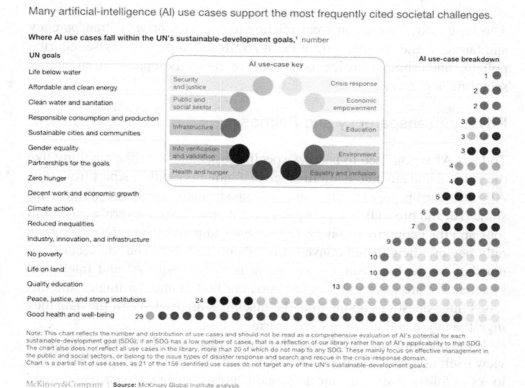

Where AI use cases fall within the UN's sustainable-development goals,¹ number

Note: This chart reflects the number and distribution of use cases and should not be read as a comprehensive evaluation of AI's potential for each sustainable-development goal (SDG); if an SDG has a low number of cases, that is a reflection of our library rather than of AI's applicability to that SDG. The chart also does not reflect all use cases in the library, more than 20 of which do not map to any SDG. These mainly focus on effective management in the public and social sectors, or belong to the issue types of disaster response and search and rescue in the crisis-response domain.
¹Chart is a partial list of use cases, as 21 of the 156 identified use cases do not target any of the UN's sustainable-development goals.

McKinsey&Company | **Source:** McKinsey Global Institute analysis

another to be frustrated with an underperforming enterprise-grade AI that requires a significant monthly subscription, especially when that investment, if done right, has the potential to make an order-of-magnitude difference to both top and bottom lines.

Companies that do not bother to take the time needed to meticulously integrate their AI solutions for full impact should think again. Without a strategic plan, it will be too easy to become disoriented by the endless noise and marketing hype. Conversely, if companies do not act fast, AI will infiltrate their business via other channels leading to missed opportunities to leverage AI investments aligned to business objectives, even as they change. When combined, the capabilities outlined in Figure 3 may help a company to introduce AI incrementally 'failing fast' to better manage risk, business priorities and expenditures.

Case Study: Security and Justice

This case study focuses on areas relating to data (i.e. privacy, transparency and fairness) and the weaponisation of AI. Its sub-topics comprise security, policing and criminal-justice issues that are distinctly separate from public-sector management.

Privacy, Transparency and Fairness

Today's AI is confined to narrow, specific tasks and is unlike anything like the general and adaptable intelligence that humans exhibit. Apart from this, AI's influence is growing, and, like any transformative technology, it carries some risk and presents complex policy challenges across several areas, from jobs and the economy to safety, regulatory and privacy questions. We have only begun a heightened conversation about the ethics and the security of our data as we increasingly instrument ourselves with AI and intelligent systems. We are instrumenting our cars, our bodies and our homes and this raises huge questions about what the machines might make of the data they ingest, analyse and utilise for self-learning.

If the phenomenon of *big data* has encouraged nearly every company to view itself as a data company, thereby revving up the privacy profession, AI looks to follow a similar trajectory and is poised to be the next major trend that will keep privacy professionals busy navigating privacy, transparency and fairness topics. Today's auditors, consumers and regulators will struggle to understand, predict and explain the behaviours of increasingly sophisticated AI and machine-learning (ML) systems. Without *black-box* algorithms being explainable, businesses will incorporate 'privacy by design' processes into development and training programmes or will refresh accountability frameworks to address risks and challenges presented by the rapid development of 'narrow AI' (Krigsman, 2017). Privacy and AI are both complex topics. There are no easy answers, because solutions lie at the shifting and conflicted intersections of technology, commercial profit, public policy and even individual and cultural attitudes. AI's nascency is an opportunity for society to take early control of what we want to remain private while also addressing fairness and transparency concerns.

Weaponisation of AI

When people think of weapons, they typically think of systems created and deployed by the military. The dangers of weaponising AI are perhaps more sinister. Campaigns against 'morally reprehensible weapons' already exist and include the likes of the 'Future-of-Life Petition'[1] to ban AI weapons signed by Stephen Hawking, Max Tegmark, Elon Musk and many others. The letter accompanying the petition highlights the danger of AI weapons and urges immediate action. Experts and senior military officials have said that 'killer robots' will be widespread in warfare with the global spending on robotics set to double from £71.8B in 2016 to £188B in 2020. Although the UN has been pursuing a new international treaty to ban fully autonomous weapons systems, no policies have been agreed upon, because countries like the US and Russia actively block them (Busby and Cuthbertson, 2018).

Perhaps a more worrying reality is the weaponisation of AI systems via software that can exist across all devices available to everyone. Information is shared everywhere in seconds, helped by social-media platforms and bolstered by internet and mobile technologies. History shows that a computing device tends to eventually yield to a motivated hacker's attempts to repurpose it. The weaponisation of AI systems and intelligent machines is unlikely to be an exception. If an AI system can be cheaply and easily converted into an effective and indiscriminate weapon, either as a form of a mass-killing device or software used in a cyber-attack, then there should be an international convention against it. Such systems are not unlike radioactive metals. They can equally be used for reasonable and beneficial purposes. However, we must carefully control them, because they can also be converted into devastating tools, both in our physical and virtual worlds. Importantly, repurposing an AI system for destructive purposes will be far easier than repurposing a nuclear reactor, something that hackers and cyber criminals are allegedly already doing today, according to Deepak Dutt, founder and chief executive officer (CEO) of Zighra, a mobile security start-up. There is a high likelihood that sophisticated AI will be used for cyberattacks in the near future, and that it might already be in use by countries, such as Russia, China and some eastern-European countries. The major data breaches that plagued 2017, including WannaCry to Equifax and Uber, were wake-up calls for corporations wherein security systems are lax (Dutt, 2018).

Figure 3. AI capabilities for social good

Artificial-intelligence (AI) capabilities mapped to their potential uses in ten domains where they may be of societal benefit.

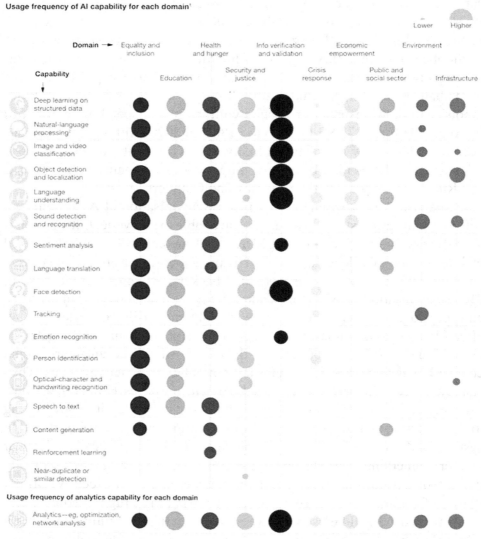

Usage frequency of AI capability for each domain[1]

Lower   Higher

Domain → Equality and inclusion | Health and hunger | Info verification and validation | Economic empowerment | Environment

Capability | Education | Security and justice | Crisis response | Public and social sector | Infrastructure

Deep learning on structured data

Natural-language processing[2]

Image and video classification

Object detection and localization

Language understanding

Sound detection and recognition

Sentiment analysis

Language translation

Face detection

Tracking

Emotion recognition

Person identification

Optical-character and handwriting recognition

Speech to text

Content generation

Reinforcement learning

Near-duplicate or similar detection

Usage frequency of analytics capability for each domain

Analytics—eg, optimization, network analysis

Note: Our library of about 160 use cases with societal impact is evolving and this heat map should not be read as a comprehensive gauge of the potential application of AI or analytics capabilities. Usage frequency estimates the number of times that models trained using AI would be used in a year to predict an outcome.
[1]Log base 10 scale. Deployment frequency capped at once per hour per year to prevent skewing; capping affected only a small number of use cases.
[2]Excluding sentiment analysis, speech to text, language understanding, and translation.

McKinsey&Company   **Source:** McKinsey Global Institute analysis

Marc Goodman, author of 'Future Crimes: Everything Is Connected, Everyone Is Vulnerable and What We Can Do About It' (Goodman, 2015), says he is not surprised that so many *black-hat* attendees see weaponised AI as being imminent and that it has been part of cyberattacks for years. Today, the more common approach to hacking is to automate attacks with tools of AI and ML. This includes everything from scripted distributed denial-of-service attacks to ransomware, criminal chatbots and more. Herein lies the immediate danger of AI weapons: they are easily converted into indiscriminate weapons, far more dangerous than if the same weapon were human managed. What counts as intelligence, and what counts as a weapon? As AI matures and becomes more of a commodity, the 'bad guys' will start using it to improve and automate the performance of attacks while also cutting costs.

Case Study: Equality and Inclusion

This case study is associated with challenges to equality, inclusion and self-determination. The focus is on the latter: bias that extends to race, sexual orientation, religion and citizenship.

Social, Racial and Gender Bias

We often assume machines are neutral. However, AI is not truly objective. Underlying algorithms can reflect the biases of their creators, and even those that are unbiased at inception can learn the biases (Sharma, 2018) of their human trainers over time. We should remind ourselves that AI is only as good as the data that powers it. Its quality depends on how well creators programmed it to think, decide, learn and act. As a result, AI and intelligent systems can inherit or even amplify the biases of its creators, who are often unaware of the problem (Byrne, 2018).

Many companies have already begun introducing AI into business processes that affect recruitment and talent-management functions. Typically, algorithms sort through numerous factors to profile people and make predictions about them. AI hiring and talent-management systems have the potential to move the needle on gender equality in workplaces by using more objective criteria in recruiting and promoting talent (Stone, 2018). But what happens if the algorithm is actually relying on biased input to make predictions? Can machines and AI develop unintentional biases, creating the same inequities as people with unconscious biases? There is mounting evidence that humans are programming their own biases, including those of gender and race, into the algorithms behind AI. In research published by Time Magazine, Joy Buolamwini, a computer scientist and founder of the Algorithmic Justice League, uncovered large gender and racial biases in AI systems sold by tech giants, like IBM, Microsoft and Amazon. Given the task of guessing the gender of a face, all companies performed substantially better on male faces than female ones. The companies evaluated had error rates of no more than 1% for lighter-skinned men. For darker-skinned women, the errors soared to 35%. AI systems from leading companies failed to correctly classify the faces of several celebrated women of colour, including Oprah Winfrey, Michelle Obama and Serena Williams. When technology denigrates even these iconic women, it is time to re-examine how these systems are built and who they truly serve (Buolamwini, 2019).

Given the clear bias problem and AI's trajectory to touch all parts of our lives, we should remain optimistic and *act now* to build ethical and inclusive AI systems that respect our human dignity and rights. The most important achievement will include a diversity of backgrounds in teams designing, architecting and governing AI systems across race, gender, culture and socio-economic background.

Case Study: Health Management

The application of AI in the healthcare industries has been steadily rising in recent years. For these systems, the focus has been on faster, more effective diagnoses and cost-savings in treatment. Industry attention is predominantly focused on using AI to improve research and development success rates, including pharmaceutical titans, like Pfizer and GlaxoSmithKline, both of whom signed AI deals last year (Tyer, 2019).

Importantly, AI is increasingly being used to help in areas related to mental health and well-being. An example of this is in the area of dementia, specifically Alzheimer's, a neurodegenerative disease that is the leading cause of dementia for the elderly, eventually leading to loss of memory and cognitive functions. Research teams are using huge amounts of data to identify changes to the physical structure of the brain in detailed scans. They are also looking for changes to the energy use and chemical make-up of the brain that cannot be seen by the human eye. The most promising AI applications are MLs that use algorithms to learn from patterns in data, allowing dementia sufferers and their families to plan more effectively for the future (Ananthaswamy, 2017).

Although AI will never replace person-to-person care, when used in the appropriate circumstances, it could enhance care and support people affected by dementia to live at home longer. Home care for elderly and the mentally ill should be supported by human caregivers. We must ensure that we maintain some form of human contact to avoid people feeling isolated or lonely. Researchers are exploring the possibility of using sensors around the house to intelligently monitor a person's behaviour. This could allow them to be notified when they are doing something risky or if there are signs of deteriorating health.

The Alzheimer's Society is working hard to make sure AI is used to make an impact for everyone affected by dementia. The 'TADPOLE challenge' is a competition wherein researchers across the globe were challenged to build a computer programme to predict changes to thinking and memory scores and brain shrinkage. Additionally, research based at the Imperial College London is using AI to locate patterns in changes to the energy producing batteries of brain cells in people with mild cognitive impairment and Alzheimer's disease.

Case Study: Public and Social Sector Management

It might seem that the personal skills and empathetic nature of social work could never be replaced by a machine. However, deciding which families need what kind of help most urgently is precisely the kind of classification that AI systems promise to do better and more quickly than unaided human beings. They are great at detecting significance from a mass of confusing information often in ways that are hard to explain, similar to *intuition*. When computers do it, it is called 'ML'. If we look back at the use cases and capabilities previously outlined in Figure 2 and Figure 3, we find that AI technologies could help automate a caseworker's typical schedule to reduced backlogs, implement cost reductions and improve efficiency, freeing them up to spend more time with clients, inject greater intelligence into scores of processes and systems and handle many other tasks that humans cannot easily do on their own. Additionally, the need to fetch data from multiple systems to manually verify beneficiaries' eligibility could be reduced and potentially removed by introducing automation technologies, such as robotic process automation (RPA). AI could go a long way toward addressing some of the long-standing challenges confronting caseworkers and the individuals and families they serve. These challenges include:

- **High turnover rates:** caseworkers often quit due to burnout, leading to increased training costs, larger caseloads on those who stay and significant instability for individuals and families who rely on caseworkers for help.
- **Large, unmanageable caseloads:** caseworkers come to human services wanting to help individuals and families. When they cannot do the right work on the right case at the right time, they may become seriously discouraged and demotivated.
- **Administrative burdens:** too often, caseworkers are shackled by paperwork and kept away from the hands-on work that actually transforms lives.
- **Long wait times:** most calls answered by call centres relate to checking the status of an application, a redetermination or some similar matter. These status questions could easily be handled by a chatbot (a computer program that simulates human conversation through voice or text chat), thus freeing up call centre workers to handle more complex inquiries.
- **Delays in service delivery:** individuals and families often have little idea how long it might take to receive the benefits and services for which they are eligible. Delays are often caused by inefficient processes, staff shortages and outdated error-prone technologies.
- **Language barriers (for non-English speakers):** in the UK and other multi-cultural societies, there are often individuals and families who do not speak English, which often causes language barriers and thereafter delays receipt of benefits and services.

Herein lies the true promise of AI-enabled human services. Caseworkers and computers can combine their strengths to achieve better results faster, often doing what humans simply could not do before, providing the insights necessary to do the right work for the right people at the right time, thus achieving meaningful results for individuals and families served (Eggers et al., 2017).

Case Study: Environment Management

The increasing population, urbanisation and industrialisation, which our planet faces, have forced society to consider whether human beings are changing the very conditions essential to life on earth (Thomson, 1997). Managing the environment is a huge undertaking. Massive quantities of new information from monitoring devices, sensors, treatment systems controls, monitoring devices and legacy databases are now pouring data into environment management companies with few tools to analyse them on arrival. Most companies lack a single system of record to accommodate them.

An effective protection of our environment is largely dependent on the quality of the available information used to make an appropriate decision. Problems arise when the quantities of available information are huge and nonuniform (i.e. coming from many different disciplines or sources), and their quality could not be ascertained in advance. Another associated issue is the dynamical nature of the problem. According to (Cortés et al., 2000), a new discipline known as Environmental Informatics, which combines research ðelds, such as AI, geographical information systems, modelling and simulation, user interfaces etc., are emerging. This is further supported by AI knowledge-based techniques and development of environmental decision-support systems.

AI techniques applied to environmental problems typically fall into three broad categories:

- Data interpretation and data-mining techniques: involve screening data to detect patterns, to identify potential problems or opportunities or to discover similarities between current and past situations. These processes help improve our understanding of the relevant factors and their relationships, including the possible discovery of non-obvious features in the data. From these processes it is also possible to learn new situations.
- Problem diagnosis techniques: try to recognise characteristic symptoms to develop and conðrm hypotheses about possible causes. They can also be used to suggest strategies for repair or recovery based on available knowledge (not always complete) and/or on past experiences.
- Decision-support techniques: involve evaluating alternatives to explore possible consequences, compare their relative costs and beneðts and recommend appropriate action plans.

These categories are not mutually exclusive and leverage AI use cases and capabilities previously outlined. For convenience, these are summarised in Table 1 (Eggers et al., 2017).

Table 1. Key AI technologies

Technologies	Definition
Rules-based systems	Capture and use expert knowledge to provide answers to tricky problems that are governed by fixed rule sets.
Speech recognition	Transcribe human speech automatically and accurately. The technology improves as machines collect more examples of conversations.
Computer vision	The ability to identify objects, scenes and activities in naturally occurring images.
ML	Takes place without explicit programming. By trial and error, computers learn how to learn, mining information to discover patterns in data that can help predict future events.
Natural-language processing	Refers to the task of organising and understanding language in a human way. Combined with ML, a system can scan websites for discussions of specific topics.
RPA	RPA robots are software programs and hardware designed to automate transactional, rules-based tasks by mimicking human interactions.

Case Study: Infrastructure Management

This case study includes the application of AI to infrastructure challenges managed by government agencies responsible for the public good in categories such as energy, water and waste management, transportation, real estate and urban planning. AI has beneficial applications in traffic management as well, with data collected in real time from traffic lights, security cameras and other sources, enabling traffic-flow optimisation and customer service. Additionally, algorithms and ML techniques are employed to analyse large amounts of data to detect statistical patterns and to develop models that can be used to make accurate predictions.

A Boston Consulting Group benchmarking study (Carrasco et al., 2019), identified a series of AI use cases from respondents who were asked about the AI applications they would support, their attitudes about government oversight and their views on AI ethics and privacy. Key findings are listed below:

- Citizens were most supportive of using AI for tasks, such as transport and traffic optimisation, predictive maintenance of public infrastructure and customer-service activities. The majority did not support AI for sensitive decisions associated with the justice system, such as parole boards and sentencing recommendations.

- People in less developed economies and places where perceived levels of corruption were higher also tended to be more supportive of AI. For example, citizens surveyed in India, China and Indonesia indicated the strongest support for government applications of AI, whereas the citizens surveyed in Switzerland, Estonia and Austria offered the weakest support.
- Demographic patterns tended to mirror general attitudes toward technology. Millennials and urban dwellers, thus demonstrated the greatest support for government use of AI, whereas older people and those in more rural and remote locations showed less support.
- Citizens were most concerned about the potential ethical issues and the lack of transparency in decision making, and they expressed significant anxiety about AI's potential to increase automation and the resulting effects on employment.

Strong support emerged for less sensitive decisions, such as traffic and transport optimisation. Additionally, the use of AI was well-supported for the predictive maintenance of public infrastructure and equipment such as roads, trains and buses. Support was strong for using AI in customer-service channels, including virtual assistants, avatars and virtual and augmented reality. The study found that people in EM tended to be more positive about government use of AI. Citizens in mature economies tended to show less support for government use of AI than those in EMs. For example, citizens surveyed in Estonia, Denmark and Sweden were the least receptive to the use of AI. The top-three most supportive countries were China, the UAE and Indonesia.

Support for government use of AI correlates moderately with trust in government. Trust in institutions is essential if governments are to gain the support needed to roll out AI capabilities. Countries where citizens are most supportive of AI were India, China, Indonesia, Saudi Arabia and the UAE. This aligns closely with countries having highest levels of trust in government. The study found that governments should select carefully how and where they launch pilots and to scale them over time. When identifying use cases that deliver the greatest benefit from experimentation, governments should balance the difficulty of implementation with the benefits, including the potential impact on citizens, the reusability and applicability of a use case to other needs and the opportunity to reduce costs and free-up resources for other uses. Pilots should be publicised, tracked and reported, not only to demonstrate the value of AI, but to also build public trust and create transparency. Communication and education will play a large part in building this trust as governments roll out increasingly advanced applications of AI to their policy and delivery environments. Governments must underscore the role of humans in government decision making. In some cases, AI alone can be used to make decisions. In many others, however, AI should augment human judgement and support decision making. Checks need to be put in place with mechanisms through which citizens can raise concerns. Governments should be transparent about the quality of the AI recommendations.

Case Study: Education

The potential of AI and ML in education includes maximising student achievement and improving teacher productivity. It has immediate potential to change the way we learn, memorise, access and create information. However, it is important to understand the current limits of AI technology and to admit that it is not (yet) ready to replace teachers. AI serves as a catalyst for transformation in the field of digital teaching and learning by introducing novel solutions to revolutionise all dimensions of the educational process, leading to individualised learning experiences, teachers playing a greater role as mentors and the automation of all administrative processes linked to education (Habib, 2019). This promises better student experiences, better student outcomes and more efficient teachers, administration and infrastructure.

The role of AI in education is about enhancing human thinking and to augment educational processes, not to reduce it to a set of procedures for content delivery, control and assessment. With the rise of AI solutions, it is increasingly important for educational institutions to stay alert and see if the power of control over hidden algorithms that run them is not monopolised by tech-lords that include the likes of Apple, Google, Microsoft and Facebook who are investing heavily in new applications and research. Those who control algorithms that run AI solutions have now unprecedented influence over people and every sector of a contemporary society (Popenici and Kerr, 2017). In his book, 'The Black Box Society', Frank Pasquale noted that 'decisions that used to be based on human reflection are now made automatically. Software encodes thousands of rules and instructions computed in a fraction of a second' (Pasquale, 2015).

Recent advancements in non-invasive brain-computer interfaces and AI have opened new possibilities to rethink the role of the teacher and make steps toward the replacement of teachers with 'teacherbots' (Bayne, 2015; Botrel et al., 2015). Personalised learning with a 'teacherbot' or 'cloud-lecturer' could be adopted for blended delivery courses or fully online courses. On reflection, 'teacherbots' are solutions for the administrative parts of teaching (i.e. teacher assistance), dealing mainly with content delivery and basic and administrative feedback and supervision. An ongoing critique and inquiry of AI solutions must take place to guarantee that universities and learning institutions can maintain, promote and develop knowledge and wisdom among students and teachers alike.

GOVERNANCE AND ACCOUNTABILITY

Today, we live in an era where governments are arguably paying lip service to important matters, such as climate change, democracy and the right of free speech. There are violent protects and wars infiltrating many parts of the world. Perhaps it is a good time to take stock and ask ourselves what do we really expect and want from AI? Will AI-enabled technology to address the biggest issues that affect people's daily lives? Will members of society become even more disconnected from one another as it becomes dependent on AI making key decisions and carry out the more mundane jobs? Any technology can be abused when placed in the wrong hands. However, who should judge between right and wrong?

Although governments have often demonstrated a relatively poor historical performance in shaping technological development, they have an important role in the area of AI (Whitby, 2003). This includes providing an appropriate legislative framework, assessing overall risks and benefits and assuming the ultimate responsibility for social decisions. The intervention of key persons in authority, including governments, legislators and the judiciary, can have positive effects on technology-related goals. One example is that of Present John Kennedy, who, in 1961 made a public declaration of the US commitment to a manned lunar mission[2]. In this case, this substantially accelerated the pace of scientific and technological developments with a positive outcome: the Apollo 11 lunar landing of 1969[3].

Role of Government

Fierce international competition in the digital space means that the European Union (EU) continues to lag behind China and the US in terms of digital progress. Exploiting scale and new technologies, such as AI and blockchain, research and development and improvements to education and training allow the workforce to exploit new job opportunities and lead to greater innovation to ensure regions remains competitive. However, the EU leads the US and China when it comes to enforcing tech regulation. The European Commission, the executive arm of the EU, has imposed a combined USD 9.5B in antitrust fines against Google since 2017, and is actively targeting Facebook, Amazon and Apple (Schulz, 2019). Rather than break up the tech giants, the European Commission has opted for fines and mandates. Facebook has been subjected to probes from competition and data-protection authorities across the EU, since the region's strict new set of privacy rules, called the General Data Protection Regulation (GDPR), went into effect last year. According to (Parsons, 2019), between 2017 and 2019, Google has been fined *three* times:

1. June 2017, £2.1B for breaching antitrust rules regarding its online shopping service
2. July 2018, a record £3.9B for using its Android operating system to cement 'the dominance of its search engine'
3. March 2019, £1.27B related to practices around the firm's advertising business.

The total fines levied upon Google by the European Commission was a staggering EUR 8.25B, as noted by Jonas Koponen, the competition partner at the global law firm, Linklaters.

The EU has outlined three pillars of its approach to AI, including preparing the public for the socio-economic changes. The EU is not alone in aiming to establish guidelines for AI. The Organisation for Economic Co-operation and Development (OECD) is working on a similar project. Meetings of the G7 and G20 have featured proposals from Japan and others for an international code of conduct for the development and use of AI (McCarthy, 2019). Industry has been involved in this project as well. The industry trade associations, the Software and Information Industry Association and Technology Industry Council, have both released proposed guidelines for AI. Individual companies, including Google, Microsoft and Facebook have developed their own public standards for their uses of AI-systems (McCarthy, 2019).

What is the proper role of these guidelines for AI? One approach is to not regulate it. Rather, we should observe the contexts in which AI raises new issues and then consider cases for new domain-specific legislations and regulatory laws. Many firms, including those that do not regard of themselves as traditional tech firms, consider the prospect of AI both an intriguing possibility and a potential new area of risk. The application of existing AI technologies raises significant new issues in some of the most fundamental areas of law, including ownership and property rights, the creation, allocation and sharing of value, the misuse, errors and responsibilities for resulting harm, individual liberties, personal privacy and economic collusion. We next examine how businesses are already managing some of these risks through contracts. We then examine some of the considerations involved in public regulation of AI-related risks. We then propose a four-layer model for thinking about AI regulation in the broad sense (Lohr et al., 2019).

REGULATING AI

As technologies emerge and mature, the need for regulation grows. AI is no exception. In this climate of polarisation, which features techno-optimists such as Mark Zuckerberg and pessimists headed by Elon Musk, it is difficult for governments to strike the right balance between fostering innovations while mitigating risks. Internationally, leading global inter-governmental organisations have issued public policy frameworks for AI, typically with input from a range of experts and stakeholders. These are intended to be models for use by governments and other parties around the world. The OECD has adopted principles for 'trustworthy' AI to establish expectations for all actors participating in the AI-system lifecycle. The OECD is also developing practical guidance on ways to act consistently with these principles. In the 2019 G20 Leaders' Summit, the G20 endorsed the OECD framework with some variations on details.

Recognising the ever-growing strategic importance of AI, the European Commission (EC) stressed that the socio-economic, legal and ethical implications of this transformative technology must be carefully considered. In its 2018 communication, the EC defined a European approach to AI based on three pillars:

- Being ahead of technological developments and encouraging uptake by the public and private sectors
- Preparing for socio-economic changes brought about by AI
- Ensuring an appropriate ethical and legal framework

According to Finkel and Schembri (2019), the EC appointed the High-Level Expert Group on AI ('AI HLEG') subsequently published the official Ethics Guidelines for Trustworthy AI on 8 April 2019. These guidelines set out a framework for achieving trustworthy AI, including the adherence of AI systems to four ethical principles:

- respect for human autonomy
- the prevention of harm
- fairness
- explicability

Although human-rights law covers a broad classes of risks and harms, they are not equipped to address all known and unknown concerns pertaining to AI. Gaps will indeed remain between rights, principles, designs, developments, deployments and uses of AI systems. Moreover, one should keep in mind that implementing and monitoring the compliance with the principles enshrined in the proposed ethical framework is definitely easier said than done. In particular, the current state-of-the-art AI, based principally on deep-learning techniques, is largely incapable of explaining outcomes, which is necessary under the proposed ethical framework. New approaches are needed.

From the regulatory perspective, ethical considerations provide a fundamental basis from which new regulations and laws can be created and justified. From a developmental perspective, ethics and value judgements underpin fundamental concepts, such as agency, responsibility, identity, freedoms and human capabilities. With supervised AI-learning models, the possible choice outcomes must be provided to the system before it starts to learn. This means that the world becomes described in closed terms, based on predefined interests and categories. Furthermore, the categories are based on data collected in the past. AI systems categorise people in clusters where data from other people, considered similar by the system, are used to predict individual characteristics and behaviour.

From political and ethical perspectives, this is highly problematic. Human agency implies that we can make choices about future acts and thus become responsible for them. When AI systems predict our acts using historical data averaged over a large numbers of datasets, they cannot see the people that make true choices and break out from historical patterns of behaviour. AI could therefore also limit the domain wherein humans can express their agency.

Recent successes in AI have, to a large extent, been based on the availability of vast amounts of data. AI-based products and services can be created across domains only if appropriate data is available. At present, some of existing datasets can be considered natural monopolies, and they are often controlled by few large corporations. An important policy challenge is how such large datasets that are needed for the development and use of AI-based systems can be made more widely available. One potential solution is to build on the current GDPR, which requires that data subjects obtain copies of their personal data from data controllers in a commonly used electronic forms. Technically, this would make it possible for users to access their personal data, anonymise it locally and submit it in an appropriate format to platforms that are used for AI learning, educational, marketing and commercial purposes. Such functionality could be relatively easily embedded if platforms for data aggregation were available. One possibility is to pilot aggregation platforms that operate regionally and nationally.

Layered Approach to Regulation

AI can be broadly used in a range of applications, from voice assistants to autonomous vehicles to medical diagnoses to credit and other financial decisions. A big question remains whether countries will adopt a 'one-size-fits-all' approach or one tailored to individual sectors. Apart from differences among AI applications, the US, the UK and countries across Europe and Asia have shown openness to adopting principles and standards across sectors. In certain applications, such as AI-powered facial recognition, lawmakers and regulators have pushed for swifter and sector-specific actions. Ultimately, the successful use of AI requires trust. Transparency and legal compliance will help build trust, ensuring that any personal data used will be ethically sourced and GDPR compliant, further ensuring that the algorithms avoid unfair biases, integrating security to their design and working with regulators (where relevant) from early stages. However, there is still no universal agreement among governments on a common approach to AI regulation.

In their 'Algorithmic Regulation' (Yeung and Lodge, 2019), the authors argued that the power of algorithms and algorithmic systems underpinning AI technologies could, themselves, be regulated. They offered a unique perspective that cut across worlds of research, policy and practice. Given that AI systems are proliferating, an urgent public debate is required to review underlying values and trade-offs that could help society better expose and manage challenging social implications.

Jason Lohr, Winston Maxwell and Peter Watts (Lohr et al., 2019) proposed the creation of a framework layered and differentiated without being overly complex. The primary challenge of regulating AI and other emerging technologies is that they are emerging and present unprecedented challenges. To be effective, any form of regulation must be dynamic, building on previous laws and fundamentally open to changes and experimentation.

According to (Sheir, 2019), the layered regulatory model begins with a foundation of existing laws that govern liability, private property and contracts. These laws need little explanation and are well-established. The second layer, corporate governance, is also a more well-established field. Companies continually update internal policies to reflect competition and antitrust laws and will do the same for AI. With these foundational layers comes sector-specific regulations, in which government agencies would be tasked with addressing pertinent AI concerns in their sector. This approach may seem counterproductive, but AI has a diversity of applications and consequences that a centralised framework would probably under- or over-regulate.

The UK Government already has such an agency: the Office for AI, which includes the CEO of Google DeepMind, Denis Hassabis, as the first adviser. White papers published by this office discuss larger principles of accountability and transparency (Blaikie and Donovan, 2018).

The Centre for Data Ethics and Innovation appointed to advise the UK Government stated that 'Government should work with industry and experts to establish a UK AI Council to help coordinate and grow AI in the UK'. The recommendation was based on the perceived need to facilitate engagement between industry, academia, government and the public, because 'AI in the UK will need to build trust and confidence in AI-enabled complex systems'. Lohr, Maxwell and Watts recommended that this type of agency measure significant social consequences in regulating AI, such as media disinformation or privacy, in terms of explicit key performance indicators. These can then serve as a yardstick for when sanctions might be applied, or actions might be taken by sector-specific regulators. Avoiding over-centralisation seems to be key to effective regulation that avoids choking innovation while scrutinising technologies whose impact are as yet not fully known. Regulating AI and imposing appropriate measures to achieve this goal should be the focal point of any policy agenda. Businesses and government departments will have to act in concert to ensure the furtherance of AI in a responsible manner. Safety and entrepreneurship need not be at odds if these partnerships are effective and bipartisan. As we look to the future, we need only remember that extremes and broad declarations are rarely as helpful as practical, sustainable policy frameworks, although it may only be the former which makes the news (Lohr et al., 2019).

FUTURE RESEARCH DIRECTIONS

It may be easy to think that AI is rapidly becoming super-intelligent and will gain all the good and evil powers awarded to it in popular culture. This, of course, is not the case. The current AI systems are severely limited, and there are technical, social, scientific and conceptual limits to what they can do. That said, it is our belief that there is a need for research on the ethical implications of the current control on developments of AI and the possibility to dilute the richness of human knowledge and perspectives with the monopoly of the tech companies. We also believe that it is important to focus further research on the new roles of many professions, such as teachers, on new learning pathways for higher-degree students with a new set of graduate attributes and a focus on imagination, creativity and innovation: a set of abilities and skills that can never replicated by machines.

As AI scales, it can effectively routinise old institutional structures and practices that may not be relevant for the future. Future-oriented work, therefore, is needed to understand the potential impact of AI technologies. How this potential is realised depends on how we operationalise the AI capabilities described at the start of this chapter. There is a risk that AI might be used to scale up bad pedagogical practices. If AI is the new electricity, it will have a broad impact in society, economy, education, government and more. Moreover, it must be treated with care. Future-oriented policy experimentation is needed so that we can fully understand and tackle the social implications of AI.

CONCLUSION

When AI systems predict our actions using historical data, they cannot (presently) account for people who make unique choices or who from historical patterns of behaviour. AI can therefore also limit the domain in which humans express their agency. AI is currently high on the political agendas around the world. Several EU member states have declared it a political priority. Influential studies now suggest that perhaps one-in-two occupations in the industrialised countries is likely to become automated using already existing AI technologies (European Commission, 2017). Policy makers at the European Parliament have highlighted the importance of the issue, and the European Commission in its 2018 annual work programme set its wish to make the most of AI, which will increasingly play a role in our economies and societies. AI is now often called 'the next electricity.' The transformative impact of general-purpose technologies, such as AI, however, becomes visible only gradually as societies and economies reinvent themselves as users. Technological changes bring social and cultural changes that are reflected in lifestyles, norms, policies, social institutions, skills and the content and forms of education (European Commission, 2017).

Wide availability of cheap processing power and vast amounts of data in recent years have enabled impressive breakthroughs in ML and have created extraordinary commercial and research interest in AI, including computational models based on the structure and functions of biological neural networks. Neural AI and ML methods are now used for real-time natural-language processing and translation, image analysis, driverless cars, autonomous vehicles, automated customer service, fraud detection, process control, synthetic art, service robots and many others. Although some of this excitement might be based on unrealistic expectations and limited knowledge of the complexities of the underpinning technologies, it is reasonable to expect that the recent advances in AI and ML will have profound impacts on future labour markets, competence requirements and learning and teaching domains. AI could make some cross-society functions (e.g. education) obsolete while emphasising others (e.g. infrastructure). It may also enable new methods of teaching and learning. To influence and shape the role of AI for social good and to reduce negative social implications, it is our opinion that we must invest time and support for organisations, such as 'Partnership on AI'[4], which are intended to benefit people and society. These organisations benefit society by conducting research, organising discussions, sharing insights, providing thought leadership, consulting with relevant third parties, bringing together diverse and global voices, responding to questions from the public and media and creating educational material. Together with businesses (e.g. Google, Facebook and Amazon), government, national and international agencies must work harder to introduce new policies, practices and regulations that serve the interests of citizens and communities in areas, such as

- Safety-critical AI
- Fair, transparent and accountable AI
- Labour and economy
- Human and AI systems collaboration

- Social and societal influences of AI
- AI and social good

The stakes are high. If AI is to improve our everyday life, it must address questions of safety, accountability, inclusiveness and around trust more broadly. Overall, we expect AI regulatory approaches to advance on both the domestic and international fronts during the coming months and years. Stakeholder participation is key as lawmakers and regulators continue their discussions and move beyond discussing to propose potential laws or regulations. As with privacy law, input by industry participants before laws or regulations are passed is critical for avoiding unintended consequences that can stifle beneficial AI innovation.

REFERENCES

Ananthaswamy, A. (2017). *AI spots Alzheimer's brain changes years before symptoms emerge.* https://www.newscientist.com/article/2147472-ai-spots-alzheimers-brain-changes-years-before-symptoms-emerge/

Bayne, S. (2015). Teacherbot: Interventions in automated teaching. *Teaching in Higher Education, 20*(4), 455–467. doi:10.1080/13562517.2015.1020783

Blaikie, D., & Donovan, N. (2018). Will the UK Regulate AI? *Slaughter and May. Technology Practice.* https://www.slaughterandmay.com/media/2537013/will-the-uk-regulate-ai.pdf

Blumenthal, D. (2011). Digital Ignorance and the Society of Abundance. *Social Media Today.* https://www.socialmediatoday.com/content/digital-ignorance-and-society-abundance

Botrel, L., Holz, E. M., & Kübler, A. (2015). Brain painting V2: Evaluation of P300-based brain-computer interface for creative expression by an end-user following the user-centred design. *Brain-Computer Interfaces, 2*(2–3), 1–15. doi:10.1080/2326263X.2015.1100038

Buolamwini, J. (2019). *Artificial Intelligence Has a Problem With Gender and Racial Bias. Here's How to Solve It.* https://time.com/5520558/artificial-intelligence-racial-gender-bias/

Busby, M. C. (2018). *Killer robots' ban blocked by US and Russia at UN meeting.* https://www.independent.co.uk/life-style/gadgets-and-tech/news/killer-robots-un-meeting-autonomous-weapons-systems-campaigners-dismayed-a8519511.html

Byrne, W. (2018). Now is the Time to Act to End Bias in AI. *Fast Company.* https://www.fastcompany.com/40536485/now-is-the-time-to-act-to-stop-bias-in-ai

Carrasco, M., Mills, S., Whybrew, A., & Jura, A. (2019). The Citizen's Perspective on the Use of AI in Government. *BCG Digital Government Benchmarking.* https://www.bcg.com/publications/2019/citizen-perspective-use-artificial-intelligence-government-digital-benchmarking.aspx

Chui, M., Harrysson, M., Manyika, J., Roberts, R., Chung, R., Nel, P., & Van Heteren, A. (2018). Applying artificial intelligence for social good. *McKinsey Global Institute.* https://www.mckinsey.com/featured-insights/artificial-intelligence/applying-artificial-intelligence-for-social-good

Cortés, U., Sànchez-Marrè, M., Ceccaroni, L., R-Roda, I., & Poch, M. (2000). Article. *Applied Intelligence, 13*(1), 77–91. doi:10.1023/A:1008331413864

Dutt, D. (2018). *2018: the year of the AI-powered cyberattack.* https://zighra.com/blogs/2018-the-year-of-the-ai-powered-cyberattack/

Eggers, W. D., Fishman, T., & Kishnani, P. (2017). AI-augmented human services. *Deloitte Insights.* https://www2.deloitte.com/content/dam/insights/us/articles/4152_AI-human-services/4152_AI-human-services.pdf

European Commission. (2017). *An agenda for a more united, stronger and more democratic Europe.* Communication from the Commission to the European Parliament, the Council, the European Economic and Social Committee and the Committee of the Regions Commission Work Programme 2018 - (COM(2017) 650 final).

Finkel, O., & Schembri, T. (2019). Regulating Trustworthy AI: a Fundamental-rights Based Approach. *WH Partners.* http://whpartners.eu/news/regulating-trustworthy-ai-a-fundamental-rights-based-approach

Goodman, M. (2015). *Future Crimes: Everything Is Connected, Everyone Is Vulnerable and What We Can Do About It.* Doubleday.

Habib, M. K. (2019). *Revolutionizing Education in the Age of AI and Machine Learning.* IGI Global.

Krigsman, M. (2017). *Artificial intelligence and privacy engineering: Why it matters NOW.* https://www.zdnet.com/article/artificial-intelligence-and-privacy-engineering-why-it-matters-now/

Linde, R., & Neuvonen, A. (2017). The abundant society. *SITRA.* https://www.sitra.fi/en/articles/the-abundant-society/

Lohr, J.D., Maxwell, W.J., Watts, P. (2019). *Legal Practitioners' Approach to Regulating AI Risks.* DOI: doi:10.1093/oso/9780198838494.003.0010

McCarthy, M. (2019). The EU Should Not Regulate Artificial Intelligence As A Separate Technology. *Forbes.* https://www.forbes.com/sites/washingtonbytes/2019/02/08/the-eu-should-not-regulate-artificial-intelligence-as-a-separate-technology/

Parsons, J. (2019). Here are all Google's fines from the European Commission. *Metro.* https://metro.co.uk/2019/03/21/googles-fines-european-commission-8962424/?ito=cbshare?ito=cbshare

Popenici, S. A. D., & Kerr, S. (2017). Exploring the Impact of Artificial Intelligence on Teaching and Learning in Higher Education. *RPTEL, 12*(1), 22. doi:10.118641039-017-0062-8 PMID:30595727

Schulz, E. (2019). If you want to know what a US tech crackdown may look like, check out what Europe did. *CNBC.* https://www.cnbc.com/2019/06/07/how-google-facebook-amazon-and-apple-faced-eu-tech-antitrust-rules.html

Sharma, K. (2018, Feb.). Can We Keep Our Bias From Creeping Into AI? *Harvard Business Review*, 9.

Sheir, S. (2019). *A Layered Approach to Regulating AI.* https://aibesummit.com/blog/regulating-ai/

Stone, M. (2018, Mar. 14). Want a More Diverse Workforce? How AI is Combating Unconscious Bias. *Dell Technologies Perspectives.*

Thomson, A. J. (1997). Artificial intelligence and environmental ethics. *AI Applications, 11*(1), 69–73.

Tyer, D. (2019). *No longer artificial – AI in pharma and healthcare.* https://pharmaphorum.com/views-and-analysis/ai-pharma-healthcare/

Waddell, K. (2019). The dangers of "AI washing". *Axios.* https://www.axios.com/ai-washing-hidden-people-00ab65c0-ea2a-4034-bd82-4b747567cba7.html

Whitby, B. (2003). *Social Implications of Artificial Intelligence. Doctor of Philosophy by Publication. School of Computer Science.* London, UK: Middlesex University.

Whitby, B. R. (1988). *AI: A Handbook of Professionalism.* Chichester: Ellis Horwood.

Yeung, K., & Lodge, M. (2019). *Algorithmic Regulation.* Oxford University Press. doi:10.1093/oso/9780198838494.001.0001

Yoshiyuki, S., Suzuki, K., & Hasegawa, Y. (2014). *Cybernics: Fusion of Human.* Machine and Information Systems. doi:10.1007/978-4-431-54159-2

ENDNOTES

[1] Autonomous Weapons: an Open Letter from AI & Robotics Researchers. This open letter was announced on 28 July at the opening of the IJCAI 2015 conference (Source: https://futureoflife.org/open-letter-autonomous-weapons).

[2] The Decision to Go to the Moon: President John F. Kennedy's May 25, 1961 Speech before a Joint Session of Congress (Source: https://history.nasa.gov/moondec.html).

[3] Apollo 11: First Men on the Moon. (Source: https://www.history.com/this-day-in-history/armstrong-walks-on-moon).

[4] (Source: https://www.partnershiponai.org/).

Chapter 9
The Future Is Already Here

ABSTRACT

In Japan, the world's most technologically sophisticated society, the future has already happened with public displays of AI-powered systems and robots underpinned by big data and fast being incorporated along with other emerging technologies such as the internet of things (IoT), augmented reality (AR), virtual reality (VR), blockchain, and cryptocurrency. Hence, the building blocks of the future already exist today, perhaps within niches, and in the coming years, they will spread to make the 'normal' of the future. The human race needs to forge a society that collectively and fairly controls how AI will 'write' the future to avoid it being unequally spread and affected by inequalities, cancers, and the dysfunctional habits of today.

"The future is already here – it's just not evenly distributed." –William Gibson, An American-Canadian Writer

INTRODUCTION

This penultimate chapter may be summed up by a simple question: *'What Will Our Society Look Like When Artificial Intelligence Is Everywhere?'*

We live in extraordinary times. New advances in technology such as artificial intelligence (AI) underpinned by Big Data along with other emerging

DOI: 10.4018/978-1-7998-4607-9.ch009

technologies such as the Internet of Things (IoT), Augmented Reality (AR), Virtual Reality (VR), Blockchain and Cryptocurrency, allow our society to understand the world that surrounds us in new and unprecedented ways. Today, we carry in our pockets computers more powerful than those that sent Apollo 11 to the moon. We are at the brink of an *abundant future* never before experienced that promises both exciting opportunities and disconcerting challenges.

While western media is full of stories told by adults about the future of AI – things like self-driving cars, virtual assistants and robotic caretakers for senior citizens – today's children likely imagine an even wilder set of prospects especially those born in our technology filled world. As these new tools come into use, we wonder if AI systems will be effective, trustworthy and reliable both for ourselves and for tomorrow's generation. How can we work towards a future where children's creativity and curiosity is combined with adults' wisdom, maturity and duty of care, to deliver the best possible future for all? How can we develop responsible AI for our children?

AI allows us to see ourselves in unusual new ways by revealing subtle aspects of the relationships that exist between us and the world around us. We must ask ourselves how AI systems could shape the way we interact, such as by undermining personal privacy standards or by over-engineering our daily social dynamics.

In recent years we have observed large changes in economy in general and marketing in particular as a result of internet expansion, globalisation of businesses run by Google, Amazon, Facebook and others and ubiquitous information availability. One of the scientific fields which gained momentum as a result of this was data analysis under various names: 'statistics', 'data mining', 'machine learning', 'data analytics' and 'knowledge discovery'. Many new data analysis techniques have emerged that exploit availability of more and different data from several sources underpinned by supercomputers which fuse high-performance computing (HPC) and AI to deliver 'peta-scale' performance (Zubaşcu, 2019), to accelerate scientific discovery with NVIDIA's GPU-accelerated apps[1].

Everyone agrees that 'AI' will change the world and it is the most important technology of the 21st century that will help us better understand our global ambitions as well as tackle topics as diverse as space exploration to countering terrorism and even creating art.

For the first time in recent history, in regards to AI, we have observed a multitude of initiatives, strategies and actions by dozens of governments around the world with very different goals and approaches. It remains an issue that politicians and leaders of all nations have to deal with.

While politics provides the framework conditions for research, financing, education, data, promotion and regulation, in the medium-term AIs must be developed by companies and brought onto the market. First of all, national interests have to be considered.

According to Forbes,

- ***China has a clear vision*** of how country wants to master artificial intelligence. From China's point of view, artificial intelligence is an important tool for strong foreign policy, military dominance, economic success and for controlling one's own population.
- ***The USA benefits from a strong research cluster and the super corporations*** Google, Microsoft, Facebook and Amazon, each of which is in the lead of the AI development.
- ***The USA has been promoting the research and implementation*** of AIs for decades through its countless secret services and ministries.
- ***Canada and Israel have become equally important*** but smaller players in the global competition for AI rule.
- ***Israel has more AI companies*** than Germany and France put together. Additionally, Israel has always been technologically strong leveraging a network of universities, close access to Asian and American capital markets as well as close cooperation with its military and government.
- ***Other countries including Japan, South Korea and India***, also have good prerequisites for playing a relevant role in the AI industry in the coming years.

It is abundantly clear that AI is becoming increasingly smarter, more knowledgeable, more capable and faster with each passing day. Contrary to our own biological nature, there are no limits to the AI. Hence, we find ourselves actively exploring progressive AI, namely, Narrow-, General- and Super-AI.

However, society still faces significant hurdles and challenges that will have to be overcome before the expanding potential of AI can be achieved. Many see meeting those challenges as a task of utmost priority right now for the tech industry, governments, research institutions as well for-profit and non-profit businesses – across all nations and countries, globally.

Most significantly, these challenges are fundamentally *human*.

Social Inequalities

AI systems are only as robust as the data sets and inputs that humans provide. Ideally, to identify patterns, an algorithm needs to assess large volumes of structured and/or unstructured data. While developing these data sets, researchers make conscious decisions about which data to include and which to exclude, often based on their own sets of conscious and unconscious biases. Thus, the outputs of AI systems are limited to the quality and quantity of its data inputs limited; perhaps, made worse by human decisions as to what is and is not relevant and the availability of data from the real world.

In simple terms, algorithms essentially work to recognise a pattern that exists in a data set and then make decisions based on these patterns. There is inherent bias in the data sets including gendered biases and social inequalities which have been shown to be flawed and simplistic. Unless the culture itself changes and systemic reforms are implemented, it is unclear how AI will help to fix these types of biases and social inequalities. After all, it is only replicating existing patterns (Ebadi, 2018).

The issue of perpetuating bias and inequality is likely to be more pronounced in fields where gender disparity is especially prominent – for example, security and military environments.

According to (Ebadi, 2018), research and work on AI in the security field has focused on its military applications, as opposed to peacebuilding. The following examples highlight the issues at hand:

- China's State Council released their 'Next Generation Artificial Intelligence Development Plan' in July 2017. Upon assessing a translated version of the plan, security applications of AI do not include peacebuilding, mediation or negotiations. While these terms make no appearance in the plan, the term 'military' appears 12 times, while 'defence' appears 10 times.
- France's AI strategy, For a Meaningful Artificial Intelligence: Towards a French And European Strategy, makes only one mention of 'peace', in relation to the impact of AI exports on 'regional peace and security' while it mentions 'defence' 24 times, 'military' nine times, 'security' 25 times and 'weapons' 17 times.
- Canada's Pan-Canadian Artificial Intelligence Strategy is really a basic overview making it difficult to examine which applications of AI are being prioritised in the security field.

Given the above examples, it is becoming clear that bias is built into much more than algorithms; the very security structures and systems in which AI tools operate have been conceptualised by humans.

To truly arrive at an AI-powered society, we cannot simply rely on AI to fix these challenges on their own or miraculously make existing inequalities disappear especially since the data supplied is derived from a human world filled with these inequalities along with conscious and unconscious bias. Increased investments in AI should also be accompanied by increased investments in inter- and cross-disciplinary research, programming and social innovation to better understand and address real world inequalities – between research institutions, profit and non-profit businesses as well as government agencies – in order to stand up solutions that take inputs from diverse domains such as politics, economics, security and law to help recognise blind spots and improve our own understanding of the societal implications of AI.

Without this kind of interdisciplinary approach, AI could simply replicate and potentially magnify societal inequalities, injustice and tribalism.

Structural Inequalities

According to (Audley and Ginsburg, 2019), 'structural inequalities' is 'the condition in which certain people are seen as less than in terms of other people and in turn said inequality is perpetuated by commonly accepted notions of inequality inherent in society'. This is the very foundation that reproduces widespread income gaps, the foundation of income inequality.

It is not an abstract idea. We *experience* structural inequality; we *see it* in the quality (or lack) of local schools and their test scores, *we smell it* in the access to healthy food (or not), *we feel it* in a sense of safety or danger as we walk the streets.

When we think about income inequality, we think about ways to make more money. Likewise, when we think about structural inequality, we're concerned with how to get people the resources for lasting economic opportunity including money. These two components of inequality, though linked, require different policy answers. Unfortunately, this masks the extent to which these unequal outcomes are consequences of common sets of processes within a single economy.

Greater resources in the surrounding environment may help the working class or poor overcome other, more personal, deficits by offering wider options. For example, attending a strong school with engaged teachers and classmates is a resource for the child of an alcoholic or depressed parent. The institution itself helps to foster resources within her to strive for and explore productive options.

The challenge is that a growing number of countries now confront the same economic instability that their poorer citizens face. Cities and towns are experiencing declining tax bases because of high unemployment and foreclosure rates, while their pension, education and infrastructure costs soar. Like their residents, these places struggle to remain middle class. Other communities are simply overmatched by the fiscal demands of increasing poverty. With dwindling help from state budgets, they cannot hope to become middle class.

But the problem of unequal opportunity is obviously far larger. The schools, home values, job networks, infrastructure, food stores and transportation options of an area all contribute to a sense of opportunity; the same applies in reverse through instability and isolation.

As resources dwindle, more of us experience the instability known by much poorer families. Economic uncertainty forces us to adjust our standards: in the colleges we attend, the debts we incur, the risks we will take. We get less at greater expense and make less at greater cost.

This is structural inequality at work. The patchwork of have and have-not neighbourhoods and towns corresponds to the distribution of have and have-not households. We are not our environments per se but when it comes to opportunity there's a striking resemblance. Too often it is down to race and skin colour. The more you are perceived as an outsider with nothing to contribute, the harder it is to be a full part of a neighbourhood or community.

In 2019, a new project (Morris et al., 2019) commissioned to explore structural inequalities, 'Exploring Inequalities igniting research to better inform UK policy', sought to cut across standard research and policy boundaries by bringing together a broad range of experts from academia, the charity sector, NGOs, government and business to review, synthesise and deepen our understanding of inequality in the UK.

The project was intentionally broad in scope, addressing multiple and inter-related inequalities across four key policy areas: education; employment; health; and housing.

In the forward of the report, written by Charlene White, is a quote which sums up the personal devastating reality of 'structural inequalities'

'you must work twice as hard as your neighbour', rang in my ears daily during my school years. My parents just kept going on and on about it. And

I'll admit . . . I found it annoying. I just wanted to be like some of the other girls and not have to work harder to be heard and understood. Fast forward to my adult years and I finally got it. It all finally made sense. My entire career thus far has been a whirlwind of working harder than my neighbour in order to reach my goals. 7-day working weeks filled with double and triple shifts. And the unfairness I felt as a schoolgirl has never left. If I'm clearly good enough to do something, why is my currency lessened because I have a vagina, darker skin and am a proud South East Londoner?

Structural inequality has been long in the making and therefore it will not be quickly addressed. Undoing it requires that we, the public, make clear that we want each other's success for the greater good of future society. Else, we are destined to keep making the same mistakes over and over again and no emerging technology (even AI) will be able to help unlock the deadlock some citizens find themselves in.

Protecting the Future Against Inequality

More than fifty years after equality commissions were first established in the UK, there has recently been increased attention on issues of structural and relational inequality in society. Despite the demographic, socio-economic and cultural transformations that have occurred over the last few decades, vast inequalities remain.

Our view is that governments and local authorities should put an emphasis on the underlying causes of structural inequalities whereby social groups based on ethnicity, race, tribe, gender, or cultural differences are systematically disadvantaged compared with other groups with which they coexist. These inequalities prevent many developing countries from realising their full potential and may undermine the sustainability of development outcomes. Furthermore, inequalities in the distribution of health by social class, gender and ethnicity have been measured using many different outcomes including infant deaths, mortality rates, morbidity, disability and life expectancy.

The cost of unemployment is a social cost: but it is mainly being carried by poor communities. This has a further dis-equalising effect on society. It raises the cost of labour: not good for a labour absorptive growth path. It erodes the value of social grants in the hands of those meant to benefit.

We invite the reader to think of social policy in terms of increasing access to productive assets, infrastructure and goods and services; strengthening governance and accountability; enabling the rights and obligations of citizens to promote equitable access to development opportunities; and managing the social dimensions of conflict, natural disasters and climate change.

As the issues are structurally entrenched and are not solved simply by gaining employment, solutions will need to tackle restructuring of tax and social laws to gradually address the imbalance.

However, intergenerational and structural inequalities leave large gaps, ones which need far more holistic attention than a simple cash boosts or changes in legal and social policies. Reversing some of the structural inequalities is a theoretical possibility, but wounds always take longer to heal than they do to open up. It would be a slow and painful effort.

As structural remedies take time, it is therefore vital that those who are already being left behind are given some relational support in the present moment, After all social mobility has, at its most reductionist, two conceptions; a person's position within their 'structure', i.e. their 'class'; or their relationship to others, i.e. their 'culture'. If we cannot fix class based 'social capital', we should focus on cultural capital to help people understand their own strengths, worth and the possibilities open to them; that they are given guidance, advice, or even a place of belonging.

It is in this light that 'civil society' of the future, potentially supported by AI-powered technologies, should work. It should not just be a 'bridging' exercise; where those with more help those with less; it should also be an exercise in which the gap is closed somewhat. More than ever, governments and community groups need to help in areas that structural inequalities open up, whether regional, economic, or social; especially as many of the skills needed to navigate life in these new societal structures are not ones taught at school and are not ones that can be experienced easily from a position of inequality.

In all cases, while igniting research about inequalities is incumbent on all members of society and important from an education and awareness standpoint, without embedding learnings and acting, we could be in danger of simply proliferating social, intergenerational and structural inequalities to future generations – which, in our opinion, is something to be avoided at all costs. Otherwise, we run the risk of creating dystopian futures irrespective of the role or effectiveness of AI in any of its forms (i.e. narrow-, general- or super- intelligence).

ARTIFICIAL INTELLIGENCE 2.0 (AI 2.0)

The surge of AI-powered systems and machine learning is supported by profound changes to the information environment. This is inextricably linked to the spread of the Internet, the flood of sensor networks, the rise of big data, the increase in size of the information community and the increasing fusion of data and information throughout society with physical and virtual (cyber) realms.

As new emerging technology breakthroughs continue, AI enters a new stage: AI 2.0. The formation of AI 2.0 will be increasingly interlinked with social demands and the abundant information environment (Pan, 2016).

Foundations of AI 2.0 are built upon the volume of acquisitions over the past decade. According to a CB Insights report (CB Insights, 2019), tech giants like Facebook, Amazon, Microsoft, Google and Apple (FAMGA) have all been aggressively acquiring AI start-ups in the last decade. Among the FAMGA companies, Apple leads the way, making 20 total AI acquisitions since 2010. It is followed by Google (the frontrunner from 2012 to 2016) with 14 acquisitions and Microsoft with 10 as shown in Figure 1.

However, tech giants are not the only companies snatching up AI start-ups. Since 2010, there have been 635 AI acquisitions, as companies aim to build out their AI capabilities and capture sought-after talent (as of August 2019). Many of these companies are switching from 'mobile first' toward 'AI first' strategies.

Figure 2 presents a heatmap, courtesy of CB Insights, of AI acquisitions sorted across 15+ core industries that start-ups operated in prior to acquisition (such as healthcare or finance), or by one of 12 cross-industry applications (like sales or cybersecurity).

Retail & CPG topped all other industries in the number of AI acquisitions (67 since 2010), due to record-level M&A activity last year. These acquisitions have added AI-driven customer analytics, in-store inventory management and personalised e-commerce experiences to retailer's capabilities.

Recent examples include McDonald's $300M acquisition of personalisation platform Dynamic Yield, Ulta Beauty's acquisitions of virtual makeover start-up GlamST and customer engagement software company QM Scientific and Nike's acquisitions of inventory management company Celect and guided shopping experience platform Invertex.

Under cross-industry applications, Speech, NLP/(G) and Computer Vision has been a leading area of focus. The category, which includes start-ups working on computer vision and natural language processing, has seen 66 acquisitions since 2010.

Figure 1. The Race for AI amongst Tech giants
(CB Insights, 2019)

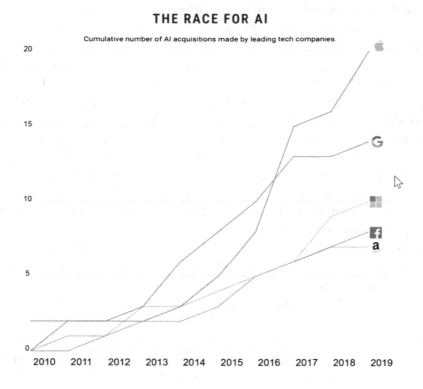

Large tech companies have scooped up smaller start-ups in this category to boost their internal AI R&D. For example, Apple acquired facial recognition firm RealFace and voice assistant start-up Novauris Technologies, Google acquired human-computer interaction company Api.ai and Microsoft acquired speech recognition & NLP start-up Semantic Machines and voice assistant company Maluuba.

Figure 2. Concentration of AI Acquisitions by Category (2011-2019 YTD)
(CB Insights, 2019)

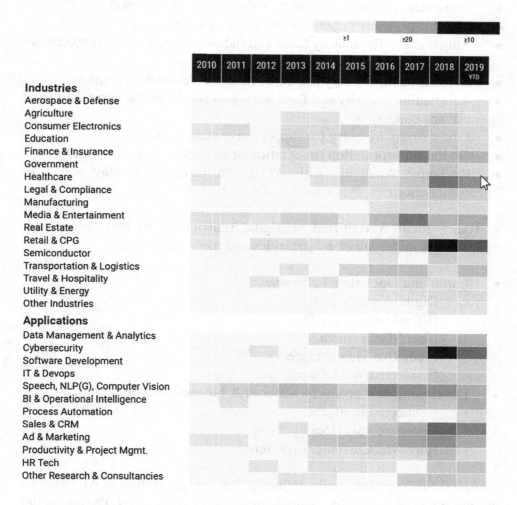

AI AND EMERGING TECH

The rise of emerging technologies ('emerging tech') have been hampered by the failure to move beyond pilots. That said, this time is different as a result of new mindsets, methods and investments. While individual emerging technologies may be at different stages of maturity, collectively, when interlinked they present fascinating opportunities.

For any emerging technology to be successful requires

- Diverse talent (to reproducible high-quality products and services)
- Investment (from governments, industry and consumers)
- Scalability (many organisations fail to move beyond pilots)
- Adherence to Regulatory Laws and Industry Standards (to demonstrate compliance)
- Referenceable industry use-cases (to drive demand-and-supply)
- Information Security and Data Standards (to assure data protection and privacy concerns)
- Low barriers for entry (to support easy adoption)
- Digital transformation (integration of into all areas of a business)
- Predictive Analytics with AI driven insights (to stay ahead of competition)

Today, focus has shifted to digital transformation and 'connected' technologies underpinned by strategies and metrics relating to

- Improving Operational efficiency:
  - Digital Factory
  - Digital Supply Chain
  - Fleet Management
  - Predictive Maintenance
  - Connected Work force
- Developing new products, services & business models:
  - Connected Products
  - Connected Services
  - Improved Customer experience

AI 2.0 can be preliminarily defined as the new generation of AI, based on the new information environment and new development goals. The remainder of this section outlines some of the other emerging technologies as we move increasingly towards 'Big Data based' intelligence – which combines data-driven and knowledge guidance into autonomous machine learning that is both explainable and more general.

Internet of Things (IoT)

Internet of Things (IoT) is about connecting machines and making use of the data generated from those machines. AI is about simulating intelligent behaviour in machines of all kinds. Clearly an overlap. As IoT devices will generate vast amounts of data, then AI will be functionally necessary to deal with these huge volumes if we're to have any chance of making sense of the data (Brunkard, 2018).

From an IoT perspective, data is only useful if it creates an action. To make data actionable, it needs to be supplemented with context and creativity. IoT and AI together is this context, i.e. 'connected intelligence' and not just connected devices. Traditional methods of analysing structured data and creating action are not designed to efficiently process the vast amounts of real-time data that stream from IoT devices. This is where AI-based analysis and response becomes critical for extracting optimal value from that data.

The opportunity to combine IoT and AI is made possible by

- Advancements in electronics enabled the sensor and computing technology to become more affordable.
- There are many connectivity options from cellular, to short range (low power), to satellite, to even sound.
- Innovation of OEMs means there are many connected devices for use in IoT solutions including drones, robots, cameras, etc.
- Cloud computing provides scalable capabilities to deal with increasing amounts of data.
- Numerous IoT PaaS and SaaS platforms for very specific use cases make IoT deployment much easier.

IoT and AI combined could be the trigger to really drive smart city business cases – creating not just the connected city but the connected intelligent city.

Augmented Reality (AR)

Augmented reality (AR) and artificial intelligence (AI) are two of the most promising technologies available to mobile app developers. While they are distinct technologies, when used together they can create unique experiences.

AR is an experience that blends physical and digital environments. Think Pokemon Go or Snapchat.

Most augmented reality experiences today revolve around overlaying the physical world with known information. Maps and games have garnered much attention in the consumer tech space. In the industrial world, the AR capabilities being leveraged would be constituted as visualize, instruct, or guide.

Computer generated objects coexist and interact with the real world in a single, immersive scene. This is made possible by fusing data from multiple sensors – camera(s), gyroscopes, accelerometers, GPS and so on – to form a digital representation of the world that can be overlaid on top of the physical one (Toole, 2019).

Smaller, faster and more accurate AI models will be the engines of AR functionality, given their ability to track and understand the 3D world. They'll also continue to enhance AR experiences, adding effects and interactivity to AR scenes.

Virtual Reality (VR)

Technologies depicted by Hollywood in sci-fi movies such as 'Star Wars', 'The Matrix' and 'Blade Runner' are no longer as far-fetched as we once imagined. The 'New Realities' (Kallman, 2019) comprised of virtual reality (VR), augmented reality (AR) and mixed reality (MR) mean that we can 'holoport' ourselves across geographic locations, use our brains to interface with computers and combine these technologies with AI to take them into yet more realities and dimensions.

Moreover, today, wearable computers and 'smart headsets' integrated with IoT connect allow consumers to access smart items in the home and control the physical world from within the virtual one.

VR and AI are also converging in training applications to generate scenarios based on real experiences and data. Virtual customer service agents in the metaverse will leverage AI to respond to customer inquiries and issues; virtual companions will also come to exist. When integrated with biosensors, AI may determine when new realities users need to take a break or have a drink of water, even pausing the experience as a result. Using a person's biodata, things like heart rate, blood pressure, sweat response and brainwaves, AI algorithms can generate completely new and individual experiences for users in the metaverse. This means that no two people would have the same digital reality experience.

To make virtual experiences indistinguishable from the real world, some believe the next step of human evolution is integrating these technologies into the brain. Neuro-reality refers to brain-computer interface (BCI) – the use of brainwaves to generate and navigate experiences through thought alone, processing both conscious and subconscious responses. Whether through implants or external electrodes, companies like Elon Musk's Neura-link and

Boston-based start-up Neurable are already leaders in this area. Soon we may all be able to turn on and off parts of the brain like we would a mobile phone. One thing we'll have to start thinking about is the fact that BCIs and neuro-reality will challenge basic human rights, as thoughts and privacy will no longer be inseparable and people could become vulnerable to exploitation in new ways.

These technologies are changing and challenging the ways we communicate, collaborate, socialise, market and learn. They have the potential to democratise training, skills and experiences, similar to what the internet did for sharing information. Yet innovation always brings new and unforeseen risks, from mental and physical implications, to new dangers around data and personal privacy. While the new realities offer plenty of new commercial opportunities, these technologies also have the power to change us individually and as a society. It's on all of us to make sure we develop these technologies and apply them responsibly.

Blockchain

Blockchain is defined as a distributed, decentralised, cryptographically secured ledger, where each new block contains a reference to the previous block, as well as all the confirmed 'transactions' since that previous block was approved. However, blockchain is not just for cryptocurrency.

After the introduction of blockchain, the term 'smart contract' was used more widely as software that runs computations on the blockchain. Today, a smart contract can be any kind of software, as long as it's based on blockchain technology. It can be used not only to complete 'transactions' but to secure data. A smart contract could specify that your physician has access to your medical history, but she can't see your financial history (Schmelzer, 2019)

The expression 'smart contracts' was coined by Nick Szabo (Szabo, 1997) long before blockchain technology was refined. He envisioned a technology meant to replace legal contracts, where the terms of a contract could be digitized and automated. An action (i.e. 'payment') could be completed as soon as the condition (i.e. 'delivery') was met.

Both AI and blockchain have a widely hyped market, with technology providers and customers claiming all sorts of capabilities that may or may not be possible. However, both technologies are starting to show tangible value across a range of applications and industries. The potential benefits of combining AI and blockchain look very compelling.

Given the hype, how can blockchain help with AI? One benefit would be the ability to share machine learning models among all parties without an intermediary or 'middleman' (or system). A good example is with facial recognition software. If one device knows what a person looks like and uploads it to the chain, other devices hooked up also know what that person looks like. When other devices upload their own facial recognition data, the other devices will gain the ability to use that for the facial recognition model. Since this happens on the blockchain, there is no central control over facial recognition and as such no one company owns or stores the data. This approach also allows for everyone to learn faster and collaboratively through the use of integrated AI with blockchain. This could help alleviate the many concerns about AI and data privacy.

Equally, blockchain can benefit AI in areas such as 'machine intelligence and learning systems' in a 'hub and spoke' arrangement likened to a 'shared brain'; individual AI systems ('spokes') would each 'learn' independently and then share that learning to a central blockchain bot ('hub'). In this scenario, there is no single ownership or government control over the bot or the shared brain – meaning it would not be opened to any form of malicious exploitation.

Another opportunity for combining AI and blockchain is the ability to address the challenge of 'explainable AI' in which AI is a 'black box' without any real transparency or explainability of how it works. By using blockchains, we can record how individual actions result in a final decision in a non-reputable manner, which allows us to go back and see where things went wrong and then fix the problem. The blockchain would be used to record events, such as autonomous vehicle decisions and actions in a way that will not be modified later. This can also increase trust since the blockchain element is unbiased and is just for storage and analysis, anyone can go in and see what has happened.

Blockchain smart contracts could provide businesses more precise control over who has permission to see their data and under what conditions. This would enable suppliers avoid the need to reveal information about their operations, pricing and sourcing and participate in digital supply chains securely.

Below are further examples of how companies can benefit from using blockchain and smart contracts:

- **Design a fully automated supply chain management system:** When a certain condition is reached, the appropriate action is taken. Imagine a factory that automatically orders supplies when it threatens to run out of them.

- **Manage huge paper trails:** Each step in the paper trail can be added as a new block in the chain and checks can be placed to ensure all conditions have been met that are needed to proceed.
- **Exchange vital business information in real time:** Every node can contribute to and access all the information in the blocks.
- **Eliminate the middleman when dealing with others:** The parties can interact directly and securely (without an intermediary) by relying on the blockchain technology.
- **Eliminate fraud:** Irreversibility makes it fraud resistant. In a proper setup, there is no way to make unauthorised changes in already approved blocks. This has applications across many industries.

Cryptocurrency

We are now living in an age when cryptocurrency has become just another form of currency – and in some places, apparently it is even more readily accepted than cash. From the time the enigmatically pseudonymous Satoshi Nakamoto published his now infamous paper (Nakamoto, 2008) which outlined a tamper-proof, decentralised peer-to-peer protocol that could track and verify digital transactions, prevent double-spending and generate a transparent record for anyone to inspect in nearly real-time. A year later, in 2009, saw the release of the first Bitcoins, setting new records ever since (Huillet, 2019).

Here are some impressive stats worth noting,

- **Since the creation of the very first block on the Bitcoin blockchain on Jan 3, 2009** – known in more technical language as its 'genesis block' – miners received combined revenue of just under $15 billion.
- **Bitcoin's first-ever recorded trading price was noted on Mar. 17, 2010** — on the now-defunct trading platform bitcoinmarket.com, at a value of $0.003. The cryptocurrency's appreciation thus stands at a staggering 304,033,233% as of press time, with Bitcoin currently trading at $9,120.
- **As of August 2019, 85% of Bitcoin's supply in circulation had been mined** — leaving just 3.15 million new coins for the future.

So how would AI benefit cryptocurrency? AI is to tech what 'blockchain' is to the cryptocurrency industry; a concept where genuine applications are significantly outnumbered by the projects interested solely in latching onto buzzwords and surfing them up for the sake of marketing exploits.

That said, AI isn't a panacea that can be liberally applied to every facet of the cryptocurrency industry nor is it going to render the smartest human traders redundant overnight. Nevertheless, it is already pulling strings within the sector, albeit behind the scenes in algorithmic technologies, facilitating everything from faster order execution to detecting bots and scammers.

According to (Hansen, 2019), more than a handful of crypto exchanges have already been victimised by substantial acts of theft, ranging from $5 million to $400 million. On a smaller scale, such companies are always trying to stay ahead of users looking to reap additional mining rewards by participating in unfair practices. Such security concerns have haunted the use of cryptocurrency since its inception.

This has led to express interest in applying AI to improve the security of high-volume transactions resulting from blockchain technology to help alleviate rising concerns of fraud via spiteful cyber-attacks. By removing the human dependency of the network and utilising self-learning technology, AI is able to play a significant role in making sure malicious actors don't get the upper hand on the blockchain.

That is precisely the sort of thinking that undergirds much of machine learning; the ability to predict based on patterns. It is what enables Amazon and Netflix to make recommendations and it enables Siri and Alexa to understand what you say. It is what is behind Uber's self-driving cars and algorithmic trading across financial institutions and investment banking.

Since AI (specifically machine learning systems) is self-learning, it is able to evolve and ultimately make it harder for potential hackers to find loopholes or vulnerabilities. The ability to recognise abnormal behaviours in the blockchain can help raise the alert of hacking attempts before they have a chance to be successful – providing an early warning tool to proactively reduce attempts to defraud a business.

Data Analytics

Each of the emerging technologies outlined above are dependent on one fundamental – an abundance of data and the need for smarter unified data analytics.

At the most basic level, data analytics is the process of transforming a raw dataset into useful knowledge. By drawing on new advances in AI and machine learning, there are opportunities to develop systems that will help to automate the data analytics process. Marketing managers have readily engaged with data analytics, benefitting (and most likely suffering) from the mountains of data at their fingertips. This has included everything from user-tracking data on apps and websites, newsletter conversion rates and online advertising click-throughs, to CRM data analysis.

This has given rise to unified data and analytic platforms (UDAP) which are the culmination of a multi-decade trend toward functional convergence. For companies afflicted with proliferating data silos and analytical tools, UDAP products are a welcome relief. They provide a comprehensive and wholly integrated data and analytics experience that accelerates insights, user adoption and return on investment. Essentially, they make good on the promise of 'faster, better, cheaper' when it comes to data and analytics (Eckerson, 2020).

With UDAP products, businesses can quickly prepare and clean data at massive scale with no limitations. The platform also enables the ability to continuously train and deploy machine learning models for AI applications.

UDAP provides the following three key benefits:

- Innovate faster with big data
- Make big data simple
- Unifying data science and data engineering

UDAP products are revolutionary. By offering an out-of-the-box, wholly integrated data and analytics environment that is easy to deploy and use, UDAP products break from tradition. They are designed to reduce deployment times and reduce total cost of ownership. However, it's important to recognise that UDAP products are not a silver bullet. Many UDAP products are sold by start-up or 'young' firms whose future is not assured, although many large software vendors are now beginning to crowd the market.

UDAP products are here to stay. They are the culmination of an inexorable trend toward convergence between data and analytics functionality and the need for a single platform to govern delivery and consumption.

Data analytics leads naturally to predictive analytics using collected data to predict what might happen. Predictions are based on historical data and rely on human interaction to query data, validate patterns, create and then test assumptions. Assumptions drawn from past experiences presuppose the future will follow the same patterns. 'What/if' assumptions are informed by human understanding of the past and predictive capability is limited by the volume, time and cost constraints of human data analysts.

Predictive insights derived from data analytics are extremely useful to marketers. They can help predict campaign effectiveness, inform decision-making on collateral, geographic markets and demographics to target. But the more detailed the desire to target and segment, the higher the time and cost demands, making successful, personalised campaigning nearly impossible.

To summarise:

- Data analysis refers to reviewing data from past events for patterns.
- Predictive analytics makes assumptions via testing based on past data to predict future 'what/ifs'.
- AI technologies (specifically based on machine learning) analyse data, make assumptions, learn and provide predictions at a scale and depth of detail impossible for individual human analysts.

Hence, given the choice between data analytics and predictive analysis, AI technologies have the potential to further enable CMOs and human analysts make decisions that have significant implications for businesses seeking to learn more about the consumer base and hence improve opportunities to deliver better experiences of their brands, products, solutions and services – while remaining ahead of competitors all vying for opportunities to attract new customers and steal portions of the market.

FUTURE RESEARCH DIRECTIONS

Future research needs to be two-fold,

1. Further study and resolutions to social and structural inequalities that a prevalent today.
2. Explore ways in which we can mature and embed AI in ways that do not take away control from humans that may lead to detrimental situations that impact society in ways that may be irreversible.

Regarding the first point, while it is incumbent on all to protect the future against any form of inequality, we should 'stop talking and start doing' and avoid procrastinating. Taking inspiration from a quote about 'Habits of Excellence' by Will Durant, often misattributed to Aristotle (Huntress, 2017),

'We are what we repeatedly do. Excellence, then, is not an act but a habit.'

If we are able to take action, develop a habit of actively remediating any forms of inequality, remain undeterred by failures along the way and, above all, remain focused on what we can do (rather what can't be done), then perhaps we have a chance to address all the many problems with today's society in the hope of creating a better future society that is civil, fair and equal.

Regarding the second point, it is our belief, that the pursuit and realisation of AI 2.0 will help with the development of an 'AI for good' that is both explainable and more general. This will endeavour will help to develop intelligent social and political systems, intelligent economies and intelligent cities, made possible only by augmenting AI and humans to create a future 'connected' society built upon autonomous machine learning systems.

Taking inspiration from the Chinese Academy of Engineering (Pan, 2016), research directions include:

1. **Internet crowd intelligence:** Building on the success of 'crowd-funding' techniques, research into 'crowd-based intelligence' should be explored to exploit the 'connectedness' offered by the Internet and mobile technologies to expand and develop practical solutions by investing in theory development, management methods and organisational change management.

2. **Cross-media intelligence:** Research on perception, learning, inference and the creation of cross-media technology platforms to establish new intelligent technologies that can 'see and hear better'. Potential applications include intelligent security, innovative design and digital creativity.

3. **Human-machine hybrid-augmented intelligence:** Research into human-machine hybrid intelligence requires the integration and cooperativity of biological-intelligence systems with machine-intelligence systems, resulting in higher levels of intelligence – by driving towards greater collaboration between humans and machines. Potential applications include wearable devices, robotics, aided education and products related to human-machine integration.

4. **Autonomous-intelligence systems:** Research into autonomous-intelligence systems includes the development of autonomous machinery, intelligent manufacturing and smart vehicles. It also involves a focus on technology, architecture, platforms and design standards. Potential

applications include unmanned vehicles, service equipment, robotics, aided education and intelligent factories.

5. **International collaborative research:** Research via thinktanks, government agencies and research institutions should be combined across national and international borders to help develop AI 2.0 that also includes social, economic and ethical causes. Without this approach, we are likely to miss an opportunity to develop the future AI-powered society that is underpinned by **FATE: F**airness, **A**ccountability, **T**ransparency and **E**thics (Hecktman and Spicknall, 2018).

All of the above will be accelerated with arguably the most exciting emerging technology, 'quantum computing' which will revolutionise Artificial Intelligence, Machine Learning and Big Data through increased computational power and data availability, as well as algorithmic advances. Today, this has launched trending research known as 'Quantum Machine Learning' or QML (Huggins et al., 2019).

QML will help reduce the time required to train a neural network and by doing so introduce an entirely new framework for deep learning. Although quantum computing is a physical reality today, it is still some years away from being able to compete with and thereafter quickly surpass, classical computers. When that time comes, it will herald a paradigm shift that will pave the way for Artificial General Intelligence.

Will we continue on current trajectories of growing inequality, or will current radical niches (social, technological or economic) spread and dominate? What will determine the path(s) we take? One thing is for certain, particularly in the context of climate change, 'business as usual' is not an option.

CONCLUSION

Using technology to empower social, cultural and economic change is just as important in every conversation we have nationally and internationally about protecting any downsides and unintended consequences. Breaking cultural barriers, empowering under-represented races, inspiring curiosity and creativity and empowering societies – all of these values and initiatives can be supported by combining AI with other emerging technologies such as IoT, VR, AR and Blockchain.

However, if we backtrack to the William Gibson's quote, 'The future is already here – it's just not very evenly distributed', we also need to address social and structural inequalities prevalent across society throughout countries across our world. While we attempt this, we should keep in mind that social and structural inequalities vary from person to person, group to group, policy area to policy area and place to place.

In the UK, much has changed over the last decade. The combination of an unprecedented squeeze on wages, sustained austerity for public services and a shrinking social security safety net has resulted in the year-on-year progress in household living standards stopping abruptly. The economic disillusionment and rise of in-work poverty this has created has contributed to the sense of anger and division that has accompanied much of the debate around BREXIT – the UK's exit from the EU – with individuals appearing to increasingly adopt a 'them and us' view of society.

The inequalities to which we refer to are enacted at a group level – covering gender, race, disability, sexual orientation, trans status and class, for instance. Individuals are subject to extra layers of structural inequalities as a direct result of their membership of these groups. It's why gender pay gaps and disability employment gaps persist, even when we control for factors such as education level. The implication is that it isn't enough to focus on improving the rules of the game when the playing field itself is inherently uneven.

The language of inequalities also often contains negative connotations – being bound up with notions of a battle, 'them and us' and seen to have deficit implications. This affects social attitudes, policy formation and creation and doesn't sufficiently articulate the benefits of creating an equal society. In advocating for a truly cohesive society the language of equality should also unite communities regardless of their ethnicity, race or economic circumstances. If we are to act as advocates of equality ourselves, we need to somehow develop and share an understanding of what we mean by the language of inequalities. Otherwise, we will fail to sincerely tackle the structural inequalities in UK (or indeed any) society.

Presently, there are inconsistencies in the ways monitoring, collection and use of data at local and national levels of government and across the devolved nations. A lack of alignment of data methods and sources can also lead to evidence gaps, complications in tracking change over time and difficulties in building a holistic picture of inequalities across the country. Local government should be supported to change this to ensure that they are systematically collecting and analysing the data they hold for the benefit of their communities and improving service provision.

As well as addressing inconsistencies in data collection, there is also a need to better link data, for example across central government services, to gain a deeper understanding of the types of inequalities. Reduced funding for data collection results in trimming of sample sizes which further reduces the effectiveness, appropriateness and usefulness of data sets.

Additionally, there is a need for analysts and researchers to consider how best to future-proof evidence collection to ensure access to continuous, comparable data. For example, to understand the effect of social media on (mental) health and its relationship to education and work, surveys and data questions need to be adapted to fit changing lives and shifting definitions of mental health and to keep pace with advances in technology and medicine. Adopting new methodologies that provide opportunities for more sophisticated and impactful analysis should also be explored. In particular, computational models could be used in conjunction with machine learning to undertake more accurate analysis of which variables are causing inequalities in particular policy areas. Taken together, this opens the door for AI to help.

However, government investment and support is required to support data collection and human resources to support analysis and reporting. Certainly, we have more information and knowledge at our disposal than ever before and there is an overabundance of experts – in academia, government, local communities and business – all working on inequality issues. AI could potentially be used to analyse and make sense of the volumes of data that are at our disposal. However, paradoxically, we run the risk of bias in the same AI systems that we seek to help us unlock the dilemmas brought about by inequality.

With the advent of AI 2.0, we can look forward to a world built on integrated natural intelligence and artificial intelligence to enhance our human intellectual and societal capabilities. This lays the ground for a future society where AI is closely integrated into human life (cross-media and autonomous systems) to the point of being a part of the human body (hybrid-augmented intelligence) – without humans giving up control, either willingly or unwillingly.

AI 2.0 will give rise to a future society that is capable of reading, managing and recombining human knowledge (computational knowledge engine) in order to make suggestions for social problems, including daily life, production, resource usage and the environment (intelligent cities and intelligent medicine). From the standpoint of recognition, control, translation and prediction in some specialised fields, AI is currently comparable to or exceeds human levels.

With the assistance of AI 2.0, humans will be able to obtain better insight and effective management to interact with complex macroscopic systems involving urban development, ecological protection, economic management and financial risk. This will also be conducive to solving specific problems, such as medical treatment, product design, safe driving and energy conservation. If we collectively build products, solutions and services with human values, we can create, augment and support our world for better outcomes – for all. Every product is worth designing responsibly while also addressing social and psychological issues to develop help develop ethical and trustworthy products.

As we usher in the 'Fourth Industrial Revolution', AI-powered technology has the potential to help with food sustainability, healthcare, clean water, mental health, education, retail banking and land rights. Through technological collaborations, governments need to continue to work and learning together to implement solutions that can help deliver a higher quality of life to all citizens – nationally and internationally. This is potentially good news for the underserved people who are living below the poverty line.

When the day comes, when the lives of people living in poverty are no longer plagued with disease, stress and inhumane working conditions, then our societies can truly be 'civilised' and we can look forward to a future world where business and society are shaped by 'AI for good' – for all.

REFERENCES

Audley, S., & Ginsburg, J. L. (2019). Caring as an Authoritative Act: Re-Thinking Respect for Students and Teachers. In K. Daniels & K. Billingsley (Eds.), *Creating Caring and Supportive Educational Environments for Meaningful Learning* (pp. 154–182). doi:10.4018/978-1-5225-5748-7.ch009

Brunkard, P. (2018). The Future of IoT is AI. *Tech UK*. https://www.techuk.org/insights/opinions/item/13827-the-future-of-iot-is-ai

CB Insights. (2019). *The Race For AI: Here Are The Tech Giants Rushing To Snap Up Artificial Intelligence Start-ups*. https://www.cbinsights.com/research/top-acquirers-ai-startups-ma-timeline/

Chatterton, T., & Newmarch, G. (2016). *The Future is Already Here, it's Just Not Very Evenly Distributed. Everyday Futures*. Lancaster: Institute for Social Futures. http://wp.lancs.ac.uk/everydayfutures/essay-collection/

Daniels, K., & Billingsley, K. (2019). *Creating Caring and Supportive Educational Environments for Meaningful Learning*. Hershey, PA: IGI Global. doi:10.4018/978-1-5225-5748-7

Ebadi, B. (2018). *Artificial Intelligence Could Magnify Social Inequality.* https://www.cigionline.org/articles/artificial-intelligence-could-magnify-social-inequality

Eckerson, W. W. (2020). The Rise of Unified Data and Analytic Platforms: The Case for Convergence. *Eckerson Group.* https://www.infor.com/en-sg/resources/the-rise-of-unified-data-and-analytic-platforms

Hansen, A. (2019). AI Proving to Be an Integral Part of Cryptocurrency High Volume Transaction Security. *Hacknoon.* https://hackernoon.com/ai-proving-to-be-an-integral-part-of-cryptocurrency-high-volume-transaction-security-cc20a40d23c7

Harford, T. (2017). Why didn't electricity immediately change manufacturing? *BBC World Service. 50 Things That Made the Modern Economy.*

Hecktman, A. J., & Spicknall, S. (2018). Building Ethical AI in Chicago and Beyond. *Microsoft Blog.* https://blogs.microsoft.com/chicago/2018/08/02/ethical-ai-in-chicago-and-beyond/

Huggins, W., Patil, P., Mitchell, B., Whaley, K. B., & Stoudenmire, E. M. (2019). Towards quantum machine learning with tensor networks. IOP Publishing Ltd. *Quantum Science and Technology, 4*(2), 2019. doi:10.1088/2058-9565/aaea94

Huillet, M. (2019). *11 Years Ago, Today Satoshi Nakamoto Published the Bitcoin White Paper.* https://cointelegraph.com/news/11-years-ago-today-satoshi-nakamoto-published-the-bitcoin-white-paper

Huntress, C. (2017). *My Favourite Quote of All Time is a Misattribution.* https://caelanhuntress.com/2017/08/24/my-favourite-quote-of-all-time-is-a-misattribution/

Kalman, A. (2019). *Artificial Intelligence and Virtual Reality.* https://fullycharged.show/blog/artificial-intelligence-and-virtual-reality/

Morris, S., Patel, O., Stainthorp, C., & Stevenson, O. (2019). *'Structurally unsound'. Exploring Inequalities: Igniting research to better inform UK policy.* https://www.ucl.ac.uk/grand-challenges/sites/grand-challenges/files/structurally-unsound-report.pdf

Nakamoto, S. (2008). *Bitcoin: A Peer-to-Peer Electronic Cash System.* Academic Press.

Pan, Y. (2016). Heading toward Artificial Intelligence 2.0. *Engineering, 2*(4), 409-413.

Quality-Harper, C., & Stock, D. (2019). *James Lovelock says artificial intelligence is the start of new life.* https://www.newscientist.com/article/2209648-james-lovelock-says-artificial-intelligence-is-the-start-of-new-life/#ixzz66BkePm7o

Schmelzer, R. (2019). *AI and Blockchain: Double the Hype or Double the Value?* https://www.forbes.com/sites/cognitiveworld/2019/10/24/ai-and-blockchain-double-the-hype-or-double-the-value/

Szabo, N. (1997). The Idea of Smart Contracts. *Satoshi Nakamoto Institute.* https://nakamotoinstitute.org/the-idea-of-smart-contracts/

Toole, J. (2019). *Combining artificial intelligence and augmented reality in mobile apps.* https://heartbeat.fritz.ai/combining-artificial-intelligence-and-augmented-reality-in-mobile-apps-e0e0ad2cfddc

Zubaşcu, F. (2019). New petascale computers to boost research in central and eastern Europe. *Science Business.* https://sciencebusiness.net/news/new-petascale-computers-boost-research-central-and-eastern-europe

ENDNOTE

[1] NVIDIA is powering the world's fastest supercomputers to accelerate AI-powered research and technology (Source: https://www.nvidia.com/en-gb/industries/supercomputing/).

Chapter 10
Closing Thoughts

ABSTRACT

In this chapter, the authors present final observations and concluding thoughts about the future social implications of artificial intelligence (AI). One of the major reasons why humans stand out from other creatures is because of our mental capacity and demonstration of intelligence. However, AI has the potential to eclipse human potential with the same and potentially greater capacity as it matures towards 'general' and 'super' intelligence. However, the immediate challenge remains our capacity to feel safe with AI innovations and to have faith in their capacity to conduct themselves without prejudice, to eliminate any mistakes, and to conduct themselves in an equitable manner. It is expected that humanity will have a better understanding of what principles of awareness and aptitude are. Thankfully, these are issues with a lot of relevance in the modern world; the opportunity to develop an AI future society with positive benefits is achievable – if we act collectively and multi-laterally on a global scale.

"By far, the greatest danger of Artificial Intelligence is that people conclude too early that they understand it." –Eliezer Yudkowsky

DOI: 10.4018/978-1-7998-4607-9.ch010

INTRODUCTION

There is no doubt that artificial intelligence (AI) has already impacted our daily lives and the ways we operate in Industry 4.0, manufacturing, healthcare, online security etc. AI and its sub-components of computer vision, natural language processing, machine learning (ML) and intelligent algorithms have had a great impact on new digital technology, quantum computing, data analytics and consumer services. It is likely that the upward trends of capabilities of AI systems will continue, in which systems eventually become capable of solving a wide range of tasks rather than a new system having to be built for each new problem. Additionally, the adoption of AI within many industries will continue. Evidence suggests that AI is currently unable to reproduce human behaviours or surpass our thinking capabilities. It is likely to stay a complementary workforce tool for a very long time. However, continuous improvements could reach a point where AI exceeds current expectations. The continued development of AI will depend on moral public opinion regarding its benefits and acceptability, on businesses continuing to gain competitive advantages from it and continued funding for its research and development. Simultaneously, AI is inspiring both fear and enthusiasm in equal measures. Some have likened the advances in AI to an inevitable dystopian future, perhaps because of the science fiction notion that machines will take all of our jobs, will 'wake up' and do unintended things. However, where some see danger and unimaginable disruption, others see great promise and positive social implications.

One of the greatest dilemmas we wrestle with is being able to incorporate AI-powered innovations in the most equitable, balanced and accountable manners possible. Each time there is an intense deliberation on the morals and ethics of AI innovation, we find ourselves in a stalemate that discourages advancement. The boundaries of decency, morality and good ethics should always remain at the core of human society. Our enduring search for discerning what is good and fair predates history and continues to be strongly debated by spiritual, traditional leaders and thinkers across industry, institutions and governments. However, when we consider the way AI is fast-becoming an inextricable part of our society, the study of the opportunities, ramifications and unintended consequences must continue.

When considering an AI future, perhaps the most deplorable scenario will be the one in which AI becomes sentient and self-serving with total neglect of our human and societal needs. In this scenario, creating AI is a recklessly irresponsible venture. However, in the short term, within the next decade, anticipated dangers and doubts should be clarified before AI becomes widespread to avoid arriving at this dark future. We should, therefore, seek ways to evolve together with AI innovation and remain steadfast in our goal to arrive at a future where AI will be deployed in an accountable manner that allows it to be handed down to posterity. AI has the capacity to modify our processes of assimilation and sufficiently advanced our society to ensure that we are continually in an atmosphere that supports the harmless transmission of knowledge.

AI will certainly have some human-entry prejudices. Thus, it is imperative to innovate AI to free itself from any prejudice. Ultimately, we must ensure a future in which AI and humans are closely coupled to create advances that benefit society globally, regardless of borders.

CREATING OUR CHILDREN'S FUTURE

Throughout this book, we have remarked on the potential of AI to fundamentally transform basic and fundamental aspects of our modern world across diverse industries, emerging markets etc. However, as the AI future unfolds, we, the parents and adults of this generation, must prepare our children to inhabit a future full of new challenges and opportunities with potentially fewer social and structural inequalities and better prospects in relation to jobs, health and security. The well-being of all children and young people across society should include goals of

- reducing inequalities in childhood
- ensuring children and young people have a strong voice in all matters that affect their lives
- promoting positive images of children and young people
- enhancing the health and well-being of all children and young people
- encouraging positive and supportive family and other environments

Additionally, there are environmental issues, such as *climate change*, which many of today's children and youth are concerned about. It affects their lives today, and it will transform their lives as adults. Few other topics have caused as much enthusiasm and public response, as passionately led by Swedish teenage climate activist, Greta Thunberg, who has already inspired millions of people to join her in her climate strikes across the world (BBC News, 2019). As a generation of leaders, we (adults) have failed in our responsibilities towards our children and our environment. Next, we must think and act to enable the coming generation to be more successful by

- empowering children and young people to become activists for change
- partnering with our children and young people in decision making
- helping with skills development and understanding that will enable sustainable living
- advocating for our children and young people to influence change at all levels
- making sure that the services needed by our children and young people are fit for purpose
- promoting fairness and social justice
- protecting those children who will be affected the most

Additionally, we must take a long hard look at our own lifestyles, as employees, as parents and as citizens, to ensure that our daily choices and business practices help mitigate or negate social, environmental and economic damages. Similarly, the emergence of AI is seen as an issue affecting how we live our lives sustainably and fairly. This will also require sustainable living, quality of life and social improvements to be balanced within our planet's resources, while preserving the same resources for future generations.

A future in which humans are augmented by AI technologies for the betterment of society and our young people must be underpinned by sustainable living built upon three interrelated key elements:

- **Social Sustainability:** aiming to deliver positive social outcomes, such as through education and housing
- **Economic Sustainability:** focusing on building economically viable communities and businesses
- **Environmental Sustainability:** living within the capacity of our planet's resources and preserving them for future generations.

Moreover, creating an AI-powered future society is a moral issue, one that also should consider environmental and social concerns by determining what we value and how we want to live our lives. Working together and alongside children, we can be pioneers in new thinking and action and in creating a positive and optimistic story for the future.

These things require stringent policy frameworks and government support. In the UK, DfES[1] has established 'Every Child Matters' (ECM) (DfES, 2004), an overarching framework for the development of a national children's policy and for the structure and delivery of children's services. ECM outcomes are also enshrined in legislation through the definition of child well-being provided in the Children Act 2004. Although the definition is focused on the social and economic aspects of children's lives and makes no specific reference to the relationship between well-being and environment, these links are important and are gaining greater recognition. The Department for Children, Schools and Families (now the 'Department for Education') has endorsed the Sustainable Development Commission's Every Child's Future Matters (SDC, 2007) report, demonstrating the relevance of the environment to ensuring children's well-being and arguing for the use of sustainable development as a valuable framework through which to achieve improved outcomes for children. Below are examples of how sustainable living is integral to achieving child well-being as defined in the 2004 Act.

- **Physical, mental and emotional health:** promoting health and well-being through providing things to do and places to go, such as open and green spaces, and promoting active and sustainable travel, such as dedicated cycle routes and easy access to reasonably priced healthy local produce.
- **Protection from harm and neglect:** creating safe and pleasant environments/communities where people want to live, work and play, supporting community cohesion and attracting business growth and investment, such as child- and family-centred urban planning.
- **Education, training and recreation:** providing opportunities for education, training, employment and volunteering, which instil values and skills that cultivate quality of life and ecologically responsible lifestyles grounded in a sense of care of themselves, one another and the environment around them while promoting economic well-being.
- **Contributing to society:** matching children and young people's desires to improve their environments with opportunities to act and enabling them and their families to shape their community and foster a sense of mutual care and respect for themselves, each other and their environment.
- **Social and economic well-being:** creating sustainable communities where strategies are in place for environmental management, including

the reduction of waste, careful use/preservation of natural resources and reduction in carbon emissions.

Jobs and Skills

Most adults were raised on the idea that, as long as you chose a good area of study, put in the hours and do well in exams at school and university, you re guaranteed a decent job that will most likely turn into a lifelong career. However, today, much like our parents, one of our primary concerns when it comes to our children is making sure they secure the skills and tools needed to succeed as they enter the workforce. To prepare our children for a future that will involve technologies such as AI, we must first come to grips with the current educational system, understand the ways in which it *cheats* our children of their personal and professional development and take steps ourselves to equip them with the tools they need to succeed in the age of AI.

Our modern-day educational system is outdated, unfitting and no longer works. Often referred to as the *factory model of education*, the current system essentially prepares young people to become identically programmed commodities by teaching them a very rigid set of theories and skills. Thus, it pushes out identical versions of the same product. This may have been effective in the past, because the purpose was to train civil servants requiring limited and specific skill sets. However, it is grossly inadequate for the needs of children who will be working in 4th Industrial Revolution and beyond. Simply put, our current education system is preparing our children for jobs that will be irrelevant by the time they are adults. Most researchers believe that up to 65% of children in primary school will end up working in jobs that do not yet even exist (Davidson, 2012). Moreover, our children will not have the luxury of a stable career and job security. Worryingly, today's younger generation is showing diminishing feelings of loyalty to their current employers and are in constant search for learning opportunities, growth and flexibility.

In research carried out by Price–Waterhouse, the factor that most highly correlated with potential job automation is the education level of the individual worker that currently performs it. Thus, to ensure our children have 'future-proof' skills, some form of government intervention will almost certainly be needed. This could potentially include a revision of the UK's primary-school curriculum, both in terms of technical content (i.e. data literacy, logic, problem solving) and teaching methods (i.e. a focus on interpersonal skills, emotional intelligence etc.). Our belief is that parents must develop and encourage their children to face all of these upcoming challenges and, together, invest their time and energies focusing on the 4 'Cs': creativity, coding, communication and confidence (Tse et al., 2019).

Health and Well-being

With the development of new technology in recent years, most children and young people now use at least one form of technology every day. Activities include using the internet to do homework, watching online content and using social-media platforms to communicate. Increased ownership of personal devices, such as smart phones, tablets and laptops, has also affected how children and young people use technology. Thus, concerns have been raised about their usage becoming more private and more difficult for parents to monitor. Additionally, there are other concerns and unintended consequences relating to cyberbullying, social media and screen time. Hence, it is important for governments to create policies to help protect the safety and well-being online of children. Internet safety has become an integral part of child safeguarding in the UK, with the UK government announcing its intention to make it the safest place in the world for children and adults to be online.

A 2017 literature review carried out by the research group at the UK Council for Child Internet Safety (UKCCIS) noted that the proportion of children aged 5–16 using the internet had reached about 94% (UKCCIS, 2017). They also noted that the amount of time children spend online continues to rise steadily. The review highlighted risks that could be encountered online:

- 1 in 10 young children and 1 in 5 teens say they had encountered something worrying or nasty online in the past year.
- children's top worries are pornography and violence. They said that they had encountered these most often on video-sharing sites, followed by other websites, then social-networking sites and games.
- children are also concerned about the levels of advertising online, their spending too much time online, inappropriate contacts, rumours and bullying.
- the top parent concerns include online violence.

The 2017 House of Lords Communications Committee report, 'Growing Up with the Internet', examined the impact =the internet had had on children's development, well-being and mental health, highlighting several potential areas of concern which had

...centred on areas such as cyberbullying and access to unsuitable content, but there are other emerging areas of concern. Parent Zone told us that parents regularly worry about 'the commercialisation of childhood, the wholesale capturing of children's data and excessive screen time'. Our witnesses also highlighted concern about the lack of regulation, the need to protect children's rights and the importance of encouraging online parenting (House of Lords, 2017).

An inquiry by the Children's Society also highlighted the negative health impacts of cyberbullying (Children's Society, 2018). It found that children who were currently experiencing mental-health problems were more than three-times likely to have been bullied online. The charity also argued that, although offline bullying remained the most common form, 'it is clear that cyberbullying is distinct and potent, particularly due to its potential to be relentless'. The report noted that, in an online environment, a bully can attack their victim 24-hours-per-day. Furthermore, the inquiry reported that 83% of young people said social-media companies should do more to tackle cyberbullying on their platforms, with many feeling that the onus to act was on the person experiencing cyberbullying. A perceived lack of consequences for perpetrators was also a theme identified by the charity, with young people reporting that the penalties existing for offline actions do not exist for similar behaviours online. Additionally, the inquiry found that 82% of young people thought social-media companies should do more to promote mental health.

The old adage is that 'there is still no substitute for time spent playing in nature'. Those benefits have had more research and development than any of today's devices and virtual assistants, such as Amazon Alexa and Google Home. Interestingly, we should take note of the fact that many of the tech pioneers and leaders, such as Steve Jobs and Bill Gates, have banned their own children from using mobile phones and smart devices. We should be more concerned about the potential side-effects from digital technology usage and pay more attention to the emotional and psychological well-being of our children and youth.

Security and Privacy

National strategies and ethical guidelines released by the UK government, non-profit and private-sector organisations seek to maximise the benefits of AI systems in ways that respect human rights and values. However, their documents have dedicated very little attention to children and the impact of

AI on them. The rights of children, as current users of AI-enabled systems and the future inhabitants of a more AI-saturated world, must be a critical consideration in AI development. How can we ensure that AI strategies, policies and ethical guidelines protect and uphold child rights? To begin to answer this question, UNICEF hosted a workshop at its New York headquarters to inform the development of AI policy guidance aimed at governments, corporations and UN agencies. The event was attended by over 60 experts, including representatives from the governments of Finland, Sierra Leone and the UAE. The group spent one-and-a-half days exploring existing AI principles and what they meant for child rights, brainstorming how to implement these principles and generating strategies for effective engagement of all the relevant stakeholders to make child-sensitive AI a reality.

This subsequently led to a 2-year initiative to explore approaches to protecting and upholding child rights ways in an evolving AI world. For this initiative, UNICEF has partnered with the Government of Finland and the IEEE Standards Association and is collaborating with the Berkman Klein Centre for Internet and Society, the World Economic Forum and other organisations that form part of Generation AI, to do the following:

- discuss UNICEF's draft principles about AI systems being based on for children
- uphold child rights
- Prioritise children's development and well-being
- Protect and nurture children's data agency
- Ensure transparency, explainable and accountability for children
- Prioritise safety, protection and AI literacy of children
- Prioritise equity and inclusion of children

Without a child-centred foundation to AI development, children's rights to learn, play and participate freely are at risk. Yet, as Brent Barron (Director of Public Policy, CIFAR) explained in his review of 18 national AI strategies and policies, there is currently little focus on the issue of inclusion. Building on CIFAR's work, UNICEF is conducting a review of published national AI documents to better understand what is and what is not being said about children. Steven Vosloo (Policy Specialist, UNICEF) shared initial findings in the form of a heatmap that indicates the level of emphasis each AI strategy places on issues which most impact children. The data implies that many governments are considering youth as a future workforce in the context of AI. However, very few are specifically addressing children's unique rights in a rapidly changing world. More importantly, the review reveals that remarkably little is being said about children in national strategies. In comparison, in most national strategy topics, such as industrialisation, national security and economic growth, receive comprehensive discussion.

Although it is important that we prepare our education system to meet the needs of a changing job market, health and well-being cannot be sacrificed to accomplish these ends. In all events, we (adults and parents) need to listen more to our children and other youth. After all, it is they who are actively growing up with and engaging with AI-powered gadgets and toys as if they are human rather than intelligent devices.

Societal Needs (of Children)

Technology is continuously disrupting our lives and presents one of the trickiest parenting challenges in the 21st century. Our children and young people are typically immersed in social-networking websites and online games. Worldwide, parents are becoming increasingly concerned about the way their children are being raised. Healthy children should be our goal. Put simply, there are two kinds of health we should tend to: physical *and* psychological (Hall, 2008). Most parents understand the importance of physical health. However, the psychological health of children is less understood. Built upon emotional bonds and relationships, these serve as core building blocks of social competencies that inform the development of social behaviours and psychological health that serve as 'scaffolding', as coined by Soviet psychologist, Lev Vygotsky (Vygotsky, 1978), to help children grow into adults who are the teachers, scientists, business leaders and entrepreneurs of tomorrow.

Jean Piaget's theory of cognitive development suggests that children move through four stages of mental development (Badakar et al., 2017). His theory focuses not only on understanding how children acquire knowledge, but also on understanding the nature of intelligence. Piaget's stages are:

1. **Sensorimotor stage:** birth to 2 years
2. **Preoperational stage:** ages 2–7
3. **Concrete operational stage:** ages 7–11
4. **Formal operational stage:** ages 12+

Piaget believed that children take an active role in the learning process, acting much like little scientists as they perform experiments, make observations and learn about the world. As children interact with the world around them, they continually add new knowledge, build upon existing knowledge and adapt previously held ideas to accommodate new information. It is often rightly said that a child's behaviour is a reflection of their parents. However, Piaget did not consider the effects of social setting and culture on the cognitive development. This, it is important that parents of the modern technology age carefully nurture their children's psychological health. Below are a set of advices aimed at guiding parents with this.

- Children's social skills
    - The first concerns are connected with the social skills of the children.
    - Children are spending most of their free time playing video games on the computer instead of going out and spending time with friends.
    - Their communication is limited, especially with their parents .
    - Face-to-face interaction is reduced to its minimum .
    - This is a huge threat to social development.
- Traditional reading and learning
    - Reading is very limited.
    - Children spend most of their time in front of a screen (e.g. television, computer, mobile phone or tablet) .
    - Tablets are replacing the notebooks.
    - Digital learning is now preferred.
    - Children will more likely Google something instead of searching for it in a book.
- Online (Cyber) Safety
    - Children share so much information on the internet that parents often cannot control or monitor it.
    - All parents ask questions like, 'Is the internet a safe place?'
    - Parents should protect their children. The least they can do is talk to them and explain the need to be careful when sharing information about their personal life on the internet.
- Health
    - Children spend much time in front of a screen. This affects their eyesight and general vision. Today, more children and young people wear glasses.
    - Children are also spending more time at home, sitting or lying on the bed instead being active.

- ○   Exercise is important for overall health.
- What should parents do?
  - ○   Parents should set some limits to technology.
  - ○   Make time to talk to children to share your ideas and discuss any anxieties and general feelings.
  - ○   Parents should encourage playtime in or outside the home to encourage and improve creativity, learning and thinking.
  - ○   Parents should aspire to be role models. Limiting your own use of technology will more likely benefit both parents and children.
  - ○   Find ways to talk to children rather than depend on technology as a surrogate. Try to be supportive and seek other strategies to teach children how to control their emotions.

To summarise, technology has pros and cons. It is not necessarily bad for children, but it should be used pragmatically. In all cases, children should feel that they can approach a parent or trusted adult who will always support and advise them.

The Road to an AI-Future

As adults, we must be the pioneers who fundamentally challenge governments, businesses and institutions to bring about a range of educational, social, economic, health, well-being and environmental outcomes enabled by AI technologies while ensuring our children's rights continue to be met. The following activities enable a community or organisation to do this.

- increase their understanding of why the issue is relevant to their organisation and to their beneficiaries and stakeholders
- connect an organisation's mission with the 'AI-Future' agenda
- identify existing entry points into organisational responses to an 'AI-Future'

An AI-Future agenda does not have be constrained to a simple a binary choice of humans vs, AI. Instead, it can be a combination of options as explored further in the sections below.

Human-centric AI Future

Is the future of business and technology so deeply intertwined that it leaves virtually no scope in the future for the subtleties and creativity of human intelligence and behaviour? The answer is surely 'no'! AI, in its current narrow form is still one of many tools that humans use for making better decisions. Equally, as AI matures, there will still be some element of human involvement, even if this is directed and managed by AI systems and intelligent algorithms. Maintaining the human element of an AI system will most certainly inform its success. This is based on the premise that AI exists to make human life simpler and richer and that it is critical for AI practitioners, researchers, developers and data scientists to adopt a human-centric approach to the development, deployment and adoption of AI.

How do we then build in the human element? This is where humanities-centric subjects of design and behavioural sciences are crucial. Simply put, behavioural sciences involve the study of internal cognitive processes of humans and societies and how these processes manifest into external perceptible and imperceptible actions and interactions. Behavioural science typically stands at a nexus of various subjects, borrowing aspects from sociology, anthropology, psychology, economics and political science. In technology the behavioural science impact how we build, use and interact with technology using human emotional intelligence traits best described by Maslow's hierarchy of needs (Maslow, 2011). This theory establishes that people are motivated by five basic categories of needs: physiological, safety, love, esteem and self-actualisation. A variation of this is based on data-science needs and is shown in Figure 1. Consider AI as the top of a pyramid of needs. Hence, self-actualisation (AI) is great, but one must first have data literacy, collection and infrastructure, which are equivalent to needing food, water and shelter in Maslow's hierarchy.

Figure 1. Data-science hierarchy of needs (inspired by Maslow's hierarchy)

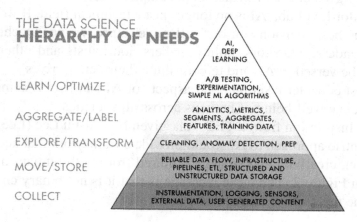

Below is a synopsis of the data-science pyramid (Rogati, 2017),

- At the bottom of the pyramid we have data collection. What data do you need, and what is available? After all, the right dataset is what made recent advances in ML possible.
- Next, how does the data flow through the system? How is it moved and stored?
- Only when data is accessible can one explore and transform it.
- Once we are can reliably explore and transform (e.g. clean) the data, we can start building business intelligence and data analytics by aggregating and labelling the data.
- Once we have labelled the data, we can use them to train AI systems and ML models. We then repeat a process where we learn and optimise the ML models to carry out some level of testing and experimentation before we are satisfied that the AI system does what we intend for it to do.

Stanford University's President, Marc Tessier-Lavigne, perhaps said it best when talking about a human-centric approach to AI, which has the potential to radically change how we live our lives. 'Now is our opportunity to shape that future by putting humanists and social scientists alongside people who are developing artificial intelligence,' he said. 'This approach aligns with Stanford's founding purpose to produce knowledge for the betterment of humanity' (Adams, 2019).

According to Fei-Fei Li, professor of computer science and former director of the Stanford AI Lab, 'AI is no longer just a technical field. If we're going to make the best decisions for our collective future, we need technologists, business leaders, educators, policy makers, journalists and other parts of society to be versed in AI, and to contribute their perspectives'.

We must consider leveraging all aspects of AI and ML systems in ways to promote the well-being of humans across all societies.

Taking inspiration from a TED Talk given by Kai-Fu Lee (Lee, 2018), a human-centric approach to AI would provide a framework that accounts for compassion, creativity and strategy required from both humans and AI, as outlined in Figure 2. The basic message is that it is not binary choices that explode the myth about humans versus AI.

Figure 2. Humans and AI, 'it is NOT a binary choice'

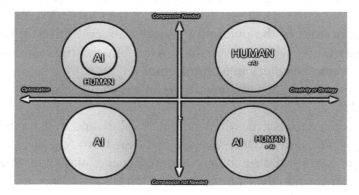

The above graph may not be perfect, but it highlights four ways that humans exist and work with AI. The axes include compassion, love and empathy: the things that AI cannot provide. 'Optimisation' remains the domain (and gift) of AI. Perhaps AI will ultimately take away routine jobs and, in due time, we may even be grateful. Eventually, with the emergence of 'General' and 'Super' AI, humans will be endowed with even smarter AI-powered tools that enable scientists, artists, musicians and writers to be more creative. This graph demonstrates a way of looking at an AI future through a human-centric lens. It allows us to maintain control over work that is creative and emotive:

- social workers to help us make this transition

- compassionate caregivers to give personalised medical care to more people
- teachers who engage and help our children giving them the necessary tools to survive and thrive in this brave new AI future world

Imagine still a future in which AI works with humans in the guise of analytical tools that allows us to rediscover our passion for exploring our world, re-focus on environmental concerns and regain control of our lives and surroundings. We may also be able to differentiate ourselves with jobs that are uniquely geared for humans that allow us to be compassionate and creative, using and leveraging what makes us human: our hearts, minds and consciousness. This could indeed be a blueprint for the coexistence of humans and AI.

FUTURE SOCIETAL CHALLENGES

We now return to the central question and theme that underpins this book:

'Is society ready for the opportunities – and challenges – of AI?'

The societal and technical challenges posed by AI are difficult and will become harder the longer we wait. They require insights and cooperation from the best minds in computer science and from experts in all domains that AI will impact. By making progress now, we will lay the foundations needed for the bigger changes that lie ahead. Some commentators have raised the prospect of human-level general AI. As Stephen Hawking and others have said, this would be the most transformative invention in human history and would need to be approached very carefully. Perhaps fortunately, we are still decades away, or possibly even centuries and we need that time to prepare. We need to start work on today's challenges of how to design AI so that we can understand it and control it and how to change our societal systems so that we gain the great benefits AI offers. We cannot assume that we will get it right the first time.

The benefits of AI cannot be understated. Developed correctly, AI will allow us to make better progress on the hard-scientific problems we will face in coming decades and might even prove crucial to a more sustainable life for our world's inhabitants. It will change the world for the better if we take the time to think and plan carefully. That said, there are non-technical challenges that lie ahead. The remainder of this chapter highlights structures and frameworks that will be required to lay the foundation for a world that comes together to collaborate, explore and create an AI future that benefits all citizens.

General Data Protection Regulation (GDPR) after Brexit

Brexit is, of course, a serious matter on many fronts, and it applies to data. First, data matters because of the free flow of information underpins much of our economy today. Organisations trade globally and suppliers are often based overseas. Sharing information is also important for security purposes to fight crime and analyse threats. However, this is only part of the problem. Although businesses can engineer solutions for data coming into the UK, the biggest risk is the effect on global competitiveness. We know data is essential to algorithms, and AI and ML are indeed shaping the way we live. AI is becoming yet another territory nations are competing upon, and we are witnessing a real race of AI nationalism. Two countries are ahead in this race: US and China. Both are home to the very few global digital businesses shaping our infosphere and future digital life (e.g. Amazon and Google). China is racing ahead with privacy-invasive AI-driven programmes, which mean constant scoring and monitoring of its citizens. Europe, meanwhile, is working on what we call 'ethical AI', rooted in the belief that AI must be human-centred, augment human capabilities and further our humanity rather than undermine it. However, missing is a coherent plan for the economic, political and ethical direction of AI. We know that AI is disruptive. No nation can stand alone to deal with the challenges of AI to maximise its benefits while minimising job losses, which are already fuelling right-wing politics. New sector-specific, cutting-edge regulations governing the digital arena are urgently needed as a solid investment in ethical AI to compete against nations having different approaches that ours.

It is now time to talk about the digital space in the same context that we talk about the environment. We know that pollution is not a matter for one nation state alone, and we know the importance of European regulations and investments in green economies. The digital space is no different. We need to care for it in the same way we must care for the environment. If we think of it that way, we will be better able to look after the opportunities and challenges of the infosphere.

GDPR after BREXIT

On 25 May 2018, the GDPR was introduced to give EU citizens more control over their personal data and how it is used. Before GDPR, if one bought goods or services online, the organisations from which the product was bought could collected information and personal data ranging from name, address, date of birth, workplace, relationship status, online viewing habits and more. The introduction of GDPR meant that organisations had to gain clear consent to collect this data, and it applied to all companies processing the data of people residing within the EU, regardless of the company's location. However, with the UK leaving the EU on 31 January 2020, its compliancy with GDPR is unclear. This is an important point to reflect on given the security concerns around data, which ultimately are the 'blood' that courses through the veins and arteries of AI systems and machines. At the end of the Brexit transition period on 31 December 2020, the UK's departure from the EU will affect the representative obligation for three types of organisations:

- UK-based companies selling to the EU, with no EU office
- International companies selling to the EU, whose only EU office is in the UK
- All companies (including those in the EU) selling to the UK with no UK office

During the transition period, the Information Commissioner's Office (ICO) has stated that existing rules on GDPR will continue to apply to the UK, and they said it will be 'business as usual for data protection'.

Overall, Brexit will have a huge effect on many businesses; not just those in the UK and EU, but around the world. One of the effects relating to data protection and GDPR is that the position in respect of the Data Protection Representative obligation to be altered for many organisations. This includes the creation of a new UK Data Protection Representative role, a requirement for companies outside the UK selling into the UK. Table 1 presents a tabulated summary of the effects of BREXIT on GDPR.

Table 1. Effects of BREXIT on GDPR (DPR Group²)

Controller/Processor Locations	Sell to UK Only		Sell to (non-UK) EU Only		Sell to UK and Rest of EU	
	Pre-Brexit	Post-Brexit	Pre-Brexit	Post-Brexit	Pre-Brexit	Post-Brexit
UK only (or UK and rest of world)	None	None	None	EU Representative required	None	EU Representative required
EU only (or EU and rest of the world)	None	UK Representative required	None	None	None	UK Representative required
Rest of world only	EU Representative required	UK Representative required	EU Representative required	EU Representative required	EU Representative required	EU & UK Representative required
UK and EU (or UK, EU and rest of world)	None	None	None	None	None	None

If negotiations have not been finalised by the end of 2020, previous government guidance would allow data to move from the UK to countries in the European Economic Area (EEA) without control over the flow of data in the opposite direction. The ICO recommends organisations consider what safeguards can be put into place to ensure data can still flow into the EU. If a data transfer agreement is not formalised by the end of the transition period, organisations relying on EEA data transfers may have to find alternative transfer mechanisms.

BREXIT and China

As a result of Brexit, China faces both enormous economic challenges and political uncertainties in future relations with its largest trading partner, the EU. Although the UK's vote to leave creates an unexpected dilemma for Chinese leadership, whose EU policy focuses largely on gaining vast market access, it also presents a rare opportunity for China to harness its policy instruments and diversify its initiatives to pursue its economic goals with European partners. As a pre-condition to achieving the desired outcome, Beijing will need to untangle its foreign policy decision-making processes. Against this backdrop, we now illuminate post-Brexit Sino–British relations and reflect on the possible impacts of Brexit upon future relations between Beijing and Brussels. We also analyse the very complex foreign policy-making mechanism in Beijing in terms of its economic policy goals with the EU.

The international system is experiencing a period of turbulent change, with two paradigmatic shifts that affect all actors and relationships: the rise of a multipolar system and the proliferation of populist/authoritarian tendencies. As a result of such shifts, it is no longer meaningful to separate the internal from the international arena, because the two spheres closely interact with each other. In this turbulent context, there are definite links between the rise of the multipolar system and the proliferation of populist/authoritarian tendencies, as reflected in the widespread analysis on the 'illiberal turn' and diffusion of power in the international system.

Global Context

The international system has experienced several systemic changes over the past century with the rise and decline of different modalities, characterised as unipolar, bipolar and multipolar systems. In the present era, we have witnessed a major diffusion of power in the international system away from the west, with the rise of new actors in the international system leading to the formation of a multipolar system. However, this time it is more complex and involves not only new state actors, but also transnational, societal and even individual actors. The multipolar system has evolved towards two primary tendencies: multilateralism, where patterns of cooperation predominate, or unilateralism, where power politics and conflict dominate the system. At present, promoting multilateralism is increasingly challenging as a result of the rise of unilateral/bilateral orientations among major actors, coupled with the proliferation of populist/authoritarian tendencies.

The change of orientation in the US from a multilateral to a unilateral one, brought on by the Trump presidency, has led to tensions in transatlantic relations and has made the post-war multilateral framework more fragile. Additionally, the rise of populist/authoritarian tendencies and Brexit have created a more conducive environment for unilateral and bilateral tendencies.

European Context

The project of European integration has faced multiple crises in recent years, ranging from economic downturn to refugee crisis and the rise of populist/ authoritarian challenges. The ensuing Brexit drama in this context has created a debate about the disintegration of the EU. It is not yet known how Brexit will evolve, but it has not yet resulted in the disintegration of the EU. It has, however, made the multilateral orientation of the EU even more fragile. Whether the UK will establish a trade deal with the EU and continue to be part of the rules-based multilateral order or if it will exit without a deal and follow policies in line with unilateral or bilateral tendencies will be a crucial factor in determining the future of the multilateral system. Thus, if the EU cannot find strong enough allies in Brazil, Canada, India, Japan and others to fight for the multilateral system, or it fails to even try, then the EU will probably disintegrate, and nationalism and conflicts will re-emerge.

To keep multilateralism alive, Europe first needs to make it work within the union itself. The presence of four ambassadors of EU member states at the opening of the US Embassy in Jerusalem shows that we are not quite there. However, Europeans should keep working together within and in defence of international multilateral institutions and agreements, such as the Iran deal, knowing that there may (hopefully) be a new US administration in place in a little more than 2 years. Globalisation and digitisation create mutual dependence, and most challenges require rules and solutions beyond borders. From internet governance to trade and from climate change to migration, agreement and cooperation towards shared solutions are essential. What can Europe do, if necessary?

- Build a web of free-trade agreements with like-minded nations and regional groupings
- Meet its Paris Climate Accord targets and set ambitious new ones, including financing climate adaptation in poor countries
- Use EU trade, aid and institution-building tools more effectively, starting with the Balkans, where the goal of membership gives us most leverage
- Leverage our rule-setting power over data protection, privacy and technical norms to build multilateral standards.

Unlike in the early 2000s, the EU is less dogmatic and outspoken in its defence of effective multilateralism, as reflected in the 2016 EU global strategy. Europe may well have to bond with China and/or Russia to keep international consensus alive. This will prove sensitive. However, the multilateral reflex is strong, and opposing Trump internally could help forge both EU unity and cohesion, as has happened before.

The Decline of Multilateralism

The world appears to be gradually moving away from multilateral to unilateral order. Given the role of the key US role in creating and largely upholding the multilateral order, it is not surprising that considerable international concern over multilateralism's future has been framed, explicitly or implicitly, around changing US rhetoric and policy under the Trump Administration. Voices from around the globe have offered a robust riposte on the importance of preserving multilateral outlooks and institutions. Even China, a troublesome actor (to some) in its own right, has capitalised on the new American rhetoric to bemoan 'international rules and multilateral mechanisms [that] are under attack.'

In part, this uncertainty stems from the fact that the American commitment to multilateralism is a voluntary self-constraint on the US' own power. As either the most powerful state among a set of countries (as in the Cold War) or as the most powerful state within the entire system (as in the post-Cold War), the bare truth is that the US has invested in multilateral systems by its own choice and its own choices alone. The resurgence of geopolitical tensions with Russia and China began to coincide with a severe weakening of support for multilateralism in its traditional transatlantic bastion. Brexit continues to damage European regional multilateralism within the EU and consumes much political bandwidth. The broader EU remains wracked by nationalist and anti-integrationist currents that are undercutting the supranational bloc's capabilities as a global actor. Russian influence operations throughout the west has stoked internal fissures to both hobble and divide the historical defenders of multilateral order. Meanwhile in Washington, if the multilateral order defined the post-Cold War was grounded in a set of 'rules, institutions, partnerships and political norms about how states do business with each other,' the Trump administration has had little interest in it.

Outside of government, a nationalist–unilateralist strand exists in the broader American body politic. A May 2019 Centre for American Progress survey classified 33% of respondents as 'Trump nationalists,' prioritising high military spending, a focus on the home front and countering immigration and 'others taking advantage of us on trade.'

Some hope that multilateral institutions can subdue geopolitical rivalries. If the return of geopolitical competition is a choice made by US, then investing in multilateral systems could stymie power politics. It requires rallying the determination to collectively will our way out of the adversarial mindset. Just as with the internet or social media, it cannot be assumed that multilateralism in any form inexorably bends the arc of history towards justice. Although the exact relationship between illiberalism and multilateralism requires further study, the evidence today illustrates a campaign by authoritarian states to redefine the rules undergirding the multilateral order, whether by assertive action within institutions or the creation of parallel structures. Here, China's ambitions loom large.

Chinese President Xi Jinping, as Liza Tobin articulated, 'intends to realign global governance across at least five major dimensions: politics, development (to include economics, society and technology), security, culture and the environment'. China 'has shifted from its traditionally more defensive posture to a more activist role' at the UN Human Rights Council. While not a new actor in this space, Beijing's actions appear increasingly forward-leaning as it seeks to 'block criticism' and 'promote Chinese interpretation of principles on sovereignty and human rights'.

The modern strategy of 'competitive multilateralism' recognises that the return of great power competition necessitates a similar balance today. Rather than focusing exclusively on protecting the cooperative dynamics that defined the post-Cold War environment, this approach seeks to expand the scope of multilateralism to recover Cold-War lessons of international institutions as tools for conflict prevention and arenas for competition. Next is a framework elaborating the three dimensions of competitive multilateralism.

- **Multilateralism as facilitating cooperation:** Issues such as counterterrorism, combatting infectious disease, poverty alleviation and most importantly, climate change will continue to bedevil humanity. Any sufficient response to these transnational threats, as Jake Sullivan wrote, 'needs to be global, bringing the US together with its rivals — including China — to face shared challenges' because 'none of [these threats] can be effectively confronted by the US alone'.
- **Multilateralism as supporting conflict prevention:** Looking to more contentious situations, multilateral institutions can remain a significant force in conflict prevention. This is particularly true via prevention's original form: that among the major powers. While rarely sufficient on their own, multilateral fora historically have served as tools to assist key states in deescalating and containing spiralling crises. Multilateral deconfliction initiatives also must consider the implications of technological developments altering the international landscape. This is particularly urgent in two respects. First, many emerging domains lack robust, or even existent, international architectures to respond to a crisis involving new technologies. Cyberwarfare, drone warfare, advances in biotechnology, space and AI all reflect critical new competitive arenas among not only great powers, but also potentially smaller states and non-state actors as barriers to entry decreases. It

remains an open question whether or not existing multilateral fora can manage potential conflict in these spaces or if the world requires original institutions to mitigate these threats.

- **Multilateralism as spaces for competition:** Democratic policymakers and the public must grapple with the reality of authoritarian powers. What differs today, however, is an international environment defined by globalisation's deepening of interconnections and interdependence of economies, information and technology between democratic and authoritarian societies. What remains to be seen is whether they will be utilised to expand authoritarianism's reach or coordinate a democratic pushback by
  - Continuing collaboration on shared challenges
  - Creating off-ramps for crises that risk spiralling into conflict
  - Competing with authoritarian regimes selectively within existing institutions and via new ones to uphold democracy

Given these political topics, it is only fitting to end with a selection of 'Asilomar AI Principles' (verbatim) developed by The Future of Life Institute (Tegmark et al., 2017). These principles were signed by 1274 AI/Robotics researchers and 2541 others.

- **Capability caution:** There being no consensus, we should avoid strong assumptions regarding upper limits on future AI capabilities.
- **Common good:** Superintelligence should only be developed in the service of widely shared ethical ideals and for the benefit of all humanity rather than one state or organisation.
- **Human control:** Humans should choose how and whether to delegate decisions to AI systems to accomplish human-chosen objectives.
- **Importance:** Advanced AI could represent a profound change in the history of life on earth and should be planned for and managed with commensurate care and resources.
- **Liberty and privacy:** The application of AI to personal data must not unreasonably curtail people's real or perceived liberties.
- **Non-subversion:** The power conferred by control of highly advanced AI systems should respect and improve, rather than subvert, the social and civic processes on which the health of society depends.
- **Recursive self-improvement:** AI systems designed to recursively self-improve or self-replicate in a manner that could lead to rapidly

increasing quality or quantity must be subject to strict safety and control measures.

- **Shared benefit:** AI technologies should benefit and empower as many people as possible.
- **Shared prosperity:** The economic prosperity created by AI should be shared broadly to benefit all of humanity.
- **Value alignment:** Highly autonomous AI systems should be designed so that their goals and behaviours can be assured to align with human values throughout their operation.

If society keeps in mind these principles and uses them in good faith, then perhaps we will succeed in realising the AI future that offers amazing opportunities that empowers people in the decades and centuries ahead for the benefit humankind universally.

FUTURE RESEARCH DIRECTIONS

It is our belief, that additional research development needs to take place to better understand the opportunities and potential of AI in the present *and* the future. The topics that are worthwhile exploring further include:

- Global governance, race conditions and international cooperation
- Economic impacts, labour shifts, inequality and technological unemployment
- Accountability, transparency and explainability
- Surveillance, privacy and civil liberties
- Fairness, ethics and human rights
- Political manipulation and computational propaganda
- Human dignity, autonomy and psychological impact
- Human health, augmentation and brain-computer interfaces
- AI safety
- Information security and cybersecurity
- Catastrophic and existential risk

Table 2. 10 steps to successful change

Features of Successful Change		Questions to Answer
Create a positive vision	· using a compelling future that people can work towards · allows for radical thinking about the urgent change needed	· Why are we working on becoming an 'AI-powered society'? · What will success look like for us as a staff team, for our organisational goals, for children and young people and for our other stakeholders? · How will we develop a shared intention that allows for local application?
Take it to the top	· to have visible commitment from leaders who champion change and give others permission to do so	· How is senior-level leadership expressed? · How will we create the time and ownership required for this project in our objectives and alongside our other priorities?
Have a plan...	· of what needs to be achieved, when · that includes some quick wins · that impacts at different levels: operations, practice with children and young people, personal and policy	· How will we create clarity of roles and accountability? · What actions would wreck this project? · How will we plan to be pioneers in a setting characterised by uncertainty? · How will we ensure that we measure the actions that really bring success? · What tools and skills will we need, and do we have them?
...and learn and respond to	· allowing people space to experiment and continuously learn · to review progress and build on what works	· How can we keep scanning for new information and opportunities? · How will we maintain energy and address failures? · How will we capture and share individual and organisation learning? · How will we recognise individuals' development in experience and skills?
Engage employees...	· so that staff are involved and motivated and it is clear what they need to do · have values, culture, organisational stories, rituals and routines to support the change	· How will we explore 'what's in it for me' with employees? · How will we build on the best features of the organisation's culture? · How will we address resistance, confusion or conflicting priorities? · How will we communicate over the change journey? · How will we listen for feedback and questions?
...and align processes	· to embed change into formal planning, budgeting, evaluation and human-resource processes	· How will we work across functional silos or geographical distance? · How will we remove any barriers? · How will we align with, and add value to, other parallel initiatives?
Build new networks	· to bring the right people together to get things done	· How will we involve the right people inside (and outside) the organisation? · How will we recognise individual performance?
Collaborate with stakeholders	· to actively engage them in finding new opportunities	· How will we reflect the voice and ownership of children and young people? · How will we work with different stakeholders: members, partners and funders? · regulatory agencies, government?
Deliver innovations	· to provide core activities in new ways	· How will we work to make an 'AI-powered society' an opportunity (not a burden) that helps us to achieve our goals in creative, forward-looking ways?
Tell the story	· to share the plan, quick wins and successes	· What will be the plan for communicating goals, progress and learning?

CONCLUSION

For humanity to arrive at a future at which AI provides benefits to society and humankind, actions must be taken to avoid procrastination or worse 'all talk and no action'. The prompt for action can come from any of the following sources:

- Individuals in an organisation who have been building their own awareness about climate change. They can join with others or take some action in their own lives in their homes with their families, friends, schools and communities.
- An ad hoc group in an organisation can explore issues relating to climate change, the environment or sustainable living and their work could be widened or deepened.
- The prompt to act may come from interactions with beneficiaries and stakeholders, such as service providers, policymakers and/or funders, which highlights the importance of and opportunities for responding.

One way to build on individual viewpoints is to recognise that people have a wide range of personal feelings about AI. These feelings are not left at home when employees come to work. Make time at work to have conversations about the issues, and about individuals' personal reactions. Conversations can also be informal, or they can be part of the normal interaction between manager and team members.

We have outlined 10 steps in Table 2 associated with successful changes that could help any community (e.g. profit or non-profit business) envision a future society which empowers all citizens and communities by supplemental autonomous AI technologies to achieve a destiny based on F.A.T.E. (Fairness, Accountability, Transparency and Ethics).

REFERENCES

Adams, A. (2019). Stanford University launches the Institute for Human-Centered Artificial Intelligence. *Stanford University*. https://news.stanford.edu/2019/03/18/stanford_university_launches_human-centered_ai/

Badakar, C. M., Thakkar, P. J., Hugar, S. M., Kukreja, P., Assudani, H. G., & Gokhale, N. (2017). Evaluation of the Relevance of Piaget's Cognitive Principles among Parented and Orphan Children in Belagavi City, Karnataka, India: A Comparative Study. *International Journal of Clinical Pediatric Dentistry*, *10*(4), 346–350. doi:10.5005/jp-journals-10005-1463 PMID:29403227

BBC News. (2018). *Greta Thunberg: The Swedish teen inspiring climate strikes*. https://www.bbc.co.uk/news/av/world-europe-47231271/greta-thunberg-the-swedish-teen-inspiring-climate-strikes

Children's Society. (2018). *Safety Net: Cyberbullying's Impact on Young People's Mental Health: Inquiry Report*. Author.

Davidson, C. N. (2012). *Now You See It: How Technology and Brain Science Will Transform Schools and Business for the 21st Century*. Penguin Books.

DfES. (2004). *Every Child Matters: Change for children*. Department for Education and Skills.

Hall, S. K. (2008). *Raising Kids in the 21st Century: The Science of Psychological Health for Children*. Wiley-Blackwell. doi:10.1002/9781444305197

House of Lords Communications Committee. (2017). *Growing up with the Internet*. HL Paper 130 of session 2016–17, p 13.

Lee, K. (2018). How AI can save our humanity. *TEDTalks* https://www.youtube.com/watch?v=ajGgd9Ld-Wc

Maslow, A. H. (2011). *Hierarchy of Needs: A Theory of Human Motivation*. https://www.amazon.co.uk/Hierarchy-Needs-Theory-Human-Motivation-ebook/dp/B004JKMUKU

Moreland, W. (2019). The Purpose Of Multilateralism: A Framework For Democracies In A Geopolitically Competitive World. *The Brookings Institution*. https://www.brookings.edu/research/the-purpose-of-multilateralism

Rogati, M. (2017). The AI Hierarchy of Needs. *Hackernoon*. https://hackernoon.com/the-ai-hierarchy-of-needs-18f111fcc007

SDC. (2007). *Every Child's Future Matters*. Sustainable Development Commission.

Tegmark, M., Tallinn, J., Aguirre, A., Krakovna, V., & Chita-Tegmark, M. (2017). Asilomar AI Principles. *Future of Life Institute*. https://futureoflife. org/ai-principles/

Tse, T., Esposito, M., & Goh, D. (2019). *The AI Republic: Creating the Nexus Between Humans and Intelligent Automation*. Lioncrest Publishing.

UK Council for Child Internet Safety. (2017). *Children's Online Activities, Risks and Safety: A Literature Review by the UKCCIS Evidence Group*. Author.

Vygotsky, L. S. (1978). *Mind in society: The development of higher psychological processes Cambridge, Mass*. Harvard University Press.

ENDNOTES

[1]   DFES existed until 2007 and was replaced by the Department for Children, Schools and Families and the Department for Innovation, Universities and Skills (Source: https://www.gov.uk/government/organisations/department-for-education-and-skills).

[2]   BREXIT - How Does It Affect the Representative Obligation? (Source: https://www.dpr.eu.com/).

About the Author

Salim Sheikh became fascinated by Artificial Intelligence (AI) whilst delivering a final year project for his undergraduate degree at Royal Holloway, University of London; creating a program to syntactically and semantically analyse text and convert it to speech leveraging natural language processing (NLP) techniques. This led to a scholarship from University of Wales, Cardiff where he gained an MSc in "Artificial Intelligence with Engineering". Additional scholarship followed at University of Wales, Aberystwyth to do a PhD focussing on qualitative modelling leveraging case based reasoning, genetic algorithms and neural networks. In his professional life, Salim has spent the past twenty years in consulting; engaging in and leading digital and technology transformation, process improvement and organisational change programmes across UK, Europe, Turkey, UAE, Hong Kong, Singapore and Australia. He previously founded and managed a boutique consultancy ("Blue-Crow") which had strong success in Local Government, Healthcare and Pharma. Salim believes that we need a new narrative, mindset and ways of working (and living!) that allows people to align with what society needs today, tomorrow and the future; augmenting humans with technology. He continues to follow all aspects of AI and is an alumni of CIO Academy (SBS, Oxford University).

Index

Ensure Quality Research is Introduced to the Academic Community

Become an IGI Global Reviewer for Authored Book Projects

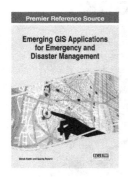

Premier Reference Source

Emerging GIS Applications for Emergency and Disaster Management

Premier Reference Source

Managerial Strategies and Green Solutions for Project Sustainability

Premier Reference Source

Comparative Approaches to Using R and Python for Statistical Data Analysis

Premier Reference Source

Solutions for High-Touch Communications in a High-Tech World

The overall success of an authored book project is dependent on quality and timely reviews.

In this competitive age of scholarly publishing, constructive and timely feedback significantly expedites the turnaround time of manuscripts from submission to acceptance, allowing the publication and discovery of forward-thinking research at a much more expeditious rate. Several IGI Global authored book projects are currently seeking highly-qualified experts in the field to fill vacancies on their respective editorial review boards:

Applications and Inquiries may be sent to:
development@igi-global.com

Applicants must have a doctorate (or an equivalent degree) as well as publishing and reviewing experience. Reviewers are asked to complete the open-ended evaluation questions with as much detail as possible in a timely, collegial, and constructive manner. All reviewers' tenures run for one-year terms on the editorial review boards and are expected to complete at least three reviews per term. Upon successful completion of this term, reviewers can be considered for an additional term.

If you have a colleague that may be interested in this opportunity, we encourage you to share this information with them.

Printed in the United States
By Bookmasters